Discipleship

By the same author

MY GOD IS REAL
ONE IN THE SPIRIT
IN SEARCH OF GOD
LIVE A NEW LIFE
I BELIEVE IN EVANGELISM
I BELIEVE IN THE CHURCH
IS ANYONE THERE?
HIDDEN WARFARE

Discipleship

by
David Watson

HODDER AND STOUGHTON
LONDON SYDNEY AUCKLAND TORONTO

To the various members of the team who have worked
with me in Christian missions and festivals throughout
the world, who have shared with me, encouraged me,
been patient with me, and have shown me more
of Christ.

British Library Cataloguing in Publication Data

Watson, David, *1930*
   Discipleship.—(Hodder Christian paperback)
   1. Christian life
   I. Title
   248′.5   BV4509.5

ISBN 0 340 33213 1

Hodder and Stoughton Editorial Office: 47 Bedford Square, London WC1B 3DP

Foreword

A jolly saint of the recent past (was it William Temple? I can't be sure) confessed to praying, 'God who made me simple, make me simpler yet.' Surely the very thought of such a prayer will jangle nerves in the modern West, where middle-class respectability, worldly wisdom and – let us say it straight out – spinelessness have muddled up and so watered down our Christianity. But in the King James Version of 2 Cor. 11:3 simplicity appears as a virtue, to be jealously guarded. 'I fear,' writes Paul, 'lest ... your minds should be corrupted from the simplicity that is in Christ.'

From Conybeare's rendering of the Greek word as 'single-minded faithfulness', Goodspeed's as 'single-hearted fidelity', and the Jerusalem Bible's as 'simple devotion', we can see what sort of thing Christian simplicity is – not naivety or dim wittedness, but sincerity and straightforwardness in facing the moral and spiritual demands of being Christ's person. Sin in our hearts, by making us complicated and devious, foments spiritual apathy and moral dishonesty; and sophistication in our culture, by relativising values and encouraging detachment as a mental attitude, reinforces both. God's grace, however – by which I really mean our Lord Jesus Christ, who is grace incarnate – reverses the process, making us increasingly honest, straightforward and childlike in our life with God: in other words, simple in the sense defined above.

Study of Scripture is the highway to this supernatural simplicity. Psalm 19:7 celebrates the Word of God as 'sure, making wise the simple' (i.e. those who lack wisdom) – but God's gift of wisdom from the Word, while banishing that kind of simplicity, leads us ever deeper into the sort of simplicity that I am speaking of now. The rule is, the wiser the simpler.

Foreword

Simplicity was seen supremely in Jesus, and is a mark of stature in his followers. If ever you have met a genuinely holy person, you know that already.

David Watson's writings seem to me to be shining examples of this kind of simplicity. They are transparently clear, and ruthlessly straightforward in facing up to the Bible's often upsetting and bewildering practical challenges. David Watson takes God at his word! So you will find breathtaking, block-busting, Bible-based simplicity on every page of this book.

He writes out of wide experience of ministry and leadership in the world of charismatic renewal, and his vision of discipleship reflects what is central in that movement. No bad thing! – for charismatic emphases have proved infinitely enriching and animating to literally millions in our time. He knows what is going on around him, and every chapter here focuses on needle issues in following Christ today. The years during which he was God's instrument of new life in the once dying Anglican parish of St Michael-le-Belfrey, York, made him one of the best-known clergymen in England, as well as widely-known elsewhere, and it is tested insights from a very fruitful ministry that he dispenses in these pages. You do not have to agree with every single statement to appreciate the authority and power of his vision of life in Christ, and to be made most uncomfortable as the searchlight of Watsonian simplicity swings your way.

I am not surprised that David Watson by his own confession found the book hard to write; vivid searching books often are, and I can well believe that the devil did not want this one written and tried all he could to stop it. But I am glad and grateful that David persevered till it was done. Now we may all get the benefit.

This is an important book. Who should read it? Anyone who wants to know what the charismatic lifestyle is at its best, and (more important) anyone who wants to be a simple follower of Jesus Christ. But be prepared to discover that you are being courteously dynamited! You have been warned.

James I. Packer

Contents

Acknowledgements

During the writing of this book, I discussed its theme with Christian leaders in different parts of the world, and I have a growing conviction that *Discipleship* is one of the vital issues for today. The Christian church has largely neglected the thrust of the Great Commission: *to make disciples*. The result is that other religions and political groups have led the way, and we see the effects of this all over the world. Further, some Christians, in an attempt to correct the church's failure to disciple its members, have swung to extremes, leaving the whole matter in an area of suspicion and caution.

I am most grateful to Edward England, whose wisdom as a literary agent is enormously valuable, for suggesting the theme to me in the first place; I have personally benefited from the reading and study that has been necessary to complete the book.

Helpful ideas have come from many sources, but I am especially grateful to Liz Attwood, a present member of my mission team, for her shrewd and honest comments throughout the painful period of writing which had to be squeezed in between Christian festivals over the year. Her perceptive remarks have been invaluable.

For the main task of typing I owe immense gratitude to Jeni Farnhill, together with Bridget Hunt who helped with the first few chapters, Jennie Lunn and Shirley Anderson who checked the final manuscript and Janet Lunt for her diagrams.

The writing of this book has been during an exceptionally busy year, including some tense problems in our church in York (which have sharpened my understanding of certain sections of this book), and I have deeply appreciated the patient encouragement given by my wife Anne.

Biblical quotations, unless otherwise stated, are from the Revised Standard Version.

Introduction

It is a widely held opinion that the battle of the '80s will be between Marxism, Islam and Third World Christianity. Western Christianity is considered too weak and ineffective to contribute anything significant to this universal struggle. Certainly the contest will be severe.

The ruthless determination of Marxism has been proved, sometimes in horrifying proportions, ever since 1917. In a speech to an audience of American Trade Unionists in 1975, Alexander Solzhenitsyn said, 'During the 80 years before the revolution . . . about 17 persons a year were executed. In 1918 and 1919 the Cheka executed, without trial, more than a thousand persons a month . . . At the height of Stalin's terror in 1937–38, if we divide the number of persons executed by the number of months, we get more than 40,000 persons shot per month.' Stalin became the greatest mass murderer in human history. The militant fanaticism of Islam has likewise been demonstrated in many Muslim countries in the world. Any convert from Islam to Christianity stands in danger of his life, even from his own family.

Numerically, Christianity is still the strongest religion of all. In a world population approaching 4,000 million, approximately one quarter of that number profess to be Christians. In terms of its message, there is no greater good news to be found anywhere than in the gospel of Jesus Christ. Who else, in the history of the world, can answer the deepest cries of the human heart? Everywhere we hear the cry for meaning in the meaningless muddle of our existence, the cry for love in a world that is rapidly falling apart, the cry for forgiveness in an age when peace of mind is rare, the cry for freedom when human misery and oppression abound on every side, the cry for hope amid the gathering gloom of the world – all summed up in the cry for

God. The clear, resounding answer to every cry is Jesus Christ! Not only has he something highly relevant to say concerning all our deepest needs, but by his living presence amongst us, he has the power to change the very heart of man.

With such numerical strength, such a relevant message and so great a spiritual power, why then is the Christian church, especially in the West, so comparatively ineffective? The Centre for Study of World Evangelisation in Nairobi recently produced a computerised survey based on an exhaustive analysis of statistics from the world's 223 countries, its 6,270 ethno-linguistic groups, its 50 major religions, and more than 9,000 Christian denominations (that last figure alone demands much sober thought when Jesus died to make us all one in him). According to the survey, during the year 1979 about 1,815,100 adult professing Christians in Europe abandoned the faith to become agnostics, atheists, or adherents of non-Christian religions or cults. North America also registered a decline of 950,000. All these were net figures, after conversions to Christianity had been noted. However, during the same period, churches in the Third World experienced phenomenal gains. In Africa the net gain was 6,152,800, or 16,600 each day. In South Asia the number evangelised was 34,813,000.[1] Why is the church in the West in such sharp decline, compared with the church in the materially poverty-stricken countries of the world? Why is western Christianity too flabby to do anything much in the strenuous battle against Marxism and Islam?

Solzhenitsyn said on BBC *Panorama* in March 1976: 'I wouldn't be surprised at the sudden and imminent fall of the West . . . Nuclear war is not even necessary to the Soviet Union. You can be taken simply with bare hands.'

Why is that? It is because Christians in the West have largely neglected what it means to be a *disciple of Christ*. The vast majority of western Christians are church-members, pew-fillers, hymn-singers, sermon-tasters, Bible-readers, even born-again-believers or Spirit-filled-charismatics – but not true disciples of Jesus. If we were willing to learn the meaning of real discipleship and actually to become disciples, the church in the West would be transformed, and the resultant impact on society would be staggering.

This is no idle claim. It happened in the first century when a tiny handful of timid disciples began, in the power of the Spirit, the greatest spiritual revolution the world has ever known. Even the mighty Roman Empire yielded, within three centuries, to the power of the gospel of Christ. All the great revolutionary leaders have struggled with this intractable problem which lies at the centre of everything: the nature of man. Che Guevara once said, 'If our revolution is not aimed at changing people, then I am not interested.' Revolutions are aptly named: they revolve. They turn one lot of sinners out, and put another lot of sinners in. The trouble with virtually all forms of revolution is that they can change everything – except the human heart. And until that is changed, nothing is significantly different in the long run. However, by the inward power of the Spirit, Christ offers a revolution of love that can transform the innermost nature and desires of every single one of us.

Something of the impact of Christ's revolution can be clearly seen on many occasions in the history of the Christian church right up to the present day – but always, in human terms, when Christians were willing to pay the price of costly discipleship. This is why Third World Christianity is comparatively so vibrant. There may be political and sociological factors at work as well, but it is often in these materially impoverished areas that we have to look today to see the clearest living examples of New Testament discipleship.

The future prospects of the affluent West are now so serious that the Christian church cannot afford to ignore the plan that Jesus chose for the renewal of society. He came with no political manifesto. He rejected all thoughts of violence. He shunned all positions of influence in public life. His plan, which was to change the history of the world in a way that has never been equalled, was astonishingly simple. He drew around him a small band of dedicated disciples. For the best part of three years he lived with them, shared with them, cared for them, taught them, corrected them, trusted them, forgave them, and loved them to the end. They, on their part, sometimes failed him, hurt him, disappointed him, and sinned against him. Yet never once did he withdraw his love from them. And later, empowered by the promised Holy Spirit, this group of trained disciples turned the world of their day upside down.

A Communist once threw out this challenge to a western

Christian: 'The gospel is a much more powerful weapon for the renewal of society than is our Marxist philosophy, but all the same it is we who will finally beat you . . . We Communists do not play with words. We are realists, and seeing that we are determined to achieve our object, we know how to obtain the means . . . How can anybody believe in the supreme value of this gospel if you do not practise it, if you do not spread it, and if you sacrifice neither time nor money for it . . .? We believe in our Communist message, and we are ready to sacrifice everything, even our life . . . But you people are afraid to soil your hands.'

Discipleship sums up Christ's plan for the world. Yet for all its brilliant simplicity, it is the one approach that most western churches have neglected. Instead we have had reports, commissions, conferences, seminars, missions, crusades, reunion schemes, liturgical reforms – the lot. But very little attention has been given to the meaning of discipleship.

This book is written in the hope that we can see again what it means to follow Jesus, and how we can help others to do the same. Together with the continuous renewing power of the Holy Spirit, this is our one real hope for the future. Nothing else can save our present world from plunging headlong into despair and destruction. God still wants his church to unite a world that is falling apart without him and to be his agent in the healing of the whole of his creation. For this to be possible, it is my strong conviction that Christ is calling to himself those who are willing to dedicate their lives fully to him, to commit themselves to all other true Christians out of love for him, and to present their bodies to him as a living sacrifice for all that he wants to do in his world today. That is what discipleship is all about, and it is what this book seeks to explore.

Notes

1. From *Evangelical Missions Quarterly*, October 1979, p. 228

CHAPTER ONE

The Call to Discipleship

'When Christ calls a man, he bids him come and die,' said Dietrich Bonhoeffer. In this startling statement we have the essence of the radical, uncompromising nature of true Christian discipleship. Certainly there are different forms of dying; not every Christian is called to literal martyrdom, as Bonhoeffer was himself. But every Christian is called to a clear and dedicated discipleship, whatever the personal cost may be.

The general concept of discipleship was by no means new when Jesus called men and women to follow him. It is therefore not surprising that, although the verb 'disciple' (*manthano*) occurs only 25 times in the New Testament (six in the Gospels), the noun 'disciple' (*mathetes*) comes no less than 264 times, exclusively in the Gospels and Acts. In secular Greek the word meant an apprentice in some trade, a student of some subject, or a pupil of some teacher. In the New Testament times we find the same primary meaning with the 'disciples of Moses',[1] who were students of the Mosaic law; and the 'disciples of the Pharisees',[2] who were preoccupied with an accurate and detailed knowledge of Jewish tradition as given both in the written Torah (the Old Testament) and in the oral Torah (the traditions of the Fathers). These disciples would submit themselves entirely to their Rabbi, and were not to study the scriptures without the interpretation and guidance of their teacher, although they expected to become teachers themselves after extensive training.

Nearer to the specifically Christian concept come the disciples of John the Baptist, who attached themselves to this New Testament prophet. Following their Baptist teacher, they fasted and prayed,[3] confronted the Jewish leaders,[4] and stayed loyal to John during his imprisonment[5] and at his death.[6] Unlike the disciples of Moses or of the Pharisees, they were fully committed to their master as well as to his message.

From all this we see that the basic idea of discipleship was widely accepted by the time Jesus began his own ministry. At the same time, when he took the initiative himself in calling people to follow him, when he called them primarily to him and not just to his teaching, when he expected from them total obedience, when he taught them to serve and warned them that they would suffer, and when he gathered around him a thoroughly mixed crowd of very ordinary people, it became obvious that Jesus had created a radical and unique pattern of discipleship. In this chapter we shall look briefly at the specifically Christian calling and then develop these themes later in the book.

Called by Jesus

In Rabbinical circles, a disciple would choose his own master and voluntarily join his school. But with Jesus, the initiative lay entirely with him. Simon and Andrew, James and John, Levi, Philip and others – all were personally called by Jesus to follow him. Even when the rich young ruler ran up to Jesus and asked a leading question of this 'good teacher', Jesus replied by spelling out the costly and total demands of discipleship, and then added 'Come, follow me.'

There may have been some who, attracted by the integrity of his person, the quality of his teaching and by the power of his miracles, wanted to attach themselves to Jesus and to his disciples, but always it was Jesus who laid down for them the strong conditions that he required. Sometimes this proved too much for them: 'This is more than we can stomach!' they once said. 'Why listen to such words?'[7] And they left him, leaving only the twelve whom he had chosen and called to himself after a whole night spent in prayer. These were the ones in particular that God had given him.[8] Yet although there is a uniqueness about the twelve apostles, this fact of God's initiative and Christ's calling lies behind all those who are his disciples. 'You did not choose me, but I chose you and appointed you that you should go and bear fruit and that your fruit should abide; so that whatever you ask the Father in my name, he may give it to you. This I command you, to love one another.'[9]

Two points of interest arise from that particular statement.

First, when we see ourselves as disciples who have been personally chosen by Jesus, this should alter our whole attitude towards him and motivate us for the work he has given us. If someone is chosen to represent his country for the Olympics, his whole attitude and approach to his event will be quite different from someone who has himself chosen to go as a spectator. With the first, there will be a total and sacrificial dedication to the task, partly because of the privilege of having been chosen. There will be a strong sense of responsibility which even the most enthusiastic tourist will not have. The Christian church today suffers from large numbers who feel that *they* have 'made a decision for Christ', or from those who think that *they* have chosen to join a certain church. Such man-centred notions spell spiritual death, or at least barren sterility. It is only when we begin to see ourselves as chosen, called and commissioned by Christ that we shall have any real sense of our responsibility to present our bodies to him 'as a living sacrifice, holy and acceptable to God'.

Certainly the apostles could not get away from this awareness of divine constraint. 'As men of sincerity, as commissioned by God, in the sight of God we speak in Christ';[10] 'Therefore, having this ministry by the mercy of God, we do not lose heart';[11] 'Paul, a servant of Jesus Christ, called to be an apostle, set apart for the gospel of God . . . To all God's beloved in Rome, who are called to be saints';[12] 'We know, brethren beloved by God, that he has chosen you';[13] 'You are not your own; you were bought with a price. So glorify God in your body.'[14] Such examples could be multiplied again and again. It was this strong sense of God's calling, of Christ's initiative, of the Spirit's sovereign work, that enabled them to be bold in their witness, to hold fast in their suffering, and to lead lives 'worthy of the calling' to which they had been called.[15]

The second point is that he calls us into a common discipleship. He calls us to share our lives both with him and with one another in love. That is why his statement 'you did not choose me, but I chose you' is followed directly by his command 'to love one another'. Indeed, it is by this love that we shall be known to be his disciples.[16] And it is only by loving one another that we shall be fruitful in his service and effective in our prayers.[17] Discipleship is never easy; often there may be pains

and tears, and frequently we shall have to re-think our values
and ambitions as we seek seriously to follow Christ. But we are
not called to face this challenge on our own. Alongside the
inward power of the Holy Spirit, God wants us to experience
the encouraging, supportive love of other disciples of Jesus. It is
in the strength of our relationships together in Christ that we
can win the battles against the powers of darkness and help one
another to fulfil the task that God has given us.

Called to Jesus

This again was something unique. The call *by* Jesus was also a
call *to* Jesus. The Jewish Rabbi and the Greek philosopher
expected disciples to commit themselves to a specific teaching
or to a definite cause. But the call of Jesus was wholly personal:
his disciples were to follow him, to be with him, and to commit
themselves wholeheartedly to him. They were to have faith in
him, and could become disciples only by repenting of their sin
and by believing in him. For example, in the Gospel record of
the call of Simon Peter and Nathanael, the all-important factor
is their response to the person of Jesus. When Simon saw
something of the commanding presence of Jesus, 'he fell down
at Jesus' knees, saying, "Depart from me, for I am a sinful man,
O Lord."'[18] When Nathanael saw the perceptive knowledge
of Jesus, he said, 'Rabbi, you are the Son of God! You are the
King of Israel!'[19]

In Kittel's *Theological Dictionary of the New Testament*
(Vol. 4), the writer makes the following comment: 'The personal allegiance of the disciples to Jesus is confirmed by their
conduct in the days between the crucifixion and the resurrection.
The reason for the deep depression which marks these days is to
be found in the fate which has befallen the person of Jesus. No
matter what view we take of the story of the walk to Emmaus,
the fact that "He" is the theme of their conversation on the way
(Luke 24:19ff) corresponds in every sense to the relation of the
disciples to Jesus before his arrest and execution. On the other
hand, it is nowhere stated or even hinted that after the death of
Jesus his teaching was a source of strength to his followers, or
that they had the impression of having a valuable legacy in the
word of Jesus. This is a point of considerable importance for a
true understanding of the *mathetes* of Jesus.'[20]

When Jesus called individuals to be his disciples, he shared his life with them. Although there was a depth of sharing with the twelve that was not common to everyone, in real measure he gave himself to all who responded to his call. By his incarnation he identified fully with them, and in his love he made himself vulnerable by opening his heart to them. Part of his great attraction was that his loving compassion was so real and open that others knew they could trust him. There was no deceit or guile about him. His transparent openness and integrity drew others into a quality of a loving relationship that they had not known before.

That is why they were all so shattered when such a perfect life of love was smashed on a cross. Indeed, after the horrifying events of the crucifixion it took some time for Jesus to restore the faith and commitment of his disciples. But he did this by leading them gently back into a renewed relationship with him. After Peter's threefold denial comes the threefold question by Jesus, 'Simon, son of John, do you love me?' Repeatedly, in his resurrection appearances, he came to his disciples, individually and corporately, to reassure them of his living presence, and of his love and forgiveness. They were to become witnesses to him – not Rabbis of his teaching. They were to tell everyone about him, and, in the sharing of their lives together, to manifest his life by being the body of Christ on earth.

When Buddha was dying, his disciples asked how they could best remember him. He told them not to bother. It was his teaching, not his person, that counted. With Jesus it is altogether different. Everything centres round him. Discipleship means knowing him, loving him, believing in him, being committed to him.

Called to obey

The disciples of a Jewish Rabbi would submit themselves as slaves to their master until such time when they could leave their schooling and become masters or Rabbis themselves. But Jesus calls his disciples to unconditional obedience for the whole of their lives. We shall never graduate this side of heaven. We shall never get beyond a life of obedience. To obey God's will is to find the fulfilment of our lives. 'Not every one who says to me, "Lord, Lord," shall enter the kingdom of heaven, but he who does the will of my Father who is in heaven.'[21] 'Why do you call me "Lord, Lord," and not do what I tell you?'[22]

To be a disciple of Jesus means to follow him, to go the way that he goes, to accept his plan and will for our lives. 'If any man would come after me, let him deny himself and take up his cross and follow me.'[23] It is a call to say "No" to the old selfish life of sin, and to say "Yes" to Jesus. Inward belief must be accompanied by outward obedience. Søren Kierkegaard once rightly said, 'It is so hard to believe because it is so hard to obey.' There is no true faith without obedience, and there is no discipleship either.

The world of today is being increasingly influenced by disciples of another kind who understand this matter of obedience much more clearly than the average Christian. A BBC radio programme about women terrorists showed that they were loyal to the uttermost, they would never betray a colleague, they were totally ruthless, and they were willing to go to any lengths to achieve their objective. Bernadette Devlin said, 'Before, there came a time where one said, "This I can't do!" Now there comes a time when one says, "This I must do!"'[24] An extremist leader of a violent revolutionary group in North America said that they were cutting down their numbers by two-thirds until they had an utterly dedicated group of trained disciples who could bring about a revolution.

Should we expect any less if we are to see Christ's revolution of love changing the world scene of today? But until we respond to this unconditional call to obey, flinging away the cautionary 'Yes, but . . .', we shall never see the light of Christ scattering the darkness of this present gloomy world. To say 'No, Lord!' is a contradiction in terms. Yet many within the Christian church want the comfortable compromise of conditional discipleship. In the long run, it is we who want to call the tune. It is we who wish to have the final word, when to say *yes* and when to say *no*. But the truth is uncomfortably clear: if Christ is not Lord of all, he is not Lord at all. There are no half-measures in the discipleship of Jesus. Malcolm Muggeridge vividly comments: 'I have a longing past conveying . . . to use whatever gifts of persuasion I may have to induce others to see that they must at all costs hold on to that reality (the reality of Christ); lash

themselves to it as, in the old days of sail, sailors would lash
themselves to the mast when storms blew up and the seas were
rough. For indeed without a doubt, storms and rough seas lie
ahead.'[25] We need urgently in the church today true disciples
who will bind themselves to Jesus Christ in unswerving
obedience and loyalty. 'The great tragedy of modern evangelism,' wrote Jim Wallis, 'is in calling many to belief but few to
obedience.'[26] Biblical evangelism should centre on the Kingdom
of God, stress the rule of God, and call people to radical
obedience.

In this painful but liberating life of obedience, however,
we are not to battle on our own. We are to exhort and encourage one another 'every day': 'Take care, brethren, lest
there be in any of you an evil, unbelieving heart, leading you to
fall away from the living God. But exhort one another every
day, as long as it is called "today", that none of you may be
hardened by the deceitfulness of sin.'[27] Once again we may
have to learn humbling lessons from some of the fighting groups
of today. The leader of El Fata, a liberation movement in
Palestine, attributed the strength of his movement in these
words: 'I can always fall out with my comrade; I can always
divorce my wife; but my brother is always my brother.' However strong and binding other human relationships should be,
none is unbreakable except the bonds of family. This is how the
liberation or terrorist groups see themselves: brotherhood
inseparable apart from death.

Within the family of God we are eternally united to one
another. If such understanding leads to qualities of love and
trust which transcend ordinary human relationships, the resulting corporate strength is immense. The Spirit of God who
enables us to call Almighty God 'Abba! Father!' is the same
Spirit who helps us to see *every* other true Christian as brother
or sister. Jesus calls us to absolute obedience, but only because
he has first laid down his life for us, placed his Spirit into our
hearts, and given us to one another in love.

Called to serve

Although the disciples were called by Jesus first and foremost to
be with him, they were also commissioned to go and preach the
kingdom of heaven, and to 'heal the sick, raise the dead,

cleanse lepers, cast out demons.'[28] As soon as Jesus called
Simon and Andrew to follow him, he told them that he would
make them into fishers of men.[29] The seventy likewise were
sent out in the name of Jesus as messengers of peace: 'Heal the
sick . . . and say to them, "the kingdom of God has come
near to you." '[30] Jesus had come to lay down his life for the sake
of others, and his disciples were called by him to do exactly the
same. Yet they did not always understand this.

Jesus repeatedly found that he had to correct his disciples as
they fell into two equal and opposite temptations which
crippled the spirit of service in their lives. The first temptation
was ambition. Several times they argued amongst themselves as
to who was the greatest. James and John asked for the places of
highest honour in the kingdom of heaven. This is the spirit of
the world: seeking for status instead of service. Jesus rebuked
them: 'Whoever would be great among you must be your
servant, and whoever would be first among you must be your
slave; even as the Son of man came not to be served but to
serve, and to give his life as a ransom for many.'[31] He later
demonstrated this spirit of service in a way they never forgot,
when he wrapped a towel around his waist and washed their
feet.

The second temptation was self-pity. 'Lo, we have left our
homes and followed you,' said Simon Peter as he began to feel
the considerable cost of discipleship. But Jesus assured him that
those who left everything for the sake of the kingdom of God
would 'receive manifold more in this time, and in the age to
come eternal life.'[32] We need to be honest and real about our
own weakness and pain, but the moment we fall into self-pity
we hinder God's working in our lives. It is only when we accept
our human frailty, knowing God's grace to be always sufficient,
and only when we are ambitious for God's kingdom alone, that
we shall be able to serve others with the loving, gracious and
humble spirit of Jesus Christ. The servant should not demand
certain conditions of service. He has given up his rights, and
may well have to forgo normal comforts and rewards. As we
grow in years it is easy to look for privilege, position and
respect. This was not the way of Jesus.

Unfortunately, some forms of evangelism today encourage
people to remain thoroughly self-centred, instead of urging them

to become God-centred. In this advertising age it is all too easy to present Christ as the one who will meet all your needs. Are you anxious? Christ will bring you peace! Are you lost? Christ will give you new direction! Are you depressed? Christ will fill your life with joy! All this is true, and it is part of the good news of Christ that he longs to meet the deepest needs of each one of us. But that by itself is only one half of the story. On its own, it mirrors the deceitful approach of the false cults. In practice many of our needs will be met as we give ourselves in service both to Jesus and to others. It is those who are willing to lose their lives who will find them. It is only when we give that it will be given to us – 'good measure, pressed down, shaken together, running over, will be put into your lap. For the measure you give will be the measure you get back.'[33] It was when the seventy went out to preach and heal that they returned filled with joy because of all that they had experienced.

The needs of the world are vast. God in his love longs to reach out to all those who, inwardly or outwardly, are crying out for help; but he has chosen to work primarily through the disciples of Jesus. If we are taken up with our own personal needs first and foremost, or if we are looking for position and status in the church, we shall be of no use to God. We are called to serve; and a servant must go where his master sends him and do what his master commands.

Called to a simple life

A disciple of a Rabbi might have given up most material benefits in order to study the Torah, but he would have known that such sacrifice was only for a limited time. Later he would be rewarded financially for his diligence when he took on the role of a teacher himself. This was altogether different with Jesus. He laid on one side all earthly securities and material comforts. Often he had nowhere to lay his head, and he lived in total dependence on his Father's love and faithfulness.

He also called his disciples to a life of humility and poverty. Although it was the Father's good pleasure to give them the kingdom, they were to sell their possessions, and give alms. They were to take with them 'no gold, nor silver, nor copper in your belts, no bag for your journey, nor two tunics, nor sandals, nor a staff; for the labourer deserves his food.' They were to trust their heavenly Father that they would 'receive without paying', and so they must 'give without pay'. Like their Master they had to be willing to leave their homes, their families, their occupations, their securities – everything for the sake of the kingdom of God. But as they sought first his kingdom, all that they needed would be provided for them. In this they had to trust their Father, and not to be anxious as the unbelieving Gentiles.

It is fair to comment that such radical discipleship applied primarily to those who were called into a life of full community with him. It was in the total sharing of their lives and possessions together that they were to look to God alone to meet all their needs. Other disciples who were not in such close-knit fellowship seemed to have kept at least some of their material possessions, since they helped to provide for Jesus and the twelve. Nevertheless, all the disciples were encouraged to live a simple life, in which they held their possessions 'in common'; and this undoubtedly became the practice of the early church.

The comparative affluence of many Christians today, especially those in the West, almost certainly is a stumbling-block to effective and radical discipleship. We must look at this more carefully in a later chapter, for it is unlikely that God will entrust us with the true riches of his spiritual life and power until we are genuinely serving him and not mammon. It is when we can be trusted with material goods, learning to live on the New Testament principle of 'enough', that God will entrust us with the gifts of his Spirit that will immeasurably enrich our own lives as well as those we serve.

Called to suffer

When Jesus called his disciples to follow him, they had to be willing to walk his way, and his way was the way of the cross. If they were to share their lives together, they must share not only their joys but also their pains. 'For it has been granted to you that for the sake of Christ you should not only believe in him but also suffer for his sake.'[34]

Jesus often tried to prepare them for this by speaking plainly both about his own sufferings and those which his followers must experience. But sometimes they could not, or would not, understand his warnings. When we read in Matthew 16:21ff that

'from that time Jesus began to show his disciple that he must go
to Jerusalem and suffer many things from the elders and chief
priests and scribes, and be killed . . .' Peter at once protested,
'Heaven forbid! No, Lord, this shall never happen to you.' For
this he received a stinging reply, 'Away with you, Satan; you
are a stumbling-block to me. You think as men think, not as
God thinks.' And in case they were under any further illusions,
Jesus began to speak plainly about their sufferings, too. 'If any
man would come after me, let him deny himself and take up his
cross and follow me. For whoever would save his life will lose it,
and whoever loses his life for my sake will find it . . .' Life for
the Master ended with rejection, pain and agonising death. The
disciple should never be surprised if following Jesus leads the
same way.

Many suffered from physical persecution. Peter and John
were imprisoned and later beaten for their boldness; Stephen
was stoned to death, and James killed with the sword. Before
long 'a great persecution arose against the church in Jerusalem,
and they were all scattered.'[35] Paul later wrote about being
beaten five times with the 39 lashes of the Jewish whip, three
times with rods, and once stoned. According to various
Christian traditions, most if not all the apostles suffered
eventual martyrdom of one form or another. During those early
years of the church waves of bitter and appalling persecution
came from a succession of Roman emperors: Nero, Domitian,
Trajan, Pliny, Marcus Aurelius, Decius and Diocletian. In
various degrees of ferocity this continued up to AD 305, and of
course has continued throughout the entire history of the
Christian church. It is sobering to remember that in recent years
countless thousands of Christians have been imprisoned and
tortured for their faith, and are still being so today in various
parts of the world. It is estimated that there have been more
martyrdoms for Christ this century than during the rest of the
church's history. 'This is not an age in which to be a soft
Christian,' comments Francis Schaeffer.

None of this should come as a surprise. Jesus constantly
warned his disciples about the physical dangers that lay ahead:
'Beware of men; for they will deliver you up to councils, and
flog you in their synagogues, and you will be dragged before
governors and kings for my sake . . . Brother will deliver up

brother to death, and the father his child, and children will rise
against parents and have them put to death; and you will be
hated by all for my name's sake . . .'[36]

Almost everyone suffered mental and emotional pain. It is
not hard to feel something of Paul's sadness when he wrote,
'Demas, in love with this present world, has deserted me . . .
Crescens has gone to Galatia, Titus to Dalmatia . . . Alexander
the coppersmith did me great harm . . .'[37] There is often much
pain within the body of Christ: some may fall away from Christ;
some may separate from other Christians on matters of
marginal emphasis; others will leave to serve Christ somewhere
else; often, too, we hurt and disappoint one another, since at
best we are a fellowship of sinners. The need to forgive seventy
times seven becomes apparent when we seriously commit
ourselves to one another as well as to Christ. Forgiveness is
always painful. It cost Jesus his death on the cross. For us, too,
it may be a crucifying experience to forgive someone who has
hurt us, or even to be forgiven when we know we have sinned.

Discipleship also involves spiritual grief. Paul once wrote
concerning his overwhelming burden for fellow Jews who did
not believe in Jesus as their Messiah: 'I have great sorrow and
unceasing anguish in my heart. For I could wish that I myself
were accursed and cut off from Christ for the sake of my
brethren.'[38] And during his ministry in Ephesus he said that 'for
three years I did not cease night or day to admonish every one
with tears.'[39] God, in his great compassion, 'spreads out (his)
hands all the day to a rebellious people.' Having made us in his
image, he longs that we should share in his love. Yet, by and
large, we have turned our backs on him; we ignore or reject his
love, and, as a consequence, so often ignore or reject one
another. Since love will never force itself on unwilling people,
he watches us fall away from him and from each other; he sees
us resenting, hating, fighting and killing one another. He sent
his Son that there might be 'peace on earth', but we will not have
this man to reign over us. So, mistrust, confusion, bitterness
and war pollute the face of this earth.

Is it surprising that a loving God is grieved, and wants us, too,
to share in his heart of grief? When Jesus weeps for his body,
the church, that is torn, wounded and broken, can we be
unmoved if we are truly his disciples? When Jesus weeps, as he

once did over Jerusalem, for those who are blind to 'the things that make for peace', can we remain indifferent? When Jesus weeps, as he once did by the grave of Lazarus, when he sees today the ravages caused by man's sin, can we be apathetic? The more we seek to love Jesus, and the nearer we come to his great heart of love, we should not be surprised if we feel the pain of his godly grief.

Suffering is inescapably woven into the fabric of discipleship – 'joy and woe are woven fine', to quote William Blake. But we shall often discover that it is in the midst of suffering that God is working most profoundly in our lives. It is a simple fact that those I've known with the greatest spiritual sensitivity and depth have also been those who have experienced most suffering. One Christian who spent over ten years in a Communist prison in Czechoslovakia for his faith in Christ said that his torturers broke his bones but not his spirit. He referred to those years as the richest years of his life. 'We must pray,' he said, 'not that persecution will not come, but that we may be worthy of it, open to the blessings God offers through it.'

Called irrespective of qualifications

Whereas the Rabbis would have accepted disciples only from the ceremonially 'clean', from the righteous according to the law, and from those with sufficient intelligence to study the Torah with a view to becoming Rabbis themselves, Jesus called to himself a curious cross-section of contemporary society. Some were down-to-earth fishermen; James and John were sons of a Zealot; the second Simon was certainly a Zealot; there was despised Levi, a traitor to his countrymen; and amongst the twelve we find Greek and Semitic names, and probably a Judean as well as Galileans. 'The circle of the disciples is in fact a microcosm of the Judaism of the time. In it we find all the powers and thoughts of the people, even in their divergence.'[40]

Most interesting of all, there was Judas who betrayed Jesus. Since Jesus knew in advance what Judas would do (Jesus called him 'the son of perdition' in John 17), it was an exceedingly strange choice, except for two supreme facts. First, Jesus loved Judas, even to the end. Second, Jesus had come to fulfil all the Old Testament prophecies about the Messiah, he therefore knew his role as the suffering Servant, and he knew also the role that Judas had to play in betraying his Master, even to the detail of the thirty pieces of silver. This foreknowledge of the treachery of Judas in no way removed his responsibility and guilt; but it is significant that, after that crucial night of prayer, Jesus chose all the disciples that his Father had given him, including that 'son of perdition'. Humanly speaking we might have chosen for the special band of apostles men with far greater qualifications than these twelve; but then God's ways are not our ways, and his thoughts not our thoughts. In his complete obedience to the Father, Jesus called those who later failed and disappointed him time and again; but never once did he withdraw his love from them. He loved them to the end.

In this thoroughly mixed and fallible band of disciples, Jesus set the pattern for the rest of the Christian church. 'For consider your call, brethren; not many of you were wise according to worldly standards, not many were powerful, not many were of noble birth; but God chose what is foolish in the world to shame the wise, God chose what is weak in the world to shame the strong, God chose what is low and despised in the world, even things that are not, to bring to nothing things that are, so that no human being might boast in the presence of God.'[41]

What we have seen about the unique concept of discipleship, introduced by Jesus, refers not just to the twelve. It refers to all those who hear the call of Jesus and who turn to follow him as their Saviour and Lord. Although there was a special and unique relationship between Jesus and the twelve, we cannot evade the strong demands made on Christian disciples by saying that these applied only to the apostles. The call to obey, to serve, to live a simple lifestyle, to suffer and, if need be, to die, is common to all those who claim to be followers of Jesus. Above all, we are to commit our lives unreservedly to him and to one another as members of his body here on earth. The Christian church is not a club that we belong to in order that our needs might be met; it is a body, a building, a family, an army – these are some of the pictures used to show that, by accepting the call of Christ, we have responsibilities that we cannot avoid if we are to be his disciples. It is not a question of our feelings and personal choices; it is a matter of taking with the utmost seriousness the conditions and demands of discipleship that Jesus lays upon us. We are no longer our own. We have been chosen by him, called by him, bought by him; we therefore now belong to him, and by virtue of this fact we also belong to one another, however easy or difficult, joyful or painful, we may find this to be.

If the cost is great, the aims, privileges and rewards are infinitely greater. 'The glory which thou hast given me I have given to them, that they may be one even as we are one, I in them and thou in me, that they may become perfectly one, so that the world may know that thou hast sent me and hast loved them even as thou hast loved me. Father, I desire that they also, whom thou hast given me, may be with me where I am, to behold my glory which thou hast given me in thy love for me before the foundation of the world.'[42] To be a part of the fulfilment of such a profound and magnificent prayer is surely worth the sacrifice of every part of our lives.

Notes

1. John 9:28f
2. Mark 2:18
3. Mark 2:18; Luke 11:1
4. John 3:25
5. Matthew 11:2
6. Mark 6:29
7. John 6:60, NEB
8. John 17:9
9. John 15:16
10. 2 Cor. 2:17
11. 2 Cor. 4:1
12. Romans 1:1, 7
13. 1 Thess. 1:4
14. 1 Cor. 6:19ff
15. Ephesians 4:1
16. John 13:34f
17. John 15:16f; cf. Matthew 18:19
18. Luke 5:1–11
19. John 1:44–51
20. Op. cit., Vol. IV, p. 446
21. Matthew 7:21
22. Luke 6:46
23. Mark 8:34
24. *More Deadly than the Male*, broadcast on 4th December 1978
25. *Christ and the Media*, Hodder & Stoughton, p. 43.
26. *Agenda for Biblical People*, Harper, New York, 1976, p. 23.

27. Hebrews 3:12f
28. Matthew 10:8
29. Mark 1:17
30. Luke 10:1–20
31. Matthew 20:26–28
32. Luke 18:28–30
33. Luke 6:38
34. Philippians 1:29
35. Acts 8:1
36. Matthew 10:17, 21f
37. 2 Timothy 4:10, 14
38. Romans 9:2f
39. Acts 20:31
40. Kittel, op. cit., vol. IV, p. 452
41. 1 Corinthians 1:26–29
42. John 17:22–24

CHAPTER TWO

Called into God's Family

Nothing is clearer in the Gospel records than the tremendous concern God has for every individual. In an age when the individual seems increasingly redundant and insignificant, it is a vital part of the good news of Jesus Christ that every single person matters to God. He knows us and calls us by name. He has a personal love for each one of us. 'Zacchaeus!' said Jesus to the startled tax collector hiding up in his sycamore tree. It was this personal approach that so quickly captured the hearts of many who were lost and lonely. Here at last was someone who really cared for them as individual persons.

Yet although that is part of the glory of the Christian gospel, it is equally obvious that Jesus calls individuals, not to stay in isolation, but to join the new community of God's people. He called the twelve to share their lives both with him and with each other. They were to live every day in fellowship with one another, losing their independence and learning interdependence, gaining new riches and strength as members of God's new society. They were to share everything together, their joys, their sorrows, their pains and their possessions, and in this way become the redeemed, messianic community of Christ the King. And it was not just the twelve men; there were several women, too, who joined the small band and helped financially to support them. Indeed all the disciples were called, at some level into a depth of sharing that they had never known before. This is what excited John, when he wrote about the reality of the shared life the apostles enjoyed with Jesus, which now was made available to all believers: 'That which we have seen and heard we proclaim also to you, so that you may have fellowship with us; and our fellowship is with the Father and with his Son Jesus Christ.'[1]

The priority of community

Today we live in an age not only of personal insignificance, but also of great loneliness. More than ever the church needs to recapture the priority of community in Christian discipleship. In his three years of intimate relationship with his disciples, Jesus has given us the model for the church. He loved his disciples, cared for their needs, taught them, corrected them, stimulated their faith, instructed them concerning the kingdom of God, sent them out in his name, encouraged them, listened to them, watched them, guided them; and he told them to do the same towards each other. The church which rediscovers something of the God-given quality of such a sharing community will speak with great relevance, credibility and spiritual power to the world of today. The church, wrote Paul, is 'built upon the foundation of the apostles and prophets; Christ Jesus himself being the chief cornerstone.'[2] He does not say that it was their doctrine, institution or religious activity that became the foundation of the church. God's revealed truth, given to us in the scriptures, is clearly of unique importance. But it was the apostles themselves and the sharing of their lives that pragmatically, if not theologically, formed the basis of the Christian church.

Although Jesus taught his disciples many truths concerning the kingdom of God, he wanted them most of all to know *him*. This is the meaning of eternal life.[3] In their corporate life together they came to know him who is the life, and in that way they were able to share that life – his life – with others. The word 'know' that is used for 'knowing God' or 'knowing Jesus Christ' is the same word as is used for a man knowing his wife. It speaks of a deep, intimate, personal union. To achieve such knowledge, Jesus therefore called his disciples into a living, loving community. He saw this as top priority as he began the task of building his church.

This pattern that Jesus lived out with his own disciples was clearly continued in the early church and became an outstanding feature of it. 'All who believed were together and had all things in common.'[4] They worshipped together, prayed together, worked together, witnessed together, and shared their possessions together as the various needs arose. The reality of their love for one another was a rich expression of the joy of their individual conversion, and certainly made an enormous impact on the world around them. Jesus said that love should be the hallmark of his disciples, and he prayed that by the loving unity of their lives together others would believe and know the truth about him. This is exactly what happened. It is not surprising with such a community of disciples bound together in love, that God added to their number day by day those who were being saved. In their commitment to one another, as well as to Christ, they became the visible manifestation of the body of Christ on earth, and experienced the power of his resurrection. God's power is always for God's people, not just for individual believers. According to the psalmist, it is 'when brothers dwell in unity' that the Lord commands his blessing.[5]

The forming of the church into the new community of God's people is, however, only the means towards the fulfilment of the much wider plan that God has for the whole of his creation. His master plan can best be summed up in Ephesians 1:9–10, where Paul writes: 'For he has made known to us in all wisdom and insight the mystery of his will, according to his purpose which he set forth in Christ as a plan for the fulness of time, *to unite all things in him*, things in heaven and things on earth.' Today it is obvious that we live in a sick society, falling apart without God. Every aspect of this world has been polluted by the sin of man and is in the power of the evil one. Creation itself is 'in bondage to decay'.[6] For this reason, Christ came to usher in the kingdom of God, and 'God's kingdom', to quote a memorable expression of Hans Küng, 'is creation healed'. God wills, therefore, to bring everything under the authority of Christ, that all things might be united and restored in him.

To accomplish his great plan, God has chosen his church to be his agent. But the church can accomplish this healing, reconciling ministry effectively only if it has first experienced this reality within its own ranks. That is why the existence of over 9,000 Christian denominations throughout the world is an insult to Christ, a denial of the gospel, and the greatest hindrance to the spread of the kingdom of God. It is only when Christians deeply repent of tearing the body of Christ into thousands of separate pieces and pray earnestly for the healing and renewing power of the Holy Spirit, that the church can ever be God's agent in reconciling all things in Christ. Until that time, creation itself remains broken and bowed, 'groaning in travail' and waiting 'with eager longing for the revealing of the sons of God'.[5]

To be both biblical and realistic, we have to realise that there is always both 'now' and 'not yet' about the kingdom of God. To the extent that Christ has come and is reigning over those people and structures that have submitted to his Lordship, the kingdom of God is already manifest. 'But we do not yet see everything in subjection to him;'[7] and because Christians are no more than redeemed sinners who still live in a fallen world, we shall not see God's kingdom in all its power and glory until Christ comes again in triumph to 'put all his enemies under his feet'.

A biblical balance is therefore important. In so far as the church can become a united and caring community of God's people marked by love, there could be 'substantial healing' within God's creation, even if we have to wait for complete restoration until the coming of Christ. God in Christ has certainly begun to reconcile the world to himself, and has entrusted to us both the message and ministry of reconciliation. But when a sick church attempts to bring about the healing of a sick world, it should not be surprised if it receives the cynical retort, 'Physician, heal yourself!' That is why it is crucial that all true disciples of Jesus repent of all negative, unloving attitudes that divide us, and determine, as an act of the will, to be totally committed to one another in the power of the Spirit of love. Only in this way will God's purposes ever begin to be realised for his world. God has never withdrawn his plan for the church. It is 'through the church' that 'the manifold wisdom of God might now be made known to the principalities and powers in the heavenly places.'[8] But until the church can unitedly manifest the wisdom, power and love of God, the world remains captive to the powers of darkness, and the Devil and all his children mockingly taunt, 'Where is your God?'

Once we see that the church is to be God's agent for the redemption of his world, we can understand why the New Testament writers were so persistent and emphatic about the urgent need for believers to be reconciled to one another, to put away all bitterness and slander, to forgive one another, and to walk in love 'as Christ loved us'. Constantly in the epistles we find this urgent stress on restoring or maintaining authentic Christian community. Until the kingdom of God can be demonstrated in our relationships of love with one another, we have nothing to say with any credibility to an unbelieving and broken world.

The unity of God's people
This is the burden of Jesus in his great high-priestly prayer in John 17. Notice his repeated plea to his Father, made all the more powerful perhaps because of his often painful experiences with his own disciples: 'Keep them in thy name . . . that they may be one, even as we are one . . . that they may all be one; even as thou, Father, art in me, and I in thee, that they also may be in us, so that the world may believe that thou hast sent me. The glory which thou hast given me I have given to them, that they may be one even as we are one, I in them and thou in me, that they may become perfectly one, so that the world may know that thou hast sent me . . .' Since the nature of the Trinity could be described as a community of perfect love, the reality of God amongst us is seen not primarily in right doctrines (important though these are), but in the church becoming herself a community of love. Instead of allowing herself to be divided by sin, the church must seek earnestly to maintain the unity of the Spirit in the bond of peace, however painful that may sometimes be. In no other way will God's reality and rule be seen. It is only when we overcome the evil around us by persistent love that the kingdom of God will be seen to be greater than the kingdom of this world.

Our unity in Christ is, or should be, an expression of the life of God. It is a vital way in which the invisible God manifests – or makes visible – his own nature here on earth. The church is, or should be, 'the word made flesh' for today. Others should be able to look at our fellowship of love and say, 'That is what God is like!' It will not be the total truth about an infinite God, of course. But it will be perhaps the most meaningful and relevant truth that can touch the minds and hearts of all people of all races, backgrounds, cultures and languages. Love is a universal language. God's love amongst God's people is always the most convincing argument for the truth of the gospel. The most fruitful church-based mission I have ever had the privilege of leading was effective for precisely this reason. There was such an obvious demonstration of the love of God within the church and flowing out into the community, that all I had to say, in effect, was 'This is what you have seen and heard . . .!' No wonder they flocked into the kingdom of God, for there it was, right in their midst. Hardly anyone could fail to see it, and a great many believed in the King.

When the early church visibly demonstrated that all racial and social barriers had been broken down by the cross of Christ, and that, through the power of the Spirit, they were now all one in Christ, there could have been no greater evidence for the truth of the gospel in that ancient world. Today, when I have seen the reconciling power of Christ draw together into a deep loving fellowship political extremists, previously bitterly opposed to one another, terrorists, Marxists, blacks and whites, oppressor and oppressed, there is no more powerful proof that I could offer concerning the reality of Christ to an unbeliever. If relationships such as these can be healed, creation itself can be healed. God's kingdom will come when we obey Christ's new commandment, and love one another as he has loved us.

That is why discipleship, based on community, is essential for effective witness. Discipleship involves much more than the training of the individual believer for personal evangelism, vitally important as this is. A purely individualistic approach is not biblical. The New Testament makes it clear that, although every Christian is inescapably a witness to Christ, not every Christian is called to be an evangelist. The church is certainly committed to evangelism, but the church as the body of Christ has many members with different gifts. It is only when the various gifts of the Spirit are allowed to develop 'as he wills' that the body of Christ can function properly, and it is only then that the church can fulfil its commission to evangelise. The reality of the gospel should first clearly be seen in the life of the church. When that is self-evident, those who are evangelists in the church simply have to explain the truth behind that reality, and can do so with the support of other members in the body who are committed to evangelism but are not gifted as evangelists.

Missiologists, such as Peter Wagner, have stressed the '3 P's' of evangelism. There must first of all be *presence evangelism*, where the church by its worship, life and witness brings to the world the sense of God's presence; and it is the present-day absence of this, due to the moral and spiritual sickness of the church, that makes evangelism in many places so difficult. Second, there is *proclamation evangelism*, when the truths of the gospel are proclaimed at every level to those who have already sensed the presence of God amongst his people. Third, there is *persuasion evangelism*, when the evangelist seeks to persuade men and women to turn in repentance and faith to Jesus Christ, on the basis that they have by now sensed God's presence and understood the proclamation of his message. They are now being persuaded to respond. However Snyder adds a fourth 'P', which is *propagation evangelism*. The ultimate goal of evangelism is not to see people converted to Christ, nor even made into disciples. 'To do justice to the biblical under-standing of the church we must go one step further and say that *the goal of evangelism is the formation of Christian com-munity . . .*'⁹ If disciples are not formed into the community of God's people, God's plan for the healing of creation cannot begin to be fulfilled.

Elsewhere Snyder makes this important comment: 'Many churches do not share the gospel effectively because their communal experience of the gospel is too weak and tasteless to be worth sharing. It does not excite the believer to the point where he wants to witness, and (as the believer uncomfortably suspects) it is not all that attractive to the unbeliever. But where Christian fellowship demonstrates the gospel, believers become alive and sinners get curious and want to know what the secret is. So true Christian community (*koinonia*) becomes both the basis and the goal of evangelism.'¹⁰

Most evangelists and church leaders will say that whereas training in evangelism is important, the most crucial factor is motivation. Christians may know what to say, but lack the desire to say it. Almost certainly this is due to the low level of Christian experience in the church itself. But when the church becomes renewed in the Spirit, the life of Jesus will 'spill out' to others. Any discerning person will at once recognize the reality – or lack of it – behind what we are saying. If we are genuinely excited by the gospel because Christ is alive within us, and if we are able to say 'Come and see' because the church manifests the life of Christ, evangelism will flow naturally.

God's alternative society

When the church commits itself to a pattern of corporate life based on radical biblical principles, it immediately challenges the moral, political, economic and social structures of the world around it. In this way, by its very existence, the church is both prophetic and evangelistic. And only in this way will the proclamation of the gospel make much impact amongst the vast majority of people who, at this moment, are thoroughly disillusioned by the church as an institution. For this reason it is impossible to separate the call to discipleship, the call to community and the call to mission. Without a strong commitment to discipleship, there can be no authentic Christian community; and without the existence of such a community, there can be no effective mission.

For many Christians in many churches, however, fellowship means little more than casual acquaintance, or at best a working relationship because we happen to belong to the same group which exists for some specific purpose. When Jesus drew men and women into discipleship he was requiring a depth of relationship that would be much more demanding and, as a result, much more enriching and powerful. He wanted them to find their identity as true sons and daughters of God, which included a total commitment both to himself and to all others within God's family. This was to be their life and their security. That is why it is so hard for a rich man to enter the kingdom of God, since his identity and security would almost certainly be in his riches together with the status and power that these would bring. But what Jesus promised his disciples, who nervously protested that they had left everything to follow him, was that 'there is no one who has left house or brothers or sisters or mother or father or children or lands, for my sake and for the gospel, who will not receive a hundredfold now in this time, houses and brothers and sisters and mothers and children and lands, with persecutions, and in the age to come eternal life.'[11]

The phrase 'with persecutions' is significant. Christ's calling is to a radical alternative society which will, by its existence and values, profoundly challenge the existing society of today. 'The church should consist of communities of loving defiance. Instead it consists largely of comfortable clubs of conformity.'[12] No one will bother to persecute dull conformity. But as soon as we adopt a lifestyle of 'loving defiance' which challenges the status quo concerning covetousness, oppression or self-centredness, there is likely to be some strong and bitter opposition. Fellowship for those first Christians 'meant unconditional availability to and unlimited liability for the other brothers and sisters – emotionally, financially and spiritually'.[13] This striking statement exposes the superficiality of many church fellowships today. It is interesting that the word for fellowship (*koinonia*) in the New Testament occurs more frequently in the context of the sharing of money or possessions than in any other. If the church is to become a community of God's people in the way that Christ demonstrated with his own disciples, it means much more than singing the same hymns, praying the same prayers, taking the same sacraments, and joining in the same services. It will involve the full commitment of our lives, and of all that we have, to one another. Yet it is only when we lose our lives that we will find them, so bringing the life of Jesus to others. In fact, this practical expression of love will speak more powerfully of the living God than anything else.

To maintain values that are fundamentally different from those of the world is never easy. Yet if the church is to be effective as God's agent of reconciliation, it must be both *in* the world, but not *of* the world. It is on this issue that many evangelicals and ecumenicals today have taken largely polarised positions, neither of which is biblical. Evangelicals have frequently seen the church as a religious ghetto, separated from the world, pre-occupied with its doctrinal and moral purity, and regarding itself as the special object of God's favour and blessing. As such, Christians go out to the world in the style of spiritual commando raids, aiming to destroy its strongholds, weaken its defences, and generally preparing the way for the gospel, but living essentially apart from the world. Social and political involvements in the world are therefore viewed with suspicion and classified as 'liberal'.

Ecumenicals, reacting strongly to this, and aware that God loves the whole world, not just the church, have all too often secularised the gospel, allowed the world to set the agenda, and so abandoned the distinctive profile of the church in the world.

The church, however, is 'God's experimental garden in the world. She is a sign of the coming age.'[14] Both gospel proclamation and social action are equally important. They are like two blades of a pair of scissors. If either is missing, the cutting-edge is lost.

To maintain the distinctive quality of salt and light in a rotten and dark society is far from easy. To withstand, therefore, the pressures of the world, as well as offering the love and life of Jesus to the world, Christians need urgently the strength and support of other committed disciples. It is all very well Paul saying, 'Don't let the world around you squeeze you into its own mould,'[15] but on your own it is frankly impossible to defy the materialistic and covetous pressures of society which assail us on every side. Ronald Sider writes: 'The values of our affluent society seep slowly and subtly into our hearts and minds. The only way to defy them is to immerse ourselves deeply into Christian fellowship so that God can fundamentally remould our thinking, as we find our primary identity with other brothers and sisters who are also unconditionally committed to biblical values.'[16] On our own we shall never stand against the principalities and powers that wage war against us. If the circumstances leave us with literally no alternative – at home, at work, in prison, or wherever – God's promise is clear; there is always 'grace to help in time of need'.[17] In normal circumstances, however, we are able to overcome in spiritual warfare only when we are strongly united in Christ.

Time to act

The training of the disciples by Jesus amounted to little more than a 'crash-course'. In less than three years he had to win their hearts, instruct their minds, bend their wills, bind them together into his new society, and equip them with the power and gifts of his Spirit. He knew that his time with them was short. He knew, too, that he would send them out into a hostile world which would oppose them, persecute and destroy them. There was no time to lose. Although he had come to bring them 'life in all its fulness', and to fill their empty hearts with his love and joy, he warned them of times of suffering that would soon come upon them: 'The hour is coming . . . when you will be scattered . . . In the world you have tribulation . . . They will lay their hands upon you and persecute you, delivering you up to the synagogues and prisons . . . You will be hated by all for my name's sake . . . Many will fall away, and betray one another, and hate one another . . . And because wickedness is multiplied, most men's love will grow cold . . .'[18] Such words were no empty threats. The persecution of the early church was appalling in its severity and cruelty. It was only the love of Christ controlling them that enabled them to conquer in his name. In their hearts, God's grace welled up within so that they were able to praise him with inexpressible joy in the midst of horrific trials.

Only a fool would fail to see the parallels of all this to this present time. Throughout this century countless millions of Christians have been imprisoned, tortured, beaten and killed for the sake of Christ. Vast numbers suffer today. Yet in many Communist countries, where the going has been tough, God's grace is so evident that the disciples of Jesus, who are patiently enduring such trials with considerable faith and love, are often a strong rebuke to the coldness, apathy and complacency of the church in the West. However there are many signs that even Christians living in comparatively safe and secure surroundings need to be alert to the sufferings that almost surely lie ahead for all of us. If we have any understanding of the restlessness and aggression increasing everywhere today, not to mention the vast nuclear stockpile, the population explosion, the dwindling of the earth's resources, the continuing economic recession, and the militancy of Marxism and Islam, we must realise that we are very near the time when men will be 'fainting with fear and with foreboding of what is coming on the world'.[19]

'Strengthen yourselves in the time of peace' is a line of a song we often sing in our church. It is essential that we prepare ourselves now in every way for the battles we shall later have to fight. We must deepen our personal knowledge and love of the Lord Jesus; we must increase our faith in our heavenly Father; we must learn how to be continuously filled with the Holy Spirit; above all, we must drop our differences, forgive and be forgiven, and renew our commitment to one another out of love for Christ. It was the Christian *community* that withstood the persecution of the first century, and it is Christian communities around the world that overcome today the pressures that come increasingly upon them. It is when Christians come together in the name of Jesus that he promises to be with them with special strength and power. It is together that we can lift up that shield of faith which can quench all the fiery darts of the evil one. Now is the time to act.

Carlos Mantica, a leader of the City of God Christian community in Managua, Nicaragua, wrote in 1978: 'Since 1973 we had been warned through prophecy that a period of trial would be coming soon, and we began to take this seriously. When the time of testing came we were not fully prepared but strong enough to withstand its first impact.' Christians in that country went through severe testings through the genocide, torture and terrorism that flared up in 1977. *Those who were deeply committed to one another in true Christian community were, however, largely able to stand fast in the midst of suffering* – an experience known to God's people throughout the 2000 years of church history. Mantica shared some of the vital lessons that they learned:

1. In war, the most important time is preparation time. For all of us the most important time is *now*. When the time of real trial arrives, preparation is over: you are either ready or unprepared. If you are not prepared, you will suffer the consequences.

2. In times of trial, spiritual warfare becomes twice as intense. The world, the flesh and the devil work against you very powerfully. Being as strong as usual is not enough . . . It is important to have some kind of fortress or stronghold.

3. This fortress is built with deep conviction, firm decisions, and strong relationships . . . Our firm decision must be to choose God's kingdom and reject any other. To accept Jesus as our absolute and only Lord. The Lord of our time. The Owner of our money and possessions. The lord of our thoughts, emotions and acts . . .

Jesus decided that community should come before suffering so that we could assist each other and many others when necessity arose. Now we understand the importance of it and feel the need to strengthen our relationships. In addition to

God's covenant with us, a covenant with our brothers and sisters is the best insurance we can get for times of hardship.[20]

The superficial fellowship of many church fellowships will not be enough. Personal belief in Jesus, regular devotional life, faithfulness in church attendance – all these again will not be enough. We need to see ourselves as members of one family, one body. We have been eternally united in Christ, and must make that unity real now by strong loving commitments to one another.

> Guard your circle brothers,
> Clasp your hand in hand.
> Satan cannot break
> The bond in which we stand.
>
> Joy is the food we share,
> Love is our home brothers,
> Praise God for the Body,
> Shalom, shalom.[21]

Notes

1. 1 John 1:3
2. Ephesians 2:20
3. John 17:3
4. Acts 2:44; 4:32
5. Psalm 133
6. Romans 8:19–22
7. Hebrews 2:8
8. Ephesians 3:10
9. *The Community of the King*, IVP, pp. 104f
10. Op. cit., p. 125
11. Mark 10:28–31
12. Ronald J. Sider, *Rich Christians in an Age of Hunger*, Hodder & Stoughton, p. 163
13. Ronald Sider, op. cit., p. 164
14. David J. Bosch, *Witness to the World*, Marshall, Morgan & Scott 1980, p. 225
15. Romans 12:2, J. B. Phillips
16. Op. cit., p. 164
17. Heb. 4:16
18. John 16:32f; Luke 21:12, 17; Matthew 24:10, 12
19. Luke 21:26
20. *New Covenant Magazine*, November 1978
21. Ann Ortlund (© Copyright 1970 by Singspiration Inc.)

CHAPTER THREE

Creating Community

Discipleship involves a life of realism and sharing. We are called to share our lives both with Jesus and with other disciples, but we cannot share what we do not really know. 'Know thyself' is an ancient and wise maxim, but the pressures of today are such that many people face an identity crisis: they do not know who they really are. Partly this is due to the emphasis today on *doing* rather than on *being*. In western society what seems to matter is what we do, how much we achieve, what we accomplish. As we concentrate on this, we may wonder who we really are; and until we have some knowledge and security about this, we cannot possibly share ourselves with others.

Another reason for this lack of personal identity is the fantasy world in which many people live for most of the time – a fantasy accentuated by television, advertising and the press, and further aggravated by the depressing hopelessness of much of the 'real' world around us. Because most individuals cannot face the complexity and enormity of today's crises, the natural defensive mechanisms are either a dazed apathy, a straight denial that any problems exist, or a retreat into a dangerous world of illusion.

The Christian is not immune from such personal conflicts. But being a disciple of Jesus means not an escape from reality, as some critics suppose, but rather the reverse. Jesus was a total realist. Far from withdrawing from the real world of sin and pain, he was born into it and fully shared the struggles, temptations, joys and sufferings of man. He faced squarely the reality of man's nature, crippled and twisted by sin, and laid down his life that man might once again be restored into the divine image. He tackled man's last enemy, death, head-on; and by dying and rising again from the dead gave man the only

solid, realistic hope in the face of death that there is in the
world. Unlike the false prophets, he did not say 'peace, peace'
when there was no peace. He warned the people of his day of
the coming judgement of God upon Jerusalem, and told us all
to expect wars, famines, earthquakes and much tribulation
before his coming again. He was also honest and straightforward with people. He knew what was in their hearts.
Sometimes gently and sometimes ruthlessly he went straight to
their greatest needs, whether the individuals concerned knew
them or not.

In the same way Jesus calls his disciples today to a life of
realism, openness and honesty. We are to take off our masks.
We are to be real with one another. We are to walk in the light,
as he is in the light; only in this way can we have fellowship with
him and with each other. And if that light of Christ exposes sin,
the blood of Jesus goes on cleansing us from all sin. In fact it is
as we bear one another's sins and burdens, learning to forgive
and accept each other, that the love of Christ will grow within
us more and more.

There is probably nothing which so shatters our fantasy
dream-world, so helps us to come to terms with our true
identity, and so enables us to be open and real with one
another, as genuine Christian community. Here I am not
referring only to a particular lifestyle, living together under one
roof, although that may often speed up the necessary process of
coming to terms with ourselves and others. I am referring to all
expressions of Christian community, especially those that might
be found – and should be found – in a local church. There may
be some, of course, who join a fellowship with a fantasy-dream
about Christian community, that here there will be heaven-
upon-earth, marked by perfect love, joy and praise. If such
dreams do exist – and undoubtedly they do – they need to be
shattered, and through Christian fellowship the disillusionment
is likely to come soon. Bonhoeffer comments: 'God's grace
speedily shatters such dreams. Just as surely God desires to lead
us to a knowledge of genuine Christian fellowship, so surely
must we be overwhelmed by a great disillusionment with
others, with Christians in general, and, if we are fortunate, with
ourselves . . . God is not a God of the emotions but the God of
truth. Only that fellowship which faces such disillusionment,

with all its unhappy and ugly aspects, begin to be what it should be in God's sight . . . When the morning mists of dreams vanish, then dawns the bright day of Christian fellowship.'[1]

In open fellowship with other Christians, we can be sure that we are being real in following Jesus, and not just playing religious games, however correct our theology may be. Christianity is all about relationships: our relationship with God and our relationship with others. But such is the nature of sin, and so powerful are the forces of darkness, we can easily be both deceived and deceitful in our relationships. Jesus reserved his sternest judgements against the hypocrites of his day. Many of them, no doubt, were startled by the charge of hypocrisy. Were they not devout men who believed in God and kept the law with great diligence? Were they not moral and upright, highly respectable members of the religious society of that day? Yet all the time they were play-acting in their relationship with God. There was no reality about it. 'This people honours me with their lips, but their heart is far from me.'[2] One of the best ways of checking our own discipleship is by being genuine and open with others. It may be painful, but always it will be fruitful.

This sense of Christian community for all disciples was so strong and fundamental in the first century that salvation outside the church was considered impossible. When individuals were added to the Lord, they were added to the church. When they belonged to Christ, they belonged equally to his body, the church. The severest punishment for gross sin was to be excluded from the fellowship of the church. This was tantamount to delivering the offender over to Satan, since God's grace was to be experienced especially in the church. And since the New Testament concept of the church is neither a building, nor an institution, nor an organization, but the people of God, this means that the disciples of Jesus should gain great strength from belonging to one another in Christ. Bonhoeffer once wrote, 'He who looks upon his brother should know that he will be eternally united with him in Jesus Christ.'[3]

Community and the cross

The true basis for all fellowship is when two or more persons kneel at the foot of the cross of Jesus Christ, trusting wholly in his mercy and love. It may well be in fellowship with other Christians that the light of Christ will shatter my self-righteousness and expose my sinful heart. At that point of reality, I see how my sins crucified Christ and how they wound his body, the church, today. Once I really face that, nothing that I can say or do should surprise me concerning the image I have about myself. Also, as I turn towards my brother, nothing he may say or do should surprise me about him. I can no longer be critical or judgemental, since there, at the cross, I have discovered the state of my own sinful heart.

Since the cross is at the heart of all fellowship, it is only by way of the cross that fellowship is deepened and matured. This will involve the frequent and painful crucifixion of all forms of self – self-seeking, self-centredness, self-righteousness – and the willingness to remain weak and vulnerable in open fellowship with other Christians. Often we try to meet each other from positions of strength. We talk about our gifts, blessings and achievements in the name of Christ. Mutual encouragement along these lines may sometimes be necessary and helpful. But true fellowship, which binds our hearts together in love, begins when we meet at the point of weakness. When I am willing to be open to you about my own personal needs, risking your shock or rejection, and when I am willing for you to be equally open with me, loving you and accepting you with unjudging friendship, we find ourselves both at the foot of the cross, where there is level ground, at the place of God's healing and grace.

John Powell once expressed the fears we have in being open to one another in these words: 'I am afraid to tell you who I am, because, if I tell you who I am, you may not like who I am, and it's all that I have.'[4] We naturally find it safer to maintain an image, to put on a mask, to hide our real selves. This is not the way of fellowship or discipleship, but it explains why many churches scarcely begin to demonstrate the quality of community life that Jesus wants us to experience, and, because of this, have so few (if any) real disciples. Keith Miller described the predicament like this: 'Our churches are filled with people who outwardly look contented and at peace but inwardly are crying out for someone to love them . . . just as they are – confused, frustrated, often frightened, guilty, and often unable to communicate even within their own families. But the *other*

people in the church *look* so happy and contented that one
seldom has the courage to admit his own deep needs before
such a self-sufficient group as the average church meeting
appears to be.'[5]

The breakthrough to genuine fellowship comes when
Christians stop relating to one another as righteous saints, and
start accepting one another as unrighteous sinners. A pious
fellowship has no place for the sinner. In such an unreal and
super-spiritual atmosphere everyone must wear a mask. We
dare not be different. If the true facts about any one of us were
exposed the shock would destroy the system; so sin remains
trapped in concealed hypocrisy. It is only when we are free to
say honestly who and what we are that we discover our true
freedom as children of God. In God's presence we can freely
admit our sin, since we know from his word that he loves us and
accepts us in spite of what we are. He never ceases to love us,
even though he knows the worst about us. But until we come to
that same point of honesty with one another, we shall never
experience the depths of God's love in our own lives, or the
reality of that accepting, forgiving and caring love expressed
tangibly through each other.

When we close our hearts to one another, we close our hearts
to God. Instead, we should recognise the Spirit of Christ in one
another. As we love and serve each other, we are loving and
serving him. Paul wrote that 'we regard no one from a human
point of view', because 'if any one is in Christ, he is a new
creation; the old has passed away, behold the new has come.'[6]
There is a sense in which we should try to see one another not as
we are naturally, but as what we are and can become in Christ. If
we could recognise the enormous potential that we all have in
Christ, we should then encourage each other to become what
we are: in God's eyes, complete in him.

Community and confession

We live today in a sick church that desperately needs God's
healing. James guides us to one important remedy in his epistle:
'Confess your sins to one another, and pray for one another,
that you may be healed.'[7] Unconfessed sin keeps us in the
darkness, and breaks our fellowship both with God and with
each other. It wounds and tears apart the body of Christ. It robs

both the believer and the community of God's *shalom*. 'When I declared not my sin,' records David in the psalms, 'my body wasted away through my groaning all day long. For day and night thy hand was heavy upon me; my strength was dried up as by the heat of summer.'[8] Christian fellowship likewise becomes sick through the sin of any one of its members. The whole body is infected. Simply because we belong to one another, the sin of one member affects the whole. Fellowship is restored and the body healed only when that sin is openly confessed and brought into the light.

This acknowledgement of sin in the presence of another brother is a safeguard against self-deception. It is a curious fact that it is invariably easier to confess our sins privately to a holy and sinless God than openly to an unholy and sinful brother. If that is true, 'we must ask ourselves whether we have not often been deceiving ourselves with our confession of sin to God, whether we have not rather been confessing our sins to ourselves and also granting ourselves absolution. And is not the reason perhaps for our countless relapses and the feebleness of our Christian obedience to be found precisely in the fact that we are living on self-forgiveness and not a real forgiveness?'[9] That is perhaps why James, in the context of open confession to another brother, gives the assurance that any sins committed will surely be forgiven. Once sin is brought out into the light, it can be forgiven and forgotten. Its power has been broken. It can no longer hold the believer in bondage, or tear the fellowship apart. The sinner can honestly be a sinner, and still enjoy the grace of God and the love of the brethren. This is the moment where fellowship in Christ becomes a profound reality. 'In confession the Christian gives up all and follows. Confession is discipleship. Life with Jesus Christ and his community has begun.'[10]

Wisdom may be needed in knowing too much to confess in any given group. Although we should have the freedom to do this with almost any Christian gathering at any time, it may not always be expedient or healthy for the group. For example, if a leader is totally honest about his failures with a young and immature group of Christians, they may not know how to handle the situation. The openness may hinder rather than help. But each Christian should have a peer group, or at least a counsellor, in whose presence he can say virtually anything. Because of certain abuses in the confessional system in the catholic traditions of the church, many evangelical groups virtually deny the value of confession to another Christian altogether. But the practice is both biblical and healthy. Significantly, a common feature in many of the great revivals in the church has been this open confession of sin to one another. As concealed sin is brought out of the darkness, the light of Christ is able to shine as never before. Fellowship and unity are restored. The Spirit is free to move with power.

Bearing with one another
The more deeply we commit ourselves to loving fellowship with others, the more we shall be hurt. As sinners we shall fail and disappoint one another time and again. Yet it is precisely as we accept, with love and understanding the foibles and frailties of others, the irritating habits that try our patience, the sins that we have to forgive, that we shall be fulfilling the law of Christ, the law of love. Jesus had to bear all this from his own disciples, and if we want to follow him we must do the same. That is why Paul urges the Christians at Philippi to have the mind of Christ. Just as he humbled himself and became a servant for our sake, so we must humble ourselves and serve one another out of love for Christ. We are to look not only to our own interests, but also to the interests of others. We are neither to judge nor to criticise; instead we are to love and to forgive. We are not to dominate others, nor to use them for some selfish advantage, nor to mould them into our image; instead we are to see others made in the image of God, to be honoured and respected.

A Christian leader with some experience of community once asked me, 'Have you come to that point in your relationships where you *have* to depend on the Holy Spirit?' He knew that we had gone through some difficulties in our extended household. Once the honeymoon period – or fantasy-dream – was over, we were all finding various aspects of our discipleship being strongly challenged. We were surprised by the degrees of selfishness and covetousness that were still very active in our hearts. Through guile and deceit we tried in vain to cover up areas of darkness in our lives. We were startled to find that such areas still existed and even more depressed to discover our natural deceitful reactions to them. In self-defence we became suspicious and critical of one another. Mutual love and trust wore thin. We saw ourselves as spiritually bankrupt in a way that we did not expect. The moment of disillusionment – and of reality – had arrived.

In any true community in Christ all darkness will sooner or later be exposed to the light. Human love, for all its powerful emotions, is basically self-centred and self-seeking. It desires to have, to possess, to capture; it does not serve. Human love will not release the object of that love for the good of the whole. It makes that object into an idol which it worships, and which tends to dominate every other thought and action. Human love manipulates both people and situations in order to achieve its end. It is restless and insatiable, and, even when disguised as spiritual fellowship, is destructive of true fellowship. 'If we say that we have fellowship with him (or with others) while we walk in darkness, we lie and do not live according to the truth.'[11]

Once we accept the total inadequacy of human love for the building up of community and confess our own natural sinfulness, we can know the joy of God's complete forgiveness, and then ask that his love, instead of ours, might be poured into our hearts each day by the Holy Spirit. His love cares for people as people. When we are controlled by the love of Christ we shall be able to forgive, as often as seventy times seven. We shall care for the needs of others and lay down our lives for them. We shall give to our brother in need. We shall sacrifice time and money for him. We shall listen to him, and let God speak to us through him. God's love is wholly concerned with maintaining unbroken fellowship, walking fully in the light, being always open to God and open to others.

Loving one another

William Barclay describes Christian love like this: '*Agapē* is the spirit which says: "No matter what any man does to me, I will never seek to do harm to him; I will never set out for revenge; I will always seek nothing but his highest good." That is to say, Christian love, *agapē*, is *unconquerable benevolence, invincible good will*. It is not simply a wave of emotion; it is a deliberate conviction of the mind issuing in a deliberate policy of the life . . .'[12] Such love is, of course, perfectly revealed within the Trinity; it is seen in the love that God has for the whole world; it is marked by the motivation of the life and ministry of Jesus; it is measured by his total self-sacrifice on the cross; it takes the initiative towards man in his sin; it calls for a response of love towards the Great Lover; it is to be found amongst those who are his disciples; it is the supreme mark of the Christian and of the Christian church in the world. Without this love, we have nothing and are nothing.

Because of the supreme value of love, it may be helpful to look first at God's love for man, second at man's love for God, then at man's love for man, and finally at the characteristic of love itself.

The essential nature of God is love.[13] It is *all-embracing* love, since God desires that all should be saved.[14] It is *unmerited* love, in that while we were yet sinners Christ died for us.[15] It is *sacrificial* love, marked by God giving us his Son and even making him to be sin for us.[16] It is *merciful* love, since God longs to wash away our sins; he does not keep his anger for ever.[17] It is *conquering* love, enabling us to overcome the trials and temptations that God in his wisdom allows us to experience for growth into full maturity.[18] It is *inseparable* love, which nothing can ever break – neither depression, disease, demonic forces, nor death itself.[19] It is *chastening* love, since this too is necessary for our 'highest good'.[20] It is *everlasting* love, as the scriptures remind us some 180 times. It is also *jealous* love, in that God expects the total devotion of our lives to him who has given himself unreservedly to us.[21]

In response to this, our love for God should be *exclusive*, since our hearts have room for only one supreme devotion.[22] It must be *obedient*, which is the ultimate proof of our love.[23] It is always *in response* to his initiative,[24] and is the *foremost sign* of the fruit of the Spirit.[25]

The Bible, however, is insistent that our love for God, although intensely personal, is not to be private. It is to be seen in the love we show towards one another. The Christian is to love those within his own *family*.[26] If he cannot show true Christian love in his own home, he is disqualified as a leader of the household of God.[27]

In this age when the breakdown of family life has reached

devastating proportions and will cause immense problems for tomorrow's world, Christian homes, and not least those of Christian leaders, seem under special attack. More than ever we need to help one another to work at our marriages, to love, to repent, to forgive, and to strengthen our marriage vows. Quality time with our children is equally important, particularly for the active Christian worker. Although a reaction to marriage-failure *can* be to make this special relationship something of an idol, Christian love between husband and wife, parent and child will often be one area where we greatly need the help of the Spirit of God.[28]

This nuclear family unit, although special and sacred in God's eyes, is not to be exclusive. Christian love must enable us all to form strong brother-sister relationships with the wider *family of God*.[29] If we fail here, we have nothing to offer to the lonely, the single, the divorced and the widowed members of the church, together with solo parents and numerous others needing a genuine and tangible expression of the love of God amongst his children. 'See how they love one another!' should be the outstanding impression of the outsider towards the Christian Church. *Agapē* love also reaches out to our *neighbours*;[30] and Jesus made it clear that anyone in need is our neighbour, regardless of differences of race, colour, creed or class. Barclay comments: 'More people have been brought into the Church by the kindness of real Christian love than by all the theological arguments in the world; and more people have been driven from the Church by the hardness and ugliness of so-called Christianity than by all the doubts in the world.'[31]

Christian love includes *enemies* as well.[32] This is one of the most striking facts of God's love shown to us in Jesus Christ. the one who prayed 'Father, forgive them; for they know not what they do' is the same one who by his Spirit can help us to forgive anyone, anything, always. This is why love is the greatest and strongest force in the world. It overcomes evil with good. It can break the hardest and cruellest heart. It is steadfast in the very worst of storms. It changes negatives into positives, pains into joys, darkness into light. 'The Christian's only method of destroying his enemies is to love them into his friends.'[33]

How, then, can we summarise the nature of this extra-ordinary quality of love – 'love so amazing, so divine'? Love is *sincere*;[34] it has an open heart and an open hand; it knows nothing of corruption and deceit. It is *generous*,[35] marked by the sacrificial giving of time, money, energy and gifts to those in any form of need. It is *active*,[36] backing expressions of love with acts of service. It is *forbearing and forgiving*,[37] turning a blind eye and a deaf ear to the faults and failings of others, and quickly releasing others from the sins that have hurt. It is *uniting*,[38] seeking always to make peace and to heal the divisions within Christian homes and churches. It is *positive*,[39] believing the best about others, not fearing the worst. It is *sensitive*,[40] taking care not to say or do anything that will cause another brother to stumble. It is *upbuilding*,[41] so that even when the truth that is spoken must sometimes hurt, always it aims to build up that person into Christ. It is the *summary* of the entire Christian faith,[42] the fulfilling of the law, and must be the Christian's first and foremost aim.

If that portrait of love leaves us somewhat breathless, it is meant to. God does not require us to strive for such qualities in our own strength. Humanly speaking this is quite impossible. But when we come to that point in our relationships where we have to depend on the Holy Spirit, God's grace will be sufficient for us. There is no escape from the pain of crucifixion. Anyone who is willing for discipleship in the context of community will know at times tears, depression, perhaps even despair. But through the ashes of our own failures can emerge the phoenix of a new quality of love, God's love assuring us of his constant forgiveness and lifting us out of darkness into his marvellous light.

Bonhoeffer is right in stressing the impossibility of Christian community without *agapē*, the love of God, and the certain destruction of such community if the weakness of human love is not clearly seen for what it is. 'The existence of any Christian life together depends on whether it succeeds at the right time in bringing out the ability to distinguish between a human ideal and God's reality, between spiritual and human community.'[43] The failure to distinguish clearly between these two is the reason why many fellowships have run into difficulties. When Christians try to open their hearts to one another, and seek to love and serve one another in their own human strength, the result is that natural desires are awakened, emotional entangle-

ments soon follow, and suspicions, jealousies and resentments
are quickly aroused. What may genuinely have begun in the
Spirit has ended in the flesh, bringing confusion and disaster.
Unfortunately the natural reaction from those who have been
hurt, or from those outside who have witnessed the carnal
chaos, is to back away from deep relationships altogether, to
withdraw to a safe distance, to erect little barriers and defences
so that no further wounds can be inflicted. This too is a fleshly
reaction and will be another way of destroying the community
of love that Christ longs to see in his church.

Covenant love

We need to remember that Jesus knows all about these human
desires and human reactions in each one of us. He saw various
expressions of them in his own self-seeking disciples when they
became ambitious for positions of influence in the kingdom of
God, when they argued between themselves as to who was the
greatest, when they were jealous, critical and indignant with
one another. Later the risen Christ saw human desires, in their
many forms, manifesting themselves in all the churches. We
sometimes think of only the Corinthian church as being carnal;
but the New Testament letters would never have been written
to any church apart from natural, human problems arising
within their fellowships. *But never once did Jesus withdraw his
love from his disciples whose lives were not perfectly under the
control of the Spirit*. Had he done so, none of us would have any
confidence in our relationship with him. Instead as he binds
himself to us in his covenant love, he calls us to do the same for
one another. Only in this way will we help one another to grow
up in Christ, with his love filling our hearts and pervading our
fellowship.

The basis of covenant love is commitment. It has nothing to
do with natural feelings and desires. We commit ourselves to
our brothers and sisters because we see Christ in them. We give
ourselves to them in loving service, laying down our lives for
them, thinking first of their needs and interests rather than
ours. Community demands great personal sacrifice. Real community will not function without covenant love, the nature of
which is to love others more than oneself and to give one's life
for them. Without a doubt, the practical experience of life in

community will sorely test and stretch the love of anyone who attempts it.'[44] It is only God's love, given to us by his Spirit, that will ever make community possible. That is why love, more than anything else, is the one unique feature – or should be – amongst those who are Christ's disciples.

Community as a means of growth

From what we have already seen about the intrinsic value of the community for discipleship, it will have become clear that the environment of community can be a major factor in spiritual growth. Paul, in Ephesians 4, states that God gives various gifts to his church 'to equip the saints (that is, all Christians together) for the work of ministry, for building up the body of Christ'. In fact, the New Testament sees all the gifts of the Spirit as having this specific purpose, that of building up the whole community, not just the individual. The only exception to this being the private gift of tongues, which is to help the believer in his personal communion with God and thus indirectly strengthen the body of Christ. It is only when I am personally edified that I can hope to edify others.

God's purpose in this is that we should 'all attain to the unity of the faith and of the knowledge of the Son of God, to mature manhood, to the measure of the stature of the fulness of Christ'. Paul's emphasis again is on our togetherness in Christ. It is as we seek together to deepen our knowledge of the Son of God, that we shall grow into spiritual unity and maturity, and thus reveal something of the glory of the fulness of Christ. No individual Christian can do all this on his own. Paul here, and in other passages, is thinking primarily of bodily growth, not individual growth. As the body grows, the individual members will naturally grow. But each member needs the life and gifts of the rest of the body before there can be true development. For this to happen, we need gladly and readily to submit to one another, learn from one another, listen to what God may be saying through one another, and count each other better than ourselves.[45] It is 'with all the saints', whatever the age, maturity or tradition, that we shall be able to know the breadth and length and height and depth of the love of God.[46]

There is an important place for solitude and for private prayer and meditation, of course, but in the western church the emphasis has been excessively and unhealthily on the individual. This is not the emphasis in the New Testament. The numerous instructions in the New Testament epistles were almost all for the churches and not for individuals. The common word for Christian, saint, occurs sixty-two times, sixty-one in the plural, and the one verse where it occurs in the singular says 'Greet every saint'! The overwhelming emphasis is on our corporate life together in Christ. We belong to one another; we are to serve one another; we are to strengthen and encourage one another.

The more we live as members of one another within the body of Christ, the more we shall experience the gifts of the Spirit to edify that body. The manifestation of the Spirit is given only 'for the common good'. It is as we live together in love that the Spirit will give his gifts as an expression of his love within his body, the church. We all need one another. No one member can say to another, 'I have no need of you.' In humility and love, we must therefore be willing to bring God's word or a spiritual gift to another brother, whoever that brother might be. Those who are older and more mature in the faith must humbly realize that they may need help, encouragement, forgiveness and maybe rebuke from someone who is possibly much younger, since, regardless of our supposed maturity, we are all sinners in constant and desperate need of the mercy and grace of God. God's grace may come through any member of the body, and has nothing to do with the spiritual maturity of the member whom God may choose. If that member makes extravagant claims about his own ministry, that is another matter; his gifts and ministry should anyway be carefully weighed and tested by the leaders of that community. But to humble us and remind us of our constant weakness, God may well use a 'weaker' brother to speak clearly to a 'stronger' one. In this way we continuously realise our indispensable interdependence, and so grow together into Christ.

I am grateful to those who are willing to speak the truth to me in love, even when it hurts; and I am even more grateful when it comes from those who are young enough to be my children. In this way we are beginning to be the body of Christ, with each member serving the others. As we shall see more fully in chapter 4, many problems arise when one Christian – the obvious leader or teacher – is regarded as the 'guru' with all the others as his disciples. Naturally, by virtue of greater know-ledge or experience, one member may have much to contribute. But essentially Christ is the Discipler; he is the Shepherd of the flock; he is the Teacher in our midst. Therefore it is the task of a Christian Community to encourage each other into maturer discipleship.

Holy Communion

The clearest expression of Christian community is to be found in the service of Holy Communion, the Lord's Supper or Eucharist. It is here above all that we thank God for the basis of all our fellowship, namely the cross of Jesus Christ. Although once we were 'separated from Christ, alienated from the commonwealth of Israel, strangers to the covenants of promise, having no hope and without God in the world', now we celebrate the fact that 'in Christ Jesus we who once were far off have been brought near in the blood of Christ.' We also rejoice that all human barriers have been broken down through the cross, 'for he is our peace, who has made us (all) one, and has broken down the dividing wall of hostility.'[47] We all come to the cross as sinners, and God accepts us as his sons. We look up to him with confidence saying, 'Abba! Father!' We turn to one another in love saying, 'My brother! My sister!' Here, at this glorious fellowship meal, we realise again that we are 'no longer strangers . . . but members of the household of God'. Here is the solemn guarantee of our eternal relationships with God and with one another. Being members of one body, we eat of the one bread and drink of the one cup. We praise and worship God who has joined us together through the death of his own Son, and now no one can put us asunder.

It is at this eucharist that we remember the matchless and measureless grace of God. We openly acknowledge that we have sinned against him and against one another 'through ignorance, through weakness, through our own deliberate fault'. We do not attempt to hide our sin. This meal is for sinners only. We are present at the table of the Lord simply because we have sinned and need his forgiveness. And in the symbols of the bread and wine we have the solemn pledge that, as we confess our sins God will remember them no more. In this eucharist we thank God that our fellowship with him and with each other is restored. Since the body of Christ was broken once for all on the cross, the body of Christ on earth today can be healed. We come therefore with expectant faith, knowing that the risen Christ is with us to draw us back to himself, to bind our hearts together in love, to feed us, strengthen and heal us, according to the unsearchable riches of his grace. As we lift our hearts to him, we can also expect spiritual gifts to be given to edify the body of Christ: gifts of prophecy, healing, faith and love. In turning to one another, we can bring each other the peace and love of Christ.

It is here, that we must sort out our relationships with one another, for, if we fail to do that, we shall be 'guilty of profaning the body and blood of the Lord', thus bringing judgment upon ourselves.[48] The situation which Paul addressed with those words concerned partly the divisions within the church at Corinth, and partly the material inequality of its members: 'For in eating, each one goes ahead with his own meal, and one is hungry and another is drunk.' Had they really loved one another, they would have shared their food together, as well as repenting of the divisions within their fellowship. Instead, by coming divided and unrepentant to the one meal which spoke so powerfully of their unity in Christ, they were experiencing God's chastening in the form of physical sickness and even death. This fellowship meal, which Jesus instituted with his own disciples, is both a means of grace and a form of discipline for all who follow him today. It will help to check that our relationships within the community are healthy and right.

At this meal we are also spiritually strengthened in order to serve God in the world. The focus on the death of Christ is a reminder that the disciple must also take up his own cross and follow him. We are to walk with Christ into this world of sin, willing to suffer for his sake in order to reconcile the world through Christ. We offer our lives especially in service of the poor and needy. As a thanksgiving for all that Christ has done for us, we present our own bodies as a living sacrifice, and ask to be filled with the power of his Spirit, that we might live and work to his praise and glory.

Not least, this fellowship meal should be a foretaste of heaven. We remember that at best it is only a shadow of the

marriage feast of the Lamb. With our hopes fixed on the glory
that is waiting for us, we do not lose heart with the 'slight
momentary afflictions' of this present time. If at this moment
our joys are mingled with tears, we take courage at this
fellowship meal that one day God will wipe away every tear
from our eyes. Until that glorious day, we remain a community
of God's people, members of his own household, encouraging
and serving one another, renewed daily by God's love, as we
work together for the kingdom of God.

Notes

1. *Life Together*. SCM, pp. 15–17
2. Mark 7:6
3. Op. cit., p. 13
4. *Why am I afraid to tell you who I am?*, Fontana, p. 12
5. *The Taste of New Wine*, Word, p. 22
6. 2 Cor. 5:16f
7. James 5:16
8. Psalm 32:3f
9. Bonhoeffer, op. cit., p. 90f
10. Op. cit., p. 90
11. 1 John 1:6
12. *More New Testament Words*, SCM, p. 16. (I am also indebted to William
    Barclay for some of the study on 'love' in this section.)
13. 1 John 4:7f
14. 1 Tim. 2:4
15. Romans 5:8, 10
16. John 3:16; 2 Cor. 5:21
17. Eph. 2:4; Psalm 103:8–10
18. Romans 8:37
19. Romans 8:38f
20. Heb. 12:6
21. Exodus 20:5
22. Matthew 6:24
23. John 14:15, 21–24; et al.
24. 1 John 4:19
25. Gal. 5:22
26. Eph. 5:25ff; 1 Tim. 5:8
27. 1 Tim. 3:1–5, 12; Titus 1:5–8
28. Note Eph. 5:18, followed by instruction on family relationships, 5:21ff
29. 1 Peter 2:17; Gal. 6:10
30. Luke 10:27; et al.
31. Op. cit.; p. 21
32. Matt. 5:44; Luke 6:27

33. William Barclay. Op. cit; p. 21
34. Rom. 12:9; 2 Cor. 6:6; 8:8; 1 Peter 1:22
35. 2 Cor. 8:24; 1 John 4:11
36. Hebrews 6:10; 1 John 3:18
37. Eph. 4:2; Col. 3:12–14
38. Eph. 4:3; Phil. 2:2; Col. 2:2
39. 1 Cor. 13:4–7
40. Rom. 14:15; Gal. 5:13
41. Eph. 4:15; 2 Tim. 2:22–26
42. Rom. 13:10; Col. 3:14; 1 Cor. 13; 1 Cor. 14:1; et al.
43. Op. cit., p. 24
44. *New Covenant Magazine*, August 1977
45. Eph. 5:21; 1 Cor. 14:31; Phil. 2:3
46. Eph. 3:18
47. Ephesians 2:13f
48. 1 Cor. 11:27–29

CHAPTER FOUR

Making Disciples

The Christian gospel is God's good news for the whole world. This was the startling truth that shook those first Christian Jews, that 'God shows no partiality, but in every nation . . . every one who believes in (Jesus) receives forgiveness of sins through his name.'[1] It took a little time for the apostolic leaders to realize the significance of this, but the last recorded words of Jesus before his ascension into heaven had been, 'Go therefore and make disciples of all nations.'[2] This was his one master plan for the salvation of the world, brilliant in its simplicity but strangely ignored by much of the church in most generations. His disciples were to make disciples who would make disciples, *ad infinitum*.

A disciple is a follower of Jesus. He has committed himself to Christ, to walking Christ's way, to living Christ's life and to sharing Christ's love and truth with others. The verb *to disciple* describes the process by which we encourage another person to be such a follower of Jesus; it means the methods we use to help that person to become mature in Christ and so be in a position where he or she can now disciple someone else. Since every Christian is a disciple of Christ we must be careful not to develop 'discipling programmes' that become so specialised and stereotyped that they develop into almost another denomination, or at least a faction within the church.

In recent years there has been a strong emphasis by a number of Christian leaders in different countries along the lines of 'shepherding, discipling and submitting'. Some of this has been disturbing and divisive, for reasons that we shall see later. Nevertheless, movements in the church which tend to go to unfortunate extremes nearly always come into being as inevitable protests to certain weaknesses in the church. In rediscovering emphases which have been largely neglected it is all too easy to push those emphases so strongly that they become unbalanced, contentious and even heretical. The New Testament word 'heresy' originally referred to a divisive party that was not necessarily linked with major doctrinal errors at all. Such a group became a heresy or faction[3] simply because of the strong personality of its leader or the over-emphasis of what at heart was a biblical truth. But we must not throw out the baby with the bath-water. If we need to be wary of over-stressing certain aspects of discipleship, we must be equally wary of over-reacting to what is still a vital biblical principle that the church has neglected to its own peril.

The need for discipling

Certain failures in the church have made the shepherding movement, with all its excesses, inevitable.

First, many Christians, especially in some of the mainline churches, have been deeply disturbed by the lack of doctrinal and moral discipline within the church. An article in *The Times* newspaper[4] on the Church of England's Doctrine Commission Report said, 'What the 18 theologians hold in common is a belief in the likelihood of God, and reverence for Jesus. They disagree about everything else.' When ordained clergymen openly deny the divinity of Christ or reject the bodily resurrection of Christ, clear discipline needs to be taken. Given the need for compassion when any Christian, including a leader, is wrestling with honest doubts on even most basic doctrines, we need also the courage to stop such a theologian or teacher from exercising a public ministry whilst working through their personal uncertainties. The Roman Catholic Church has often shown here the discipline that other churches have lacked. The attitude of many churches towards illicit sexual relationships is another disturbing example of the weakness of Christian discipleship today.

Second, there is a desperate lack of commitment on the part of numerous professing Christians, and a corresponding reluctance in Christian preaching to speak much about the cost of following Jesus. Little reference today is made of self-denial and the cross. We may rejoice that Jesus has died on the cross for us; but what about taking up our cross daily to follow him? For far too long the church has endorsed the 'club' mentality of

church-membership. A 'good' church member, reveals Juan
Carlos Ortiz, is 'like a good club member: he attends the club,
pays his dues, and tries not to embarrass the club.' Where,
however, does the New Testament speak about church-club
membership? Nowhere! We are members of the body of Christ,
and members of one another, both ideas stressing our total
commitment to Christ and to each other. Lack of commitment
is marked by shallowness of fellowship, flabbiness in evangelism, absence of body ministry, neglect of spiritual gifts,
sterility in worship, feebleness in prayer, and general lack of
love.

Who wants to belong to such a sick and ailing body? Yet in
this meaningless world of ours, increasing numbers of people
are looking for something worth living for, perhaps even dying
for. It is one reason why the cults are increasing in numbers,
when the established churches are declining: the cults call for
strong discipleship. So do all the revolutionary and terrorist
groups that are capturing so much of the world today. The
'shepherding movement' is an understandable protest about the
failure of the church to take the radical demands of Jesus
seriously.

Third, there is a depressing lack of direction in numerous
churches. Many of the debates and activities in the church are
like playing bridge on the Titanic after it has hit the iceberg.
Most people are profoundly aware of the uncertainty of this
present age, and everywhere there is a sense that time is
running out fast. Countless Christians are deeply frustrated by
lack of clear leadership from the top. Someone once commented that when an institution no longer knows what it is
doing, it tries to do everything. The need for business-like
discipling and for coming to grips with the real and urgent issues
of today seem more important than ever. Large numbers of
Christians are wanting to follow leaders who have the courage
to give a clear prophetic call to the church, and who will train
and mobilise the church for the tasks that are obviously
relevant for today. In other words, many Christians are willing
and wanting to be discipled.

Fourth, with the renewed biblical emphasis on every Christian
being involved in the ministry of the church, and with increased
openness to the gifts of the Spirit, confusion and excess

inevitably arise where there is not firm leadership and wise pastoral control. The sad fact is that, concerning this spiritual renewal, many clergy and ministers are cautious and suspicious. When the laity are often rearing to move forward, the clergy are dragging their feet. Subsequently, this new-found freedom in the Spirit frequently has taken place in home-based 'renewal fellowships' that may be lacking in experienced leadership. When the gifts of the Spirit are not carefully weighed and tested, some fleshly self-display is almost inevitable. Due to the lack of encouragement and teaching by the ministers of local churches, Christians, who may genuinely have been blessed by the Holy Spirit, will look elsewhere for spiritual guidance.

Fifth, according to the tradition of the church, there has been either gross neglect in the area of evangelism, or an over-dependence on the big-time evangelist to do the job committed to the church. Neither attitude is biblical. Although some are called to be evangelists for the benefit of the whole church, the New Testament lays the emphasis clearly on the witness of every Christian. Dr James Kennedy illustrates the value of this in the following graphic way. If you were an outstandingly gifted evangelist with an international reputation, and if, under God, you could win 1,000 persons for Christ every night of every year, how long would it take you to win the whole world for Christ? Answer, ignoring the population explosion, over 10,000 years. But if you are a true disciple for Christ, and if you are able under God to win just one person to Christ each year; and if you could then train that person to win one other person for Christ each year, how long would it take to win the whole world for Christ? Answer, just 32 years! In churches where discipling is taken seriously, there are few, if any, specifically evangelistic services with a gifted evangelistic preacher. Many, however, are still being won for Christ through the individual witness of each Christian.

The need for some discipling or shepherding programme should now be apparent. 'Unless disciples are adequately built, there will not be enough competent leadership to carry on the work of the church.'[5] If the church as a whole does not take this need seriously, it has only itself to blame for any unhelpful and divisive alternatives.

The dangers of shepherding

There are many biblical references to the leader of a church taking on the role of a shepherd. 'Take heed to yourselves and to all the flock,' said Paul to the Ephesian elders.[6] 'Tend the flock of God that is in your charge,' wrote Peter.[7] 'Feed my lambs . . . Tend my sheep . . . Feed my sheep,' said Jesus when he reinstated Simon Peter as leader of the church.[8] Yet in many churches the whole concept of shepherding is viewed with suspicion and dismay. Why is that? There are some obvious pitfalls to be avoided.

First, serious discipling has all too often become legalistic and authoritarian. Rules and regulations covering a wide range of expected behaviour (not all spelt out in the Bible) have become the norm, often marked by a narrow pietism, an unhealthy separation from the world, and an intense spirituality that shows little of the spontaneous love and joy characterised by the New Testament church. All this can lead to a hard unbending Christianity which seems far from the gracious gentleness of Jesus Christ. I have seen many Christians who once were relaxed and radiant, beginning to look cowed, anxious and fearful again, because they have come into the bondage of strict human shepherding. The pressures may not be structural, but emotional. Through the genuine and detailed care of mature Christian couples, those under their pastoral care, especially single girls, can feel strong emotional ties that are not easy to break. Similar pressures can also exist within a single sex discipleship. Strong loyalties are established, so that any deviation can seem like rebellion. If you go along completely with those over you, all is well; but if you choose differently, however slightly, there is either a major confrontation until your conform once again, or else you are out on a limb. The emotional pulls to conform are therefore immensely strong; only as you do so will the fragile security of your submissive relationships with other Christians remain intact.

Similar dangers were known in New Testament times. Paul once urged the Colossian Christians not to 'submit to regulations, "Do not handle, Do not taste, Do not touch" . . . according to human precepts and doctrines.' Such self-discipline often appeals to deeply committed Christians, but invariably it leads either to self-righteousness or to a false sense of guilt. Paul commented that such 'rigor of devotion' may seem godly and wise, 'but in actual practice they do honour not to God, but to man's own pride.'[9] The Galatian Christians, too, had fallen into a similar trap. Paul wrote, 'O foolish Galatians! Who has bewitched you?' Some of them had followed Peter who 'drew back and separated himself, fearing the circumcision party'. Due to pressure of the Judaizers, Peter and others with him had slipped from their Christian liberty into religious legalism. Paul urged them, 'For freedom Christ has set us free, stand fast therefore, and do not submit again to a yoke of slavery.'[10] Legalism and licence – those are the two main dangers which rob us of our true freedom in Christ. Yes, there must be leadership and discipline within every church; but when this effectively quenches the Spirit in people's lives, and causes Christians to draw back from one another, becoming cautious, critical and fearful, Paul's teaching is highly relevant.

Second, strong shepherding can develop into a new priesthood. In some cases, every disciple submits virtually every area of his or her life to a shepherd, and every shepherd (with not more than twelve disciples under him) submits his life to another shepherd – all in a pyramid structure. Submission is often practised more widely than within the fellowship of a local church. For example, the leaders of one church might submit their lives to the leaders of another church, which could be many miles away; and they in turn might submit to international leaders in another country altogether. Such submission can involve tithing to a shepherd, detailed accountability to that shepherd, and obediently accepting guidance from that shepherd on matters concerning marriage, family, housing, work, finance, lifestyle and so forth.

The 'new priesthood' of such a system is now clear. How can I hear the voice of God? I must listen to my shepherd. How can I know the will of God for my life? I must ask my shepherd. What is the right interpretation of this passage of scripture? My shepherd will teach me. One woman, trying to explain the blessings of all this to me, said, 'It is such a relief not to have the responsibility for making decisions yourself.' That, however, is the point of danger. When shepherding assumes detailed control over the lives of others, there will be a serious loss in personal responsibility, maturity and even significance. Since

almost every Christian finds guidance difficult, it may initially
be a relief to let someone else make the decisions instead. In the
long run, however, this will keep a disciple in an unhealthy
dependence on a human shepherd instead of a healthy dependence on the Great Shepherd. Pastors and teachers are part
of God's gift to the church to teach faithfully the biblical
principles involved in decision making, and no doubt to help us
think through complex issues more objectively; but we must
each give an account of ourselves to God. We are personally
responsible to him, and should not allow ourselves to be in
situations where we can blame others for the mistakes we have
made in our lives. Responsibility and maturity go closely
together. Paul and the writer to the Hebrews lamented the
immaturity of those who should by that stage have been
teachers and leaders themselves; instead they still needed
others to nurse them and be responsible for them.[11]

Carl Wilson comments that in certain groups the leaders 'are
beginning to claim the right to speak for Christ in telling people
what to do, without having any clear scriptural authority for
what they say. Some . . . are claiming an authority that actually
puts them between Christ and the people. They tell them when
to marry, divorce, go to school, and the like . . . If the people of
the churches concede to clergy the right to make decisions of
life and doctrine apart from the clear teaching of Scripture, it
will inflict the deathblow to disciple building in the churches,
even as it did in the early church.'[12] The apostle Peter, for this
reason, urged the elders not to be domineering over the flock.[13]

In the same way, caution needs to be exercised over strong
prophetic utterances. These may be part of God's word for a
church, but when these prophecies are held with almost greater
authority than scripture itself, serious problems can arise. It is
worth noting that the New Testament envisages prophecy as a
gift of the Spirit through any member of the congregation for
'upbuilding and encouragement and consolation . . . You can
all prophesy one by one, so that all may learn and all be
encouraged.'[14] Here there is little hint of any strong or 'heavy'
prophecy which becomes God's agenda for the church. Sometimes God may want to speak strongly and clearly to a church; if
so, we should expect it to be confirmed from a number of quite
different sources.

Third, dominant shepherding inevitably becomes divisive. When a group of disciples lean too much on one leader, the natural consequence will be a competitive and carnal spirit, 'I belong to Paul, I belong to Apollos, or I belong to Cephas.' It was precisely those factions that were about to destroy the temple of the Spirit at Corinth, and Paul had to speak clearly as to what they were doing to God's church, God's building. It was not primarily a rebuke to the leaders; it was a warning to those who were exalting leaders above their God-given role. So Paul pointedly asks, 'What then is Apollos?' Not 'who', notice, but 'what'! 'What is Paul? Servants . . .' He went on to stress that the leaders were nothing in themselves; all the growth and life came entirely from God. If the factions at Corinth continued on the divisive way, grouping themselves around various leaders (or shepherds) they would destroy God's temple; and 'if any one destroys God's temple, God will destroy him.'[15] No man can damage God's work with impunity.

It is tragic, but not surprising, that unfortunate emphases on shepherding, discipling and submission have been the cause of sharp controversy within the charismatic renewal (in particular) in different parts of the world. In many instances, groups of varying sizes have separated themselves from churches which, for all their faults, God was undoubtedly blessing. Independent house churches have arisen which may have flourished, but have also aggravated the deep wounds within the body of Christ.

In 1976 a measure of reconciliation over this very issue was reached between prominent leaders in North America. The leaders of the Christian Growth Ministries, Ft. Lauderdale, Florida – associated strongly with the 'shepherding movement' – issued a statement which began: 'We realise that controversies and problems have arisen among Christians in various areas as a result of our teaching in relation to subjects such as submission, authority, discipling, shepherding. We deeply regret these problems and in so far as they are due to fault on our part, we ask forgiveness from our fellow believers whom we have offended.' The signatories were Don Basham, Ern Baxter, Bob Mumford, John Poole, Derek Prince, and Charles Simpson.[16]

Bob Mumford later expressed the situation like this: 'In the past, we taught people to act as they "felt led". The result in many places was chaos. In an effort to help people more accurately interpret the leading of the Holy Spirit we asked people to "check out" their guidance with a pastor or shepherd for a confirming word. The result in many cases was a bureaucratic system which squashed spontaneity and removed the joy of seeing God work . . . Without question, there have been situations where leaders have "played the Holy Spirit" to believers under their care, requiring a type of allegiance that only the Lord has the right to demand . . . As leaders we must become secure enough in our people to allow them to make mistakes in learning to hear the voice of the Holy Spirit . . .'[17]

It is one of the great needs for today to keep the necessity of discipling high on the church's list of priorities, while being fully aware of the dangers of excesses, and always seeking to maintain the unity of the Spirit in the bond of peace.

Disciples and leaders
One of the most encouraging truths about the disciples of Jesus is that they were very ordinary people, with all the human faults and failings that we see only too often in ourselves. It is part of the integrity of the Gospels that we see the disciples as ambitious and selfish, sometimes arguing amongst themselves as to who was the greatest. We see them weak in faith, anxious and fearful, constantly receiving gentle rebukes for their failure to trust in God. We find them impulsive and immature in their words and actions, self-confident when warned about temptation, lazy when urged to pray, impatient with the children, weary of the crowds, bewildered and depressed by the events leading to the crucifixion, in spite of repeated teaching by Jesus that this must happen. We notice how slow they were to learn, how quickly they forgot spiritual lessons taught in the most dramatic ways. In other words, they were just like most of us! Yet these were the men that Jesus chose to be disciples and trained to be leaders.

Many ministers have told me that they have no leaders within their congregation, and they see this as a serious hindrance to their work. Perhaps they look longingly at some large and thriving church which seems to be bursting with leaders. Naturally those churches seem to have a potential for growth which other less fortunate, leaderless churches do not. In the vast majority of cases I very much doubt if this is true. We have simply missed the way in which Jesus first made disciples and then trained them into leaders out of some very raw material. How he did it, and what we can learn for ourselves, we shall see later in this chapter. But notice first that the marks of a disciple and the marks of a leader are very nearly identical. True, a spiritual leader will have the God-given *charisma* of leadership as well; but most of the other characteristics will be the same, since every true leader must first learn to be led. Until he is a learner, he will never be a leader. In taking the task of making disciples seriously, we shall also be providing the church with the leaders that are so urgently needed.

Marks of a disciple

What are we aiming at, when we talk about making disciples? Let me mention a number of characteristics that I have observed over the years. I am not claiming that this list is complete, or that every disciple will display the full range of qualities; but at least we should know what we are hoping and praying to achieve. Let me put it in the form of questions that we need to ask; and although these questions are masculine in form, they refer to either male or female.

1. Is he willing to serve? This was a repeated lesson that Jesus had to teach his status-seeking disciples, especially when he humbled them dramatically by washing their feet. (John 13; cf. Mark 10:35–45)

2. Is he learning to listen? When Simon Peter was full of bright ideas on the Mount of Transfiguration, God told him to 'listen' to his Son. (Luke 9:35) When Martha was impatiently bustling around preparing a meal whilst Jesus was talking, she was gently rebuked for not being like Mary who was sitting quietly listening to the Master. (Luke 10:41f)

3. Is he willing to learn? When Jesus spoke about his coming sufferings and death, Peter blurted out, 'God forbid, Lord! This shall never happen to you.' The stinging reply was something that Peter never forgot. (Matthew 16:22f)

4. Is he willing to be corrected? How well does he receive honest criticism, when others speak the truth in love? (Matthew 18:15)

5. How well does he submit to those who are over him? (1 Thess. 5:12f; Hebrews 13:17) Is he willing to do this, even when he does not understand all the reasons why, or when he does not naturally enjoy what he is being asked to do?

6. Can he share his life with others, in open and honest fellowship? (1 John 1)

7. Is he learning humility? Can he rejoice with those who rejoice, and be genuinely glad when others are blessed in some way or other? (Phil. 2:3f)

8. Is he learning to examine his own life before criticising others? (Matthew 7:1–5)

9. Does he know his weaknesses? Is he learning to overcome them through the grace of God? (2 Cor. 12:9)

10. Is he a perfectionist? This will lead him into either self-righteousness, self-condemnation, self-pity, or a judgmental spirit. 'We all make many mistakes' (James 3:2; cf. 1 John 1:8–10). Is he learning to accept himself, as God accepts him in Christ – just as he is?

11. Is he able to forgive? (Matthew 18:21f)

12. Has he stickability? Or does he give up easily? How does he handle discouragements? (Ephesians 6:10ff; cf. 2 Cor. 4:7ff)

13. Is he to be trusted? (1 Cor. 4:2) Is he reliable? Will he get on with a task without constant nagging? Is he willing to trust others, even when they have disappointed him and let him down?

14. Does he mind his own affairs? Or is he always wanting to pry into the lives of others, becoming a busybody or even a gossip? (John 21:21f; 1 Tim. 5:13)

15. Does he do little things well? (Colossians 3:17)

16. How does he use his leisure? Does he see that all his time is a gift of God to be used wisely? (Ephesians 5:15–17)

17. Does he aim first and foremost to please God? Or does he seek the praise of others, or gratify his own desires? (John 12:43; 2 Cor. 5:9)

18. Is he quick to obey when God speaks to him? When fisherman Peter obeyed instantly the instructions of Jesus on the Sea of Galilee, however foolish those instructions may have seemed to him, there were astonishing results (Luke 5:4–9) This proved a vital lesson (which had to be learned more than once!) in the years ahead.

19. Has he faith in God, especially when there may be no outward signs to encourage his faith? (Luke 18:1–8; Mark 11:12ff)

20. Where is his security? Is he willing to trust ultimately in the love and faithfulness of God, or does he look for more temporal and material securities first and foremost? (Matthew 6:19–34) Is he willing to move as the Spirit leads him on, to make adjustments and changes, or does he resist change?

21. Has he a clear understanding of God's priorities for his life? (Acts 6:2–4)

Making disciples

The golden rule is to start small. Although Jesus spent some time with the crowds, and at least on one occasion sent out seventy disciples on a specific mission, it is clear that he spent most of his ministry on this earth with the small band of twelve. And of those twelve, he concentrated especially on three, James, Peter and John. Those three were with him in the sickroom of Jairus' daughter, on the Mount of Transfiguration, and in the Garden of Gethsemane. No doubt Jesus risked the jealousy of the other nine by giving certain privileges to those three; no doubt he caused envious questions to be asked by other followers when he spent so much time with the twelve. But it is impossible to disciple more than a small group at any given time if those disciples are to grow into true spiritual maturity. On those twelve depended the whole future of the Christian church. One failed completely and all the others were disappointments from time to time. But as Jesus persisted with them, loving them to the end, he was laying a firm foundation for the whole church of God.

Any wise leader will likewise concentrate his time with a small group of committed Christians, twelve probably being the maximum number for effective discipling. In fact, the fewer the better. Paul clearly spent much time with Timothy, Luke, Titus, Silvanus and a few others. He told Timothy to entrust what he had learnt from the apostle 'to faithful men who will be able to teach others also'.[18] Concentrating on a few at depth, so that they in turn will be able to do the same with others, is in the long run far more effective than the much more superficial teaching of a larger group. Here especially, 'small is beautiful' – and fruitful.

One vital point is to understand exactly who is the discipler in any group. The common and natural answer is the most mature and experienced leader present. A much healthier model, however, is to see Christ as the primary Discipler, so that we all seek to encourage one another, correct one another, and build one another up in love. Those with greater knowledge and experience will of course have more input than others; but we all genuinely need one another in order to grow up into Christ in every way. He is the one we are to listen to, learn from, and obey; and he may well speak to us through any member of the group. The Spirit distributes gifts as he wills, and all are for the common good.

When any Christian leader sees himself, or is seen by others, as the 'guru' of the group, problems are likely to follow. Dominant leadership will not help, but hinder spiritual growth and development. Also, every leader needs constant encouragement or even correction; the Holy Spirit might well use a much younger and less experienced member of the group to speak clearly to that leader. Remember that it is out of the mouth of babes that we find perfect praise! The writer to the Hebrews, although urging the Christians to remember their leaders, to obey them and to submit to them,[19] also knew the vital importance of mutual ministry to one another: 'Exhort one another every day . . . let us consider how to stir up one another to love and good works . . ., encouraging one another . . .'[20]

At present I work with a small team that travels with me everywhere, as we lead Christian missions or festivals in different parts of the world. It is nearly always the same team, and naturally we spend much time together, working closely as a team, and praying together. But even at home, in between these special engagements, we meet all together at least four times a week. We usually begin with a time of worship and praise. Then we share together what God has been saying to us or doing in our lives, nearly always relating this to verses or passages from the scriptures that we have been reading during the previous day.

These 'sharing times' are neither pooling our problems nor

just picking out nice devotional thoughts from the Bible. They are times of reality when we let down our masks, say what is going on in our thoughts or lives, and link this with what God may be teaching us in our present situation. For example, I might share that I have felt under pressure recently trying to write this book; but when reading Psalm 37 this morning I felt God was reminding me to 'take delight in the Lord' and to be more aware of his loving presence always with me. Another member of the team might wish to comment by adding what he or she also had been learning from the Lord recently when under pressure, or by gently 'speaking the truth in love' to me by saying that I had allowed my work to make me tense and irritable with the team during the last few days. Our one desire is to encourage each other to grow up into Christ in every way, and to do so in the atmosphere of God's unchanging love. Occasionally these times can be painful as we have to face up to where we really are with the Lord and with one another; they could lead to deep repentance, maybe even tears. Much more often we have great fun together, and nearly always these are times of immense mutual encouragement. We all know the dangers of any public and 'platform' ministry; we know too that the credibility of what we do on the stage or in the pulpit will depend entirely on the quality of everyday relationships, with God and with each other. It is in the sharing of our lives together that the life of Jesus will be more clearly manifest amongst us; and we have nothing of lasting value to offer others apart from Jesus.

The precise patterns of our team meetings vary, of course. On some days we try to give ourselves to intercession for some forthcoming festival or tour; on other days we study the Bible more carefully together, or tackle some theme, such as counselling, personal evangelism, or anything else that may be immediately relevant. Always these are learning times, but the learning may be relational or devotional, not merely cerebral.

Is this concentration of time as a very small group a matter of spiritual indulgence? Should we not make ourselves much more widely available to a larger number of needy people? I think not. Because so much of our ministry is in reaching out to numerous people with all their various needs, our time of mutual discipling is all the more important, and the spiritual

fruitfulness of it soon becomes apparent. Further, although the
work of this particular team may be specialised, the principle of
sharing, caring, praying and working in small groups is vital for
every church. If the present programme of any church makes
such discipling impossible, the sooner adjustments are made,
the better. A man may kill himself trying to attend to the needs
of his whole parish or congregation; but if he can give himself to
a small group of disciples, many or all of whom may later
become leaders, his congregation will eventually thank him that
he was not so immediately available to everyone during those
earlier years.

In many areas today there is a growing shortage of trained
clergy and ministers. George Martin, in *Today's Parish*, suggests
a plan for the impending dearth of priests in the Roman
Catholic Church: 'Perhaps pastors should imagine that they are
going to have three more years in their parish as pastor – and
that there will be no replacement for them when they leave. If
they acted as if this were going to happen, they would put the
highest priority on selecting, motivating, and training lay
leaders that could carry on as much as possible of the mission of
the parish after they left. The results of three sustained years of
such an approach would be quite significant. Even revolutionary.'[21]

Sharing lives
There is an ancient proverb which says:

> I hear, I forget
> I see, I remember
> I do, I understand

This is precisely the way in which Jesus trained his disciples.
Luke, writing to Theophilus about his Gospel, said, 'I have
dealt with all that Jesus began to *do* and *teach* . . .'[22] The doing
came before even the teaching. Jesus had no formal curriculum,
no planned course of instruction, no classroom syllabus.
Instead, he called his disciples to be *with him*. Jesus said to
them, 'You also are witnesses because you have been with me
from the beginning . . . You are those who have continued with
me in my trials . . . I have given you an example . . .'[23] They
watched him at work, they worked with him, they asked him

questions when they failed or did not understand, they went out in pairs to practise what they had learned, they came back to report, they asked more questions, they received further instructions. In this way they slowly but surely learnt about the kingdom of God. 'The apostles returned to Jesus, and told him all that they had done and taught' (note the order again).[24]

This is disciplining at its best, when deep personal relationships are formed within a small group of Christians who are living together, working together, sharing together. According to Moses Aberbach this was also the ideal rabbi-disciple pattern of education at the time of Jesus. The disciple would spend as much time with his teacher as possible, often living in the same house. 'Disciples were expected not only to study the law in all its ramifications, but also to acquaint themselves with a specific way of life, which could be done only through constant attendance upon a master . . . The rabbis taught us much by example as by precept. For this reason the disciple needed to take note of his master's daily conversation and habits, as well as his teaching.' Following a teacher meant not only following his teaching, but literally to walk behind him. Apparently assisting one's master at the bath house was so commonly associated with discipleship that the saying, 'I shall bring his clothes for him to the bath house' became proverbial for 'I shall become his disciple.' Yet there was nothing distant about this relationship. The rabbi would try to raise his disciple as his own son, caring for him, providing for him, encouraging him, correcting him, until the day came when the disciple would become a teacher himself.[25]

All this was strikingly similar to the pattern of New Testament discipleship. Although Jesus asked more of his disciples than any other rabbi dared to ask, and although he gave more by laying down his own life for them, the principles of teaching by example, learning by looking and doing, were all very much the same. Jesus was the Good Shepherd who cared for his sheep, provided for them, called them by name, knew them, kept them, loved them. The sheep in turn knew the voice of their shepherd and followed him.

Especially vivid was the warm and tender relationship that developed between the apostle Paul and Timothy, whom he called 'my true child in the faith', 'my son', 'my beloved child'.[26] For a time Paul took Timothy with him on his various missionary journeys, so that Timothy would learn simply by being with such an experienced Christian leader. Later Paul sent Timothy off on missions of his own, and then appointed him to look after the large and flourishing church at Ephesus. He wrote to Timothy two lengthy, pastoral letters, giving him many instructions about how to handle various issues that had arisen in that key church. He told him how to pastor older men, younger men and women. He gave him specific instructions for specific situations. He guided him about his personal health. He gently rebuked him for his timidity, and urged him to stir up the gift of the Holy Spirit within himself. In every firm, loving, thoughtful way he cared for Timothy as a loving father would care for his son. All the time, in keeping with the father-son relationship of Hebrew families, Paul was forming Timothy into the position of spiritual leadership that Paul had served for so long. Just as a Hebrew father trained his son to *take over* the running of the family business, so Christian discipling means laying down our lives for others, training them to take over the responsibilities we have accepted until now.

Certainly, this seemed to be Paul's usual pattern wherever he went. Writing to the Christians at Thessalonica, he said: 'We were gentle among you, like a nurse taking care of her children. So, being affectionately desirous of you, we were ready to share with you not only the gospel of God but also our own selves, because you had become very dear to us . . . You know how, like a father with his children, we exhorted each one of you and encouraged you and charged you to lead a life worthy of God . . .'[27] Paul was also thrilled with the way they were taking on responsibilities for themselves. 'The word of the Lord (has) sounded forth from you . . .'[28] As the disciples develop in spiritual maturity, so their opportunities for Christian ministry should correspondingly grow.

Most people blossom when given responsibilities. Unless leaders train others to take over the tasks that they have done, the expansion of any church will cease at a certain limit. 'True multiplication occurs when disciples are trained in evangelism and disciple building. No matter how dynamic the pastor, no matter how financially stable and well organised the church, expansion will not continue if people are not trained to minister.'[29] This is exactly the method of Jesus: 'As the Father has sent me, even so I send you.'[30] Steadily their responsibilities grew, and likewise their maturity developed. He sent them out on their own, standing back whilst they tried for themselves; then gently correcting them, instructing them still more, until the time came when he could leave them altogether, knowing that his Spirit within them would continue to be their helper and guide. 'Jesus seems to have given his men as much responsibility as they could reasonably assume. He sent them out on their own, allowing them to have a ministry without him. Thus, he was preparing them for the time when he would no longer be present. It is best not to do for a disciple what he can do for himself. He must be given an opportunity to act independently and responsibly.'[31]

All this means that disciples must be made or formed – not just informed, as the church has tended to for so long. Just as God 'has predestined us to be conformed to the image of his Son', so Paul was willing to be 'in travail until Christ be formed in you'.[32] Imparting information is not enough, however important this may be as part of the whole process. More than that, we must share our lives with one another to such a degree that God is able to share his life in us and through us, until he forms us into the pattern that he wants us to be, into the likeness of his own Son, and until he develops the gifts and ministries he has given us into full maturity. Ultimately God is concerned, not with academic and theological knowledge, but with life – his life within us. He wants us not just to know about Jesus, but to be like Jesus, filled with the Spirit of Jesus, bearing the fragrance of Jesus, controlled by the love of Jesus. Such a quality of life is caught, rather than taught; and however important it may be to 'devote ourselves to the apostles' teaching', as did those first Christians, it is even more important that the life of Jesus be manifest amongst us.

Teaching
It would be a profound mistake, of course, to put true spiritual life in opposition to good biblical teaching. The words of Jesus are the words of life, as his disciples clearly appreciated.[33] In the context of a common life, Jesus spent considerable time teaching his disciples. Take for example his sermon on the

Mount, or his discourse during the last supper, or his forty days
of teaching about the kingdom of God after his resurrection.
Paul and the other apostles also spent as much time as possible
preaching, teaching, instructing, exhorting, or writing letters.
As Paul told the Ephesian elders, 'I did not shrink from
declaring to you anything that was profitable, and teaching you
in public and from house to house . . . I did not shrink from
declaring to you the whole counsel of God . . .'[34] The New
Testament epistles are eloquent examples of the importance the
early church gave to Christian doctrine and its practical out-
working in the various churches. Look at the way in which Paul
urged Timothy to 'attend to the public reading of scripture, to
preaching, to teaching', to 'follow the pattern of the sound
words', to 'guard the truth', to 'preach the word, be urgent in
season and out of season, convince, rebuke, and exhort, be
unfailing in patience and in teaching', to become 'a workman
who has no need to be ashamed, rightly handling the word of
truth'.[35]

   In no way do I want to minimise the enormous value of good,
thorough biblical teaching at every level. The church's failure to
take preaching and teaching sufficiently seriously – the standard
of preaching in many churches is abysmally low – is one reason
for the general spiritual malaise that we see almost everywhere
today. At the same time, when the emphasis in many church
circles is on theological study, Bible courses, conferences,
seminars and classroom work, it is important to realise that the
training of New Testament disciples was largely along very
different lines. Paul for example, could be both strong and
encouraging with Timothy because of the excellent relationship
that had developed between them over the years. Timothy's life
and ministry had largely been formed by the Holy Spirit
working through Paul. It was real, alive and powerful. Paul was
simply urging him not to let his natural nervousness pull him
back in the face of pressure from within and persecutions from
without, but to go on to wage a good warfare for Jesus Christ.
Certainly teaching was and is of immense importance for
Christian maturity. But above all we must look for God's love
and life expressed through individual Christians and through
churches.

Marks of a leader

We have already seen that good discipleship is excellent preparation for good leadership. The charisma of leadership, however, is not given to every disciple, and there are certain qualities that we need to look for and develop, in order to produce the leaders that are needed for the church. Every natural ability comes from God and can be used in his service. The apostle Paul, for example, used his considerable intellectual gifts to the full, and the theological wealth in his epistles has stretched the minds of the most able commentators ever since. We need men and women today who can discern the significant trends in modern philosophy and psychology, politics and sociology, and then interpret these trends for the benefit of the whole church. Unless we understand what the world is saying and doing we cannot speak with the cutting-edge of a relevant and maybe prophetic word. We need Christians with academic skills to grapple with the exegesis of biblical passages, to engage in serious theological debate or religious dialogue, to be alert to issues within the church that may cause moral or doctrinal disarray, and to communicate the gospel to secular man using all available media.

At the same time, it is interesting to note that the biblical picture of the disciple or leader has no specific reference to academic qualifications. Paul and Luke had plenty; Peter, James and John, very few. Most of the mainline churches place far too great an emphasis on academic training, and far too little on spiritual renewal and life. The result is that church leadership today is not lacking in intellectual credibility – and in some situations that is necessary and good; but the overwhelming and desperate need of the church almost everywhere is for spiritual renewal. A. W. Tozer remarked that 'the only power God recognises in his church is the power of his Spirit; whereas the only power recognised today by the majority of evangelicals is the power of man. God does his work by the operation of the Spirit, while Christian leaders attempt to do theirs by the power of trained and devoted intellect. Bright personality has taken the place of the divine afflatus. Only what is done through the Eternal Spirit will abide eternally.' People are hungry for life, and churches are not able to share life that they do not possess.

It is also a mistake for churches to be on the look-out *only* for natural leaders – those who would be leaders in any walk of life. Such persons may certainly be potential leaders in the church, since *all* good gifts come from God. But someone with a natural flair for leadership does not necessarily make a good spiritual leader; in fact his 'natural' strength may well have to be broken by God until he comes to genuine and humble dependence upon God for resources that he does not possess on his own. We see a hint of this when Jesus said. 'You know that the rulers of the Gentiles lord it over them, and their great men exercise authority over them. It shall not be so among you; but whoever would be great among you must be your servant, and whoever would be first among you must be your slave.'[36]

Paul, too with all his intellectual ability, natural strength and spiritual experience, had to learn through a painful thorn in the flesh – some physical handicap? – that God's power is made perfect in weakness. He went on to say, 'I will all the more gladly boast of my weaknesses, that the power of Christ may rest upon me.'[37] Spiritual leaders, like disciples, have to be *made*; they are not born. And when Jesus, the master-trainer, took three full years to make his leaders (not entirely successfully, from a human point of view) we can hardly expect to do the job ourselves in a shorter time. Nor will a course of lectures on Christian leadership be any substitute for imitating the way in which Jesus shared his life with the twelve, guiding them, loving them, correcting them, encouraging them, forgiving them and praying for them.

What especially are we to work and pray for, in order to shape a disciple into a leader? Together with all the qualities mentioned earlier, there are several particular ones that we need to encourage.

First, a Christian leader must have *the spirit of service*. A ruler *tells* people what to do, but a leader *shows* people by his own example. Jesus first washed the feet of his disciples, and then said, 'I have given you an example, that you should do as I have done for you.'[38] Paul was able to write to the Philippians, 'What you have learned and received and heard and seen in me, do.'[39] He rejoiced that the Thessalonians 'became imitators of us and of the Lord';[40] and he urged Timothy to 'set the believers an example in speech and conduct, in love, in faith, in purity.'[41]

Moreover, a true leader will serve another Christian in a way that develops his full potential. As the disciple grows into maturity, the true leader will increasingly step back to allow the disciple to step forward. The coach of a football team is not the star performer; he does not score all the goals or points; he does not steal the limelight. In most football teams the coach is not well known to the public at all, compared with the players. His task is behind the scenes, enabling those whom he serves to come into their own. Likewise if the Christian is in any way ambitious to be the star himself, he disqualifies himself as a leader. 'A true and safe leader is likely to be the one who has no desire to lead, but is forced into a position of leadership by the inward pressure of the Holy Spirit and the press of the external situation . . . The true leader will have no desire to lord it over God's heritage, but will be humble, gentle, self-sacrificing and altogether as ready to follow as to lead, when the Spirit makes it clear that a wiser and more gifted man than himself has appeared.'[42] It is clear that John the elder had trouble with Diotrephes, 'who likes to put himself first'. Evidently he was a hopeless leader, since he had not learnt this first priority of service.[43]

Second, a leader must possess *spiritual authority*. The evidence of this has nothing to do with status, but with obedience to God, and being filled with his Spirit. The seven helpers in Acts 6 who were chosen by the congregation and appointed by the elders, were marked out as being 'of good repute, full of the Spirit and of wisdom.' There was no question as to their spiritual authority. Stephen, for example, was described as a man 'full of faith and of the Holy Spirit . . . full of grace and power.' He did 'great wonders and signs among the people', and spoke fearlessly when on trial for his life. We are told that 'his face was like the face of an angel.' The mark of God's presence was manifestly with him.

Bob Mumford once wrote: 'Real authority is never taken, it is given. No leader should ever take more authority in the life of one of his charges than he is given by that believer.'[44] The danger comes when the believer gives too much authority to the leader, either to avoid personal responsibility or because of the requirements of that particular fellowship. Exercising a healthy and balanced authority within a church is not easy; it comes only from walking constantly with Jesus, controlled by his Spirit, sensitive to his people, equipped with spiritual gifts, and becoming increasingly like Christ.

Such a leader is quick to take advantage of momentum. When the Spirit seems to be moving in a certain direction, the leader must be willing to hoist his sails and go with the wind of the Spirit. He therefore needs to make clear decisions. He may need time to wait upon God and to seek the counsel of other Christians. But a good leader will make firm, and on the whole quick decisions, even though sometimes he may humbly have to acknowledge that he was wrong. He must also have vision. He must learn to listen to the Lord, to know where he is going, to impart the vision to others, and to inspire them to go with him.

Although the spiritual authority of any leader is given to him by those he seeks to lead, ultimately it comes from God; and it will come to those who are supremely concerned to 'obey God rather than men'.[45] The perfect model, of course, is Jesus himself. When Jesus walked this earth, he was Son of man as well as Son of God, and he showed us by his own example a life of absolute obedience. In John's Gospel we see this especially clearly. 'I can do nothing on my own authority' (5:30); 'I have come down from heaven, not to do my own will, but the will of him who sent me' (6:38); 'I have not spoken on my own authority; the Father who sent me has himself given me commandment what to say and what to speak.' (12:49) It was in his perfect submission that Jesus found his spiritual authority and power. That is why Jesus was so impressed with the faith of the centurion who came to him about his sick slave. As the soldier explained, 'I am a man *set under authority*, with soldiers under me: and I say to one "Go", and he goes; and to another "Come", and he comes; and to my slave "Do this", and he does it.' It is when we ourselves are willing to be 'set under authority' that we shall find we have spiritual authority over others.[46] God gives his Spirit to those who obey him, and our obedience to him might well be tested by our obedience to those whom he has set over us. Significantly, it is an immediate consequence of what it means to be filled with the Spirit that we should 'be subject to one another out of reverence to Christ',[47] especially to those who are over us in the Lord. 'Obey your leaders and submit to them; for they are keeping watch over your souls, as men who will have to give account.'[48] Just as the leader must one day give an account of his leadership, so the disciple must one day give an account of his submission to leadership.

Within the Trinity, any danger of an imbalanced submission is, of course, safeguarded by the perfect bond of love. Love again is the vital controlling factor within a Christian fellowship. 'Indeed, outside the context of committed, loving relationships, authority and submission can be incomprehensible or frightening. But we know that we are not called to go it alone. Rather, we are called to community, to the development of meaningful relationships and the sharing of our lives.'[49] Within such a context, carefully ordered structures of relationships are vital for the health and harmony both of the church and of the individuals within the church. Only in this way will the kingdom of God be seen amongst us and advanced in the world.

In a helpful article called *Where Does Authority Come From?* Steve Clark, a co-ordinator of The Word of God community in Ann Arbor, Michigan, gives some of the scriptural protections against the abuse of authority.[50] He mentions four in particular. First, authority within a church or community should always come from a group, and never just from one individual. In New Testament days whenever a church was established, elders (always in the plural) were appointed for the oversight of that church. Second, clear qualifications were given so as to ensure, as far as humanly possible, that the right people were in authority. Paul gave full instructions about the sort of men who should be chosen as leaders in the church to Timothy and Titus, for example.[51] Third, Jesus made it clear that authority must be marked by humble service, as we have already stressed. Fourth, it is God who ultimately 'executes judgement, putting down one and lifting up another.'[52] He is the one who calls leaders into their position within the church, and it is the task of the church to recognise those whom God has called. When mistakes are made, or when a leader stumbles, we need to trust that God is well able to correct and discipline, since he is finally Lord of his church.

This brings us to the third mark of a leader: *the willingness to exercise discipline*, although always to do this 'in a spirit of gentleness'.[53] A younger Christian, with whom I was working closely at the time, once said, 'I'm sorry that I've been going through a difficult time for the last few weeks. I know I haven't made it easy for anyone. But I wish you had said something to me. I needed your correction, but it never came.' Had I sufficiently loved this man, I would have taken the necessary steps of gentle discipline before he came out with this cry for help. Sometimes our reluctance to correct another Christian stems from a profound awareness of failures in our lives. God, however, has given us the responsibility of admonishing one another,[54] and this does not spring from our own righteousness or spiritual superiority. It is a vital expression of our care for each other within the one body of Christ. So, whilst not hesitating to exercise this God-given responsibility, we must do so only in humility. 'Look to yourself, lest you too be tempted.' Jesus taught us never to criticise or judge, otherwise we ourselves would be judged. If we see a speck in a brother's eye, we must first check to see if there is a log in our own eye; perhaps that speck in our brother's eye is only a reflection of the beam in our own.[55]

Whenever giving correction, it is important to concentrate on issues that are of some weight, not on the trivial matters that may happen to irritate us. Constant correction is discouraging; too little correction leads to carelessness. Alway we need to be positive. Paul, in his letters to the churches, repeatedly sought to encourage his readers with the evidence of God's grace in their lives, even when later in the letter he had some strong things to say. We live in a world which is quick to condemn and slow to encourage; so it is especially important that we speak positively about what is good. Correction should also be accompanied by teaching: what went wrong, and why? How can it be put right the next time? Even if the lesson has been taught before, we must not fight shy of constant repetition; the apostles knew the value of this, as did their Master.

The leader needs also to give clear warnings: about false teaching and teachers, about temptations and trials, about the activities of the evil one. 'Warn every man and teach every man' was Paul's constant concern.[56] Prevention is better than correction and the good church leaders will not be ignorant of Satan's devices.

The pattern of discipline within any church has been given

clearly to us by Jesus in Matthew 18:15-20. Discipline within the leadership itself will also follow the same guidelines; but Paul gives an important principle to Timothy which, if acted upon today, would save much of the destructive gossip about Christian leaders that causes such devastation within the church. 'Never admit any charge against an elder except on the evidence of two or three witnesses.'[57] I am grateful to Stanley Jebb for helping me to see the significance of this verse. We should never listen to any negative criticism against any Christian, especially a Christian leader, unless the critic is willing to repeat the charge in the elder's presence, or even if necessary to be a witness in court. Then, there must be at least two or three witnesses. Even then, we only receive the charge; we do not believe it or act upon it until further investigation has been made. Slander or false accusation is one of the commonest works of the devil to divide Christians from one another. 'Let us then pursue what makes for peace and for mutual upbuilding.'[58]

Training leaders

All that has been said already about making disciples will be relevant for the training of leaders. However, one further structural development in the small group pattern for church growth is important to mention.

Howard Snyder once noted, 'Virtually every major movement of spiritual renewal in the Christian church has been accompanied by a return to the small group and the proliferation of such groups in private homes for Bible study, prayer, and discussion of the faith.' John Wesley saw the necessity of this, and it was a powerful factor in the revival which swept England, influencing not only the personal religion of countless individuals, but causing immense social changes as well. Wesley himself was influenced by the astonishing effectiveness of the Moravian movement, which was largely due to their constant attention to their relationships with one another based on small groups. To establish and maintain true Christian fellowship at depth, Count Zinzendorf organized numerous small cells (*banden*) consisting of 8-12 people. These contributed immensely to the spiritual health of the church, and also became the springboard of evangelism. In this century, the extraordinary growth of the church in South America is partly due to two main factors: first, the emphasis on the power and filling of the Holy Spirit; and second, to the development of the cell structure, with many thousands springing up and multiplying all the time.

However, the leadership of these groups and cells is all-important to healthy growth and expansion. In our church in York, we have found value in developing a 'support group' consisting of the leaders of a number of house groups in a given area. The leader of this support group will be an elder who has pastoral oversight of all the groups represented. In so far as this support group of leaders is able to be open to God and to each other, so that same openness is likely to happen in the groups they lead. Thus the reality of spiritual life in the support group is vital: worshipping, praying, sharing, studying, caring. If these and other ingredients are increasingly to be found, they are likely to be reproduced in the rest of the fellowship. In this way, there is the continuous training of leaders, comparable to the 'in-service training' so widely practised in the secular world.

Summary

Paul, when writing to the Colossians, declared that it was his aim to 'present every man mature in Christ'.[59] This is the ultimate goal in making disciples. Since God is the God of all life, his concern is that we should become whole people, not just religious people. Sometimes the Christian church gives the impression that it is only interested in religion. In fact, William Temple once called it the most materialistic of all religions since it affected every area of life: everything was to be redeemed for Christ. Maturity in Christ refers therefore to our relationships at home and at work, our leisure, our use of time and money, our involvement in society – in other words, our whole style of living.

We must never restrict discipleship to religious events, when we gather together for prayer, Bible study or evangelism. It is the sharing of our lives together. Making disciples is not easy. Paul wrote, 'For this I toil, striving with all the energy which he mightily inspires within me.' Always it will mean hard work, coupled with spiritual wisdom and discernment that are gifts of the Holy Spirit. That may be partly the reason for the failure of the church as a whole to take discipling seriously. Few, if any, of us feel qualified for the task. Paul, however, spoke of the mighty inspiration of the Spirit when it came to making others mature in Christ. We must trust the Spirit's resources as we seek to obey Christ's Great Commission.

Notes

1. Acts 10:34–43
2. Matthew 28:19
3. 1 Corinthians 11:19
4. 16 February, 1976
5. Carl Wilson, *With Christ in the School of Disciple Building*, Zondervan, 1976, p. 25
6. Acts 20:28
7. 1 Peter 5:2
8. John 21:15–17
9. Colossians 2:20–23
10. Galatians 3:1; 2:12; 5:1
11. 1 Corinthians 3:1–4; Hebrews 5:11–14
12. Op. cit., p. 24
13. 1 Peter 5:3
14. 1 Corinthians 14:3, 31
15. 1 Corinthians 3:5–17
16. Quoted by Michael Harper in *This is the Day*, Hodder & Stoughton, 1979, p. 156
17. Quoted in *Fulness*, volume 24, 47 Copse Road, Cobham, Surrey, England
18. 2 Timothy 2:2
19. Hebrews 13:7, 17
20. Hebrews 3:13; 10:24f
21. Quoted in *Pastoral Renewal*, July 1978
22. Acts 1:1
23. John 15:27; Luke 22:25; John 13:15
24. Mark 6:30
25. Information from *Pastoral Renewal*, July 1978
26. 1 Tim. 1:2, 18
27. 1 Thessalonians 2:7f, 11f
28. 1 Thessalonians 1:8
29. Carl Wilson, op. cit., p. 101
30. John 20:21
31. Ibid., p. 209
32. Romans 8:29; Galatians 4:19
33. John 6:68
34. Acts 20:20, 27
35. 1 Tim. 4:13; 2 Tim. 1:13f; 4:2; 2:15

36. Matthew 20:25–27
37. 2 Corinthians 12:9
38. John 13:15
39. Philippians 4:9
40. 1 Thessalonians 1:6
41. 1 Tim. 4:12
42. A. W. Tozer ref. not known
43. 3 John 9f
44. Op. cit., p. 18
45. Acts 5:29
46. Luke 7:1–10
47. Ephesians 5:18, 21
48. Hebrews 13:17
49. Bob Mumford, *New Covenant*, January 1977
50. *New Covenant*, January 1977
51. 1 Timothy 3:2–13; Titus 1:5–9
52. Psalm 75:7
53. Galatians 6:1
54. Colossians 3:16
55. Matthew 7:1–5
56. Colossians 1:28
57. 1 Timothy 5:19
58. Romans 14:19
59. Colossians 1:28

CHAPTER FIVE

Life in the Spirit

For about sixteen years I have suffered from asthma. Fellow-sufferers will know what a crippling condition this can be. When you are gasping for breath you are literally fighting for life. You cannot talk, walk, work or do anything.

The church in many parts of the world today is in a chronic asthmatic condition. A century ago, Edwin Hatch wrote the hymn:

> Breathe on me, Breath of God,
> Fill me with life anew;
> That I may love what Thou dost love
> And do what Thou wouldst do.

That is a prayer we need to pray with all our heart today: that the breath of God's Spirit might bring new life to the whole church and to every Christian.

Alexander Solzhenitsyn has said that he sees Christianity as the only living spiritual force capable of undertaking the spiritual healing of Russia – or of any nation for that matter. Moreover, the world situation is now so serious that he believes that spiritual revival may be essential for our physical survival. The mood of our materialistic affluent society is that of apathy, cynicism, frustration, alienation and increasing hopelessness. In our spiritually bankrupt generation, people are looking not for religion but for reality. As an alternative to knowing God in convincing personal experience, few people want to recite a meaningless creed in a dreary service. Unless God is manifestly in our midst, the world has no time for the church. Unless we become the living, loving, caring body of Christ on earth, why should anyone believe in the Saviour?

The call of Jesus to his disciples was absolute: they had to deny themselves, take up their cross and follow him – no turning back. His commitment to them was also absolute. He gave his life for them on the cross; and he promised to give them his Spirit of life in their hearts. Without either of these supreme gifts of his grace, their discipleship would have been hopeless and disastrous. Instead they became the greatest spiritual revolution the world has ever seen. When the Spirit came upon them at Pentecost, nothing could stop them. Despite threats, imprisonments, beatings and killings, their enraged opponents had to acknowledge that these timid, ordinary men and women had turned the world upside down. It was a stupendous missionary achievement which probably has never been paralleled in the history of the Christian church. Devoid of human resources, they were totally dependent on the power of the Spirit of God. Today, the church has numerous resources: buildings, investments, treasures, theological colleges, libraries, films, cassettes – the list is impressive and could go on. Much less impressive is the evidence of the Spirit's power today, despite the need for this being much greater than ever.

In the closing hours of his ministry on earth, Jesus several times spoke of the coming of the Holy Spirit. He called him *another Counsellor*, who would be with the disciples for ever. All that Jesus had been to them during those three short years, the Spirit would be to them always and everywhere. He would guide and teach, encourage and rebuke, strengthen and empower. He would be the *Spirit of truth*, not received or understood by the world, but for ever dwelling in all those who followed Jesus. He would teach them all things, and bring to their remembrance all that he had said to them.[1] In particular there are four main aspects of the Spirit's work that are important for us to know and experience: spiritual birth, spiritual growth, spiritual gifts and spiritual power.

Spiritual birth

The wife of an Anglican clergyman wrote to me one day in these words: 'You prayed that the Holy Spirit would make my Christian life new, and he did just that . . . I was filled with new life and joy, and I saw praise and love on every page in my Bible. Now I did not know *about* Jesus; I knew him!'

During this imparting of new spiritual life, there are several stages where the sovereignty of the Holy Spirit is the key. No man can do this work for him. First, he shows us our need. 'When he comes,' said Jesus, 'he will convince the world concerning sin and righteousness and judgement.'[2] Over the past few years I have had the privilege and joy of seeing a number of terrorists and long-term prisoners come to a living faith in Christ. In their letters to me they have almost all used exactly the same words in describing their experience: 'for the first time I *feel free.*' No one can escape the relentless pain of a guilty conscience. Most of us try to hide sin by the cover-up of activity.

Our conscience, however, is that God-given faculty within us that is constantly vulnerable to the Holy Spirit's action. Suddenly and unexpectedly we may feel guilty for something we have done, or not done, in the past. 'Nothing is more characteristic of the human sense of guilt than its indelibility, its power of asserting itself with unabated poignancy in spite of all lapse of time and all changes in the self and its environment . . . The past is not dead; it can never, in this life, be buried and done with.'[3] That is why the apostle Paul refused 'to tamper with God's word, but by open statement of the truth' he aimed clearly at 'every man's conscience in the sight of God'.[4] He knew well, from his own humbling experience, how the Spirit of God could make the word of God like a two-edged sword piercing through all the barriers and defences in order to expose a guilty conscience. It is only through the awakened conscience that we shall be aware of any spiritual or moral need of God; and it is only when the Holy Spirit convinces us of this need, that we shall begin to call on God for his mercy and forgiveness.

Second, the Holy Spirit brings us new life. Since God is Spirit, we must be spiritually alive before we can know him. Naturally, through our sin, we are spiritually dead; we have separated ourselves from God by going our own way, not his. We are in the kingdom of darkness, or the kingdom of Satan. How can we come into the kingdom of God? How can we be born again, born spiritually? Jesus never really answered that question for puzzled Nicodemus, but he pressed home the point firmly: 'That which is born of the flesh is flesh, and that which is born of the Spirit is spirit. Do not marvel that I said unto you, "You must be born anew."'[5] There is no substitute for this.

Without the new birth we cannot *see* the kingdom of God. Imagine you were visiting York, and I tried to show you the beauty of the stained glass in York Minster. From the outside, you cannot see it, however accurately and eloquently I might explain it to you. It is only when we go inside that you can see what I am talking about. Until we step into God's kingdom by being born again, we cannot see the spiritual truths – we shall be blind to them. 'I once . . . was blind, but now I see' is how John Newton expressed it in his famous hymn 'Amazing Grace'.

Nor without the new birth, can we *enter* the kingdom of God. Just as the air is all around me and I need to breathe it in, in order to live physically, so the Spirit of God is all around me, and I need to breathe him in (or receive him), in order to live spiritually. Malcolm Muggeridge, after a spiritual journey lasting for much of his life, discovered the reality of Christ, and shortly afterwards described the situation in these words: 'I come back to the Christian notion that man's efforts to make himself permanently happy are doomed to failure. He must indeed, as Christ said, be born again . . . As far as I am concerned, it is Christ or nothing.'[6]

Third, the Spirit assures us of our salvation. 'When we cry "Abba! Father!" it is the Spirit himself bearing witness with our spirit that we are children of God, and if children, then heirs, heirs of God and fellow heirs with Christ.'[7] Once we have this deep, inner assurance – variously called the 'witness of the Spirit' or the 'sealing of the Spirit'[8] – then we can be ready for anything through Christ who strengthens us. It explains why Paul was able to say, 'I consider that the sufferings of this present time are not worth comparing with the glory that is to be revealed to us', and why he was so absolutely convinced that 'nothing whatever could separate us from the love of God in Christ Jesus.'[9] Yet, through the low level of spiritual experience in much of the church, Christians today often lack assurance concerning their relationhip with God or their forgiveness of sins. The result is invariably a weak and uncertain faith that, instead of shaking the world, will easily be shaken by it.

In much evangelistic work I realise that some who 'come to Christ' are simply coming into assurance of their faith. They already have a true relationship with God; and in that sense I accept the accusation that I am often 'preaching to the converted'. But William Temple used to say that 'until a man is converted *and knows it*, he is not the slightest use to God.' Therefore whether an evangelistic event is leading to conversions, or only to assurance of conversion, is immaterial. Without assurance of the real thing, we have virtually nothing to offer to God in terms of fruitful service.

Spiritual growth

When Jesus spoke of the Holy Spirit being a Counsellor, he used a word meaning 'one called alongside to help' – a helper. In every area in the spiritual growth of any Christian or any church the Spirit's initiative is absolutely essential. Some of these areas have been examined elsewhere in this book. However, a quick glance at other aspects of the Spirit's work may be helpful.

1. *Christ-likeness*. The primary and sovereign work of the Spirit is to glorify Christ.[10] One way of doing this is by opening our blind spiritual eyes to see the glory of Christ ourselves, and then by working within every part of our lives that he might, with increasing measure, reveal Christ's glory through us to others: 'Now the Lord is the Spirit, and where the Spirit of the Lord is, there is freedom. And we all, with unveiled face, beholding the glory of the Lord, are being changed into his likeness from one degree of glory to another; for this comes from the Lord who is the Spirit.'[11] This transforming, restoring work begins the moment we commit our lives personally to Jesus and receive his Spirit into our hearts. God's image in us has been marred and sullied by sin. Having redeemed us through the death of his own Son, God sends his Spirit into our hearts to start on the repair-work. It is a delicate and lengthy operation, which depends in some measure on our willingness to co-operate. Our natural self is always pulling against the Spirit. 'For what our human nature wants is opposed to what the Spirit wants, and what the Spirit wants is opposed to what our human nature wants. These two are enemies, and this means that you cannot do what you want to do . . .'[12] In this passage, Paul goes on to describe what human nature does, and then contrasts it with the fruit of the Spirit – love, joy, peace, and so forth.

Because there is such confusion about spiritual growth, and

because many Christians fall into the bondage of trying hard to become what they think they ought to become, a simple diagram may help.

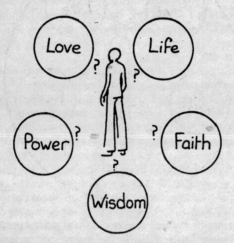

We know that we ought to be full of love, life, power, faith and wisdom; but for many it seems a hard, long and bewildering struggle. They see the situation like this – with these Christ-like qualities detached from us – the question seems to be, how can we get the love and life that we do not possess? What we need to realise is that all that we need is in Christ; and once we are truly 'in Christ' ourselves, we are complete in him. We already have in him all the love and life, all the power, faith and wisdom we need. We simply have to claim it, and begin to enjoy the unsearchable riches God has already given us in Christ. It is important to see how different this is. Instead of trying to get something that we do not possess, it is a question of letting the Spirit release from within us what we already have in Christ. Our task is to abide in him, and then trust his Spirit to work in and through us.

2. *Healing.* The healing ministry in the church has, until more recently, been largely neglected, or else left to the lunatic fringe. Biblically, however, Christ's command to the disciples to go and preach the gospel was nearly always linked with the

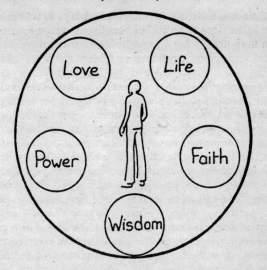

specific instruction to heal the sick. This is a vital part of God's salvation. Indeed, the English word 'salvation' is derived from the Latin *salvare*, 'to save' and *salus*, 'health' or 'help'. It means deliverance from danger or disease, and implies safety, health and prosperity. Although in new covenant times the word passed more from the physical to the moral and spiritual – but by no means entirely so – God is concerned with the 'wholeness' of every one of his children. Paul stressed that he worked with all the energy that God mightily inspired within him to 'present every man mature (*teleion*) in Christ'.[13] The word *teleios* means full-grown, whole, mature, perfect. That is God's plan: that we should be complete in Christ.

Through sin, we are naturally separated from God, and often from one another. We may also in some measure be alienated from ourselves – emotionally fractured, wounded and scarred, and so in need of inner healing. Until we are made more whole within ourselves, we shall be trapped by certain negative attitudes and reactions. It was the mark of Jesus that always, in every situation, he reacted perfectly in love. It was a holy love which God could blaze forth with righteous anger when confronted by hypocrisy or oppression; but even though he was

often sinned against, always he responded in love. God therefore seeks to work in us by his Spirit, so that we too have this
positive response of love, regardless of the situation we are in.
For this, some inner healing is necessary for every disciple of
Christ.

God's original plan for his creation is that every child born
into this world should enjoy the protective love of his parents
and family. As the child begins to develop, limited stress is
allowed into the child's experience as part of the developing
process, but harmful stresses are kept away by the protective
love of the family circle. Even Jesus had to learn obedience
through suffering, and therefore some pain is necessary for
healthy growth.[14]

Through the fall of man, however, that protective circle of
love is partially broken in every family. Thus every child
experiences some harmful stress that causes wounds – perhaps
deep wounds. Further, as the child itself is born with sinful
tendencies, it will also hurt and wound itself by negative
reaction to various situations. Thus we all grow up with
personalities that are in various ways, aggressive, defensive,
critical and moody. In other words, we do not act and react in a
Christ-like way towards one another. When the parental circle
of love is badly damaged through the breakdown of marriage
and family life, the scars will, of course, be more serious. For
example, the crime-rate amongst those from broken homes is
inevitably much higher than amongst those from loving and
united homes. Thus we have the problem, not only of 'battered
babies', but of emotionally battered children, teenagers and
adults.

As we grow up, we learn to protect ourselves from further
hurts by erecting our own defences or masks. So we keep our
distance from others; or we hide our real selves by an outward
show of self-confidence, shyness, jollity, aggression, or whatever. We become experts at cover-up; we do not like to see
ourselves as we really are, and we certainly do not want others
to know the truth. Also, these protective masks keep us from
being vulnerable. Since we refrain from opening our lives to
others, we protect ourselves from further hurts, which would
only aggravate the wounds that are hidden but still there.

Many Christian fellowships, therefore, are superficial in

relationships: we relate to one another over matters of doctrine or aspects of work, but often do not know one another and are frightened of being known. Our society teaches us not to admit our own weaknesses; and the church can make this worse when it encourages us to think we should always be victorious, radiant, loving, peaceful and strong! We may subsequently find ourselves relating to people who will both reinforce our defences ('not good to be introspective'), and refrain from probing too deeply into those inner areas that are still wounded. We join a Bible study or prayer group, or get involved in some Christian action; but still we do not face up to who we really are. We still need inner healing.

God's plan of salvation is clear. Through the death and resurrection of Christ we can be reconciled to God, and begin to know the healing of our relationship with him. Through the coming of his Spirit into our hearts, we receive a new birth and a new life – 'Christ in you, the hope of glory'.[15] As we allow Christ to be Lord of our lives, so his Spirit begins to change us into his image, from one degree of glory to another.[16] The fruit of the Spirit is thus increasingly manifest in our lives: love, joy, peace and so forth. However, it is through our new relationships in the family of God that the work of Christ and the operation of the Spirit can be applied more effectively within us. Our salvation, or wholeness, is complete in Christ, but we need to open our lives to God *and to one another* in order for his Spirit to heal our inner hurts and to renew us in God's love.

For this healing to be effective, several steps have to be taken. First, we must be willing to let those protective masks go. In fact, we may well need the help of other Christians to see what those masks are; we can be amazingly blind to our own defences! Also, it may be only in the security of accepting Christian love that we shall be willing to drop those masks, and so admit areas of failure, hurt and need. This is a humbling and often painful stage, and it may require sensitive love to melt those barriers down.

Second, we must openly confess to God our real selves, our deep desires, attitudes and reactions, humbly asking for his forgiveness and for the healing love of his Spirit. Since God is outside time, we can in prayer go back to those moments when we were hurt, and in our hearts release or forgive that person who has hurt us, or maybe confess some wrong done to another person, asking for God's help to put that thing right, if we are still able to do so. In other words, we are specifically asking for the Holy Spirit to heal those inner hurts that have been revealed to us as we let those masks fall.

Third, by the open sharing of our lives with one another in love, we work out and make real the healing of the Spirit. In a caring Christian fellowship we can speak the truth in love, be honest and real with one another, pray for each other, and so receive God's healing through the caring fellowship to which we all should belong. It is still God who heals, but his Spirit is able to move more freely through the lives of Christians who are genuinely open to one another in caring and unjudging love. 'Confess your sins to one another, and pray for one another, that you may be healed.'[17]

All three steps are vital for the wholeness that God has made possible through the gift of his Son and his Spirit. My own cultural background has been totally against that third step of openness and sharing, and I have also been very reluctant to let the masks fall! Yes, in private I could tell God everything, ask for his forgiveness, and pray for the transforming power of his Spirit. So far so good. But still my masks and defences were firmly in position. Gradually, through the gentle love and tenderness of other Christians, I allowed some of these defences to go. It was shattering to be known as I really am, and I felt sure that I would be both judged and rejected. But in an atmosphere of God's unshaken and compassionate love, shown through my brothers and sisters (who in turn needed all this just as much as I did!), I began to experience in greater depths than ever before God's deep inner healing of my whole personality. God is far from finished with me yet; but I am profoundly aware of much greater wholeness caused by the healing Spirit of Christ, as he works directly in my heart and also reaches me through other Christians, in so far as I keep my life open to them as well as to God.

Other forms of healing are also gifts of the Spirit and expressions of the love of God. Always we must bow to God's sovereignty in salvation, including healing, and usually God will work in us through medical means. Every good gift comes from above. But we must not limit God's action for today, or deny possibilities that our minds cannot understand. The same Spirit who worked many wonders and signs through Christ and the apostles is still available to us who believe. He longs, probably much more than we realise, to release us from physical sickness, from mental disorder and from Satanic bondage. And even if his immediate will seems not to bring physical healing, his Spirit within us can reveal God's strength and beauty in the midst of our felt weakness – a truth that is proved in the lives of countless Christians all over the world.

3. *Worship*. This is the first priority of every Christian. Worship is crucial to the first and great commandment. It should be our immediate desire when we come into God's presence. It should be our natural response when we first commit our lives to Christ. It is the first mark of the Holy Spirit in our hearts. Yet, if nothing is more important than worship, nothing is more impossible without the help of the Spirit of God. 'God is Spirit,' said Jesus, 'and only by the power of his Spirit can people worship him as he really is.'[18]

This is one reason why all the revivals in the history of the church have been accompanied by great singing and praise. The Spirit creates within us a desire to worship and to adore God; and, as we do so, his Spirit moves more freely amongst us. The church that is concerned about spiritual renewal or revival must be a church that takes seriously this foremost matter of worship. To begin with, our hearts may be cold and unresponsive. But if we offer to God a sacrifice of praise, the Spirit of God will begin to turn those cold hearts of stone into warm hearts of flesh.

In order for this to happen, we must take time to worship. Many forms of worship keep the congregation at a very cool level of communication with God. We stand up to sing one hymn, then sit down to pray; we stand up to sing again, then sit down to read; we stand up to sing once more, then sit for another reading; so it continues. The pattern may vary; but in this way it is hard to enter into any form of *intimate* worship, and that is what worship needs to become. By far the commonest word for worship (*proskuneo*), coming 66 times in the New Testament (the other six words come only once each), means 'I come towards to kiss'. This is the language of intimacy and love. Christianity is a love-affair with God and with his Son Jesus Christ. If I am to express my love with any feeling towards someone, I must give time to that person. So it is with God. A. W. Tozer once said that 'worship means "to feel in the heart". A person that merely goes through the form and does not feel anything is not worshipping . . . Worship also means "to express in some appropriate manner" what you feel.' With the much-needed help of the Spirit, we need to bring ourselves to that place where all that is within us will bless his holy name.[19]

The Spirit comes to give us 'access . . . to the Father'.[20] He comes to pour God's love into our hearts, for we can love him only in response to his love for us.[21] Always he takes the initiative. The Spirit comes to release us from self-consciousness, to deliver us from unhelpful inhibitions, and so make us more aware of the presence of the living God. The Spirit helps us to express our love in ways that delight our Father, honour his Son, and encourage his family: 'O magnify the Lord with me, and let us exalt his name together!'[22] It is by the power of the Spirit that we worship God and offer ourselves in his service. 'Send us out in the power of your Spirit to live and work to your praise and glory.'

4. *Generosity*. One remarkable sign of the Spirit's presence after Pentecost was the extraordinary generosity of the early church. They 'had all things in common; and they sold their possessions and goods and distributed them to all, as any had need . . . No one said that any of the things which he possessed was his own . . . There was not a needy person among them . . .'[23]

Why is the giving of most western churches abysmally small compared to this first-century church, or indeed to many Third World churches today? Proportionately, the most sacrificial giving today comes from areas where, like the Macedonian church in the New Testament days, they experience 'a severe test of affliction' and 'extreme poverty'.[24] In such circumstances, they are forced to trust God for everything; there is no alternative. But, through their genuine and active faith in Christ, the Spirit is able to perform miracles, not least the miracle of generosity. Paul speaks constantly about Christian giving as 'the grace of God' – it is always an expression of the gracious work of the Spirit of God in the lives of his people. For those of us in comparative affluence, we do not *have* to trust the

Spirit, at least for our material needs; there *is* an alternative. Consequently our faith is not so active, and the Spirit is less able to pour God's grace into our lives.

Writing about the early church, Clark Pinnock says, 'This concern for the needy, this willingness to sacrifice one's own possessions did not arise (it seldom does) from a merely human resolution to be less selfish and more ethical. It arose out of an encounter with the Spirit. Perhaps the reason that today we are afraid to risk our property, to dig into our savings, to choose less lucrative careers, is that we are not really yielded to God, not really living in the full unhindered presence of the Spirit. The love of God does not overflow in our hearts, and we fear that God is unable to take care of us.'[25]

Spiritual gifts

Jesus promised his disciples that they would do the same works that he did during his earthly ministry, and even 'greater works'.[26] He then went on to speak of the coming of the Holy Spirit. It was through the power and gifts of the Spirit that this promise was fulfilled.

Throughout the world during this century there has been a fresh discovery of some of the gifts of the Spirit that seemed lost to the church since the first few centuries. There have also been numerous spurious and counterfeit 'gifts', sometimes with tragic consequences – and this has made some Christian leaders cautious, if not critical and antagonistic. Although this is perfectly understandable, the answer to *misuse* is not *disuse* but *right use*. In order to discern whether certain manifestations are from the Holy Spirit or not, we need to look at the scriptural teaching concerning them.

To begin with, our attitudes must be positive and right, and the scriptures give us several cautionary words. First, *don't resist the Holy Spirit*. As Stephen proclaimed to the Jewish leaders, whenever God does something new there are those who will always resist what he is doing.[27] We must be very careful when we speak against some possible activity of the Holy Spirit, for, as Gamaliel once pointed out, 'you might even be found opposing God!'[28]

Second, *don't quench the Holy Spirit*. In the church at Thessalonica, it seems that some of the younger Christians were not willing to submit to the leaders of the church; Paul tells them to respect those who labour among them and to esteem them very highly in love. But some of the church leaders were critical at the enthusiasm of some of the younger members, and objected when they exercised certain spiritual gifts, especially prophecy. Paul therefore writes to the leaders, 'Do not quench the Spirit, do not despise prophesying, but test everything; hold fast what is good . . .'[29] The reason for splits in some church fellowships over spiritual gifts is usually that some people push them too hard, whilst others (often the leadership) oppose them too readily. A wiser approach is to encourage what is good, and gently correct what is wrong.

Third, *don't fear the Holy Spirit*. One woman said anxiously to her minister, 'I hope that nothing supernatural will happen in our church!' The trouble is that, through fear, it may not! Some are frightened of the dangers involved when the Holy Spirit is allowed full control. In our fears, we tend to box God up in the narrow limits of our own understanding. We tell him what we want, and what we don't want. We define the ways in which we are prepared for him to work – ways that are safe and respectable, that will not disturb or confuse, ways that we can easily grasp and keep firmly within our control. But God's ways are not our ways, and his thoughts are not our thoughts. Sometimes the Spirit is a most uncomfortable Comforter! Often he cuts right across our preconceived patterns of thought. Cardinal Suenens has said, 'The Spirit of God can breathe through what is predicted at a human level with a sunshine of surprises.' Never be afraid of the Spirit's renewing power. God is the Giver of all good gifts. Moreover he gives, not a spirit of fear, but a spirit of power, love and a sound mind.[30]

Fourth, *don't grieve the Holy Spirit*. Sometimes there can be much anger, bitterness and resentment arising over spiritual gifts – not to mention the dangers of pride or jealousy. When the Holy Spirit comes to unite us in Christ and to fill our hearts with God's love, it is tragic if we allow negative attitudes towards one another to dominate our thoughts. 'It is better to be loving than to be right.' Unless we keep our relationships harmonious, we grieve the Spirit of God, no matter how 'right' we may happen to be.[31]

Fifth, *don't be ignorant of the Holy Spirit*, particularly when it comes to his gifts.[32] The fulfilment of the prophecy of Joel at Pentecost referred specifically to the bestowing of gifts upon all who called on the name of the Lord. In particular, gifts of revelation are mentioned, to help us understand the will of God. For example, it was through prophecy that the first great missionary journey of the church was launched, and the gifts as a whole are given to edify the church for service in the world.

What, then, are these gifts? It may be helpful to focus on four main words in 1 Corinthians 12:4–7.

1. *Gifts.* Paul speaks of 'varieties of gifts'. The word 'varieties' comes three times in verses 4–6, and certainly there is a rich and wide variety. There are nine gifts mentioned in verses 8–10, three more in verse 28; and there are further lists in Romans 12, Ephesians 4 and 1 Peter 4. And there is nothing to suggest that these lists are meant to be complete; they are simply examples of what is meant by spiritual gifts. Moreover, in the New Testament, there is no sharp distinction between 'natural' and 'supernatural'. All good gifts are from God, even if some – miracles, for example – more obviously demonstrate the unusual action of God in his world. The word *charisma* means a gift of God's love; and Paul refers to many such gifts, including forgiveness, eternal life, fellowship, leadership, marriage and celibacy.

We must therefore never despise any of God's gifts or treat them as unimportant. I have heard some Christians speak scornfully of the gift of tongues, for example. But if, in love, you gave me a gift and I scornfully refused it, you would be hurt. All God's gifts are good and beautiful, even 'the least'.

Further, since these gifts come entirely from God, we must depend upon his Spirit for the right exercise of them before they become true spiritual gifts for the benefit of the church. We may naturally possess the gift of music, administration or hospitality. Such gifts can either be expressions of God's love, or opportunities for self-display. If I see the gift as 'mine' to be used for self-fulfilment, I rob others of God's intended blessing. But if I see the gift as 'his', praying that he will control it by his Spirit and use it to his glory, then it will become a true spiritual gift for the building up of the church.

2. *Service.* The word for service, *diakonia*, implies an eager readiness to serve. God will give us gifts, or use the talents he

has already given us, if we have a genuine desire to serve Christ and to strengthen his body, the church. God will never force his gifts on an unwilling servant.

It may be important here to stress the relationship between the gifts of the Spirit and the body of Christ, since Paul holds the two very strongly together in 1 Corinthians 12–14. One reason why the church has lost certain spiritual gifts may well be that it has so often failed to become, in any real sense, the body of Christ. It is only when we are much more deeply and lovingly committed to one another as members of the same body that God will entrust his gifts to us. They are varieties of service within the body of Christ.

This truth is also a valuable safeguard against an independent use of certain gifts. All should be weighed and tested within the community of God's people. For example, a man may think that he is called to preach and teach, but any such calling must first be tested and proved within the church of which he is a member. The recognition of our gifts by the congregation, and especially by the leaders of that church, is an extremely important protection against the abuse of spiritual gifts. All the warning lights should flash if any person is not willing for his or her gifts to be tested.

However, once we see that these gifts are for 'service', we need to use them. If we do not, we deny one another these expressions of God's love. As Paul wrote, 'Having gifts that differ according to the grace given to us, let us use them.'[33]

3. *Working*. Spiritual gifts are ways in which God works in and through his church today. They are 'living movements of Christ's body', to quote James Dunn. Someone is healed or converted – God at work! A generous gift of money is given – God at work! A new atmosphere of joy and love is experienced in a church – God at work!

It is vital that we should keep our hearts wide open to the fresh working of the Holy Spirit all the time, because God is always wanting to do a new thing amongst his people. He is the God of today. He speaks today, acts today, saves today. Although we may look back with thanksgiving at all that he has done in the past, we need to develop an expectant faith, believing that God wants to do something new and fresh in our midst today. In so far as we remain expectantly open to God, he will distribute his gifts according to his will, and we shall see God at work amongst us.

4. *Manifestation*. Spiritual gifts are given to manifest, or to make visible, the invisible God. We may not be able to hear God very easily, but through prophecy or exposition of the scriptures, God may speak. We may not see God, but when we love one another God abides in us and reveals his presence to us. Therefore all true spiritual gifts should manifest God's spirit amongst us.

Further, such manifestation of the Spirit is continuously being given (*didotai* – present tense in the Greek) to each Christian, providing we are open to God and willing to serve, in the ways already described. Our gifts and ministries may change in the course of time, but every person is vitally important within the whole body. Those who seem to be 'weaker' are in fact 'indispensable'.[34] In his most helpful book *Fire in the Fireplace*, Charles Hummel writes: 'Suppose you are walking near a lake and hear a cry for help. As you turn toward the water you see that a child has fallen in, whereupon you run to the spot and pull the youngster out. It is obviously absurd to argue about which member of the body was most important to the rescue – ears, eyes, feet or hands – since each met a specific need. If any of them had not functioned at the right time the child would not have been saved.'[35] Every gift is vital within the body of Christ; each needs the other. It may often be through the combined use of several different gifts that a person is literally saved – rescued from the kingdom of Satan to the kingdom of God's Son.

When spiritual gifts are exercised in an atmosphere of God's love – Paul's great chapter on love comes sandwiched between these two major chapters about gifts – they are always 'for the common good'. This word in the Greek, *sumpheron*, means literally 'for the bringing together', 'for the healing, restoring, renewing, strengthening' of the body of Christ. Love controls the gifts. Love ensures that they are always used for edifying the body of Christ, never for self-display or for manipulation over others. Love protects the fellowship from the misuse of gifts. Love encourages what is good, and gently corrects what is not so good. Love is 'the more excellent way' of bringing spiritual gifts to one another. Love cares about the needs of others, so that spiritual gifts become genuine expressions of the love of Christ for members of his body. That is why we should make love our first and foremost aim *and* earnestly desire the spiritual gifts.[36]

Spiritual power

Cardinal Newman once said that the church is like an equestrian statue: the front legs are lifted up ready to leap forward, every muscle of the back legs is standing out and throbbing with life. As you look at the statue you expect it to spring forward at any moment. Unfortunately, when you come back twenty years later, it has not moved a fraction of an inch. Yet look at the early church twenty years after the outpouring of the Spirit; they had moved forward by astonishing leaps and bounds. There was one simple reason: the power of the Spirit was with them.

How can we know this inward power? The answer, said Jesus, is that we must ask our heavenly Father for it. 'If you then, who are evil, know how to give good gifts to your children, how much more will the heavenly Father give the Holy Spirit to those who ask him!'[37] However, there may be various reasons which prevent us from either asking or receiving the renewing power of God's Spirit.

Lack of personal commitment is one common reason. Jesus gave the promise of the Spirit to those who were already committed to him as disciples. They had left all to follow him. As Peter later said, 'God gives the Spirit to those who obey him.'[38] A woman wrote to me after a service in our church: 'On Sunday I yielded all my life to Jesus, problems and all, praised him for everything and told him I was happy to accept whatever he planned for me. I was suddenly filled with the Holy Spirit, and my life since then has been transformed.'

Another hindrance to the power of the Spirit is *unconfessed sin*. The third Person of the Trinity is the *Holy* Spirit – he will not fill a vessel that is unholy or unclean. We cannot make ourselves clean, but we can repent of every known sin, trusting in the blood of Jesus to cleanse us from all sin. It may be important to ask the Spirit to search every part of our life, in order to show us anything that is displeasing to God. It is only when we have done this, humbly and honestly, and only when we have dealt with every thing that he has revealed, that we can ask God to fill us with his Spirit.

The following word of prophecy was given during a time of prayer in our church: 'I have seen in your hearts that you long to be more devoted to me; yet at the same time you feel that you cannot, because there are things that weigh you down, parts of your life that you are ashamed of, things in the past you are trying to hide. Little children, come to me with these things. Let us look at them together . . . and then they will all be gone. You are like houses with rooms that are dark and dirty, and you are trying to hide the dirt. But I am coming to help you to clear up those rooms, for anything that comes to my light becomes light. I love you so much. Come to me and talk to me. Do not hide from me, but come to me . . .' God always loves us just as we are. It is when we come to him, confessing our sins, that he will wash them away and fill us once more with the light of his Spirit.

Complacency is another common problem which keeps us spiritually lifeless. Jesus sets the promise of the Spirit in the context of the story of a man who was disturbed at midnight by a friend banging on the door, asking for some food to give to a late-night visitor. Because the friend was so persistent, the man eventually got out of bed and gave him whatever he needed. Jesus often taught by contrast. If a grumpy man at midnight will give someone whatever he needs, how much more will your loving heavenly Father give you whatever you need, especially the power of his Spirit. But there has to be some evidence on our part, that we really want this, and that we long to use God's gifts to glorify Christ and to serve other people. Before we come to this point, God may have to strip us of spiritual pride or complacency.

Some years ago I was studying the Beatitudes in Matthew 5. Over a period of two or three months, God took me, in my own experience, through the first four Beatitudes. As his Spirit moved gently in my life, I began to see how spiritually poor I really was: alone, on my knees before God, I was bankrupt – in my heart I knew it, though I had often tried to cover it up with active Christian ministry. Then God caused me to mourn or weep for my spiritual poverty. I became genuinely concerned for my lack of love for Jesus, for my low level of faith, for my disobedience in various areas in my life. In this way, God made

me meek, or humble, before him. I saw myself at the foot of the
cross, silently weeping for my spiritual poverty. Then I became
very hungry and thirsty for righteousness. I longed for a life that
would truly glorify God and please him in every way. Pride and
complacency had been stripped away. It had been a painful and
humbling experience, but God was preparing me to be filled with
his Spirit. I came to see the wisdom in all that God was doing in
my life.

Lack of physical hunger is usually a sign of sickness – similarly
if we are not hungry for God, something is wrong with our
spiritual health and we need God to break that hard shell of
complacency with our hearts.

One of the most common hindrances is *unbelief*. We do not
believe that God will do anything new in our lives. We may have
asked him to do so – perhaps many times – but nothing seems to
have happened. Jesus therefore encourages our faith by saying,
'Ask, and it shall be given you; seek, and you will find; knock,
and it will be opened to you . . .' He goes on to repeat the same
words in another form. In this way he is saying to us, effectively
six times, 'It will happen, it will happen, it will happen . . .' As
soon as we take him at his word, we need to express our faith in
him by praising God that it is now already true. Feelings and
experiences vary considerably: they come in God's way at God's
time. It is always a mistake to wait for certain types of experience
that may have been known by someone else. The vital thing is to
trust God's promise, claim it for ourselves, start praising God
that it is now true, and let the fulfilment of that promise work out
in God's way and in God's time.

Fear also is frequently a problem. What am I letting myself in
for? What changes will there be? What will God do in my life?
Jesus knew that this would always be a natural human reaction
whenever God does something new in our lives, so he said,
'What father among you, if his son asks for a fish will instead of
a fish give him a serpent; or if he asks for an egg, will give him a
scorpion?' There is no sting-in-the-tail with God. He never
plays tricks on his children. And if we, who are evil, know
how to give good gifts to our children, 'how much more
will the heavenly father give the Holy Spirit to those who ask
him?'

It is important to stress that this is not a once-for-all

experience. Those who claim that they have been 'baptised' or 'filled' with the Holy Spirit could well be asked, 'Well, where is it?' The inward renewing of the Spirit may certainly bring about a release, a fresh experience of the love of God, or a leap in spiritual reality. Something may certainly happen, however we describe it or explain it. But the scriptural command is to go on being filled with the Spirit (Ephesians 5:18 – present imperative in the Greek). Every day we need to come to Jesus for fresh cleansing of our sins, and then fresh filling of the Holy Spirit. We read several times after Pentecost that the disciples were filled (again) with the Holy Spirit. There may also be times of special 'anointing' for some specific work.

Whatever the experiences may be, we should never be afraid of opening our hearts fully to the Spirit of God and his love. James K. Baxter puts it beautifully in these words: 'Can we say it more simply? Lovers have many ways of expressing their love, but especially two. One is the words, "I love you", the other is the kiss. God's word to me, reduced to essence, is "I love, but especially two. One is the word, "I love you", the kiss. And the baptism in the Holy Spirit? That's simply allowing myself to be kissed.'[39]

It was once said of John Wesley that he had 'a strangely warmed heart allied to a strangely cool head. The latter on its own will always find deeply convincing reasons for playing it safe, remaining open-ended, instituting a dialogue, exploring in depth, setting up a commission, running a pilot scheme, circulating a paper, doing some research – in fact anything rather than going out on to the streets of Jerusalem drunk with the Spirit, and showing others how.'[40] We need urgently to recapture the vision of living daringly for the Lord, throwing ourselves totally upon the power of his Spirit, without whom we are nothing. This is the greatest and most pressing need of the church today. Everything else we do is like trying to sail a boat when the tide is out, and the wind is still.

'The crisis of the church is not at its deepest level a crisis of authority or a crisis of dogmatic theology. It is a crisis of powerlessness in which our sole recourse is to call on the help and inward power of the Holy Spirit.'[41] Nothing less than that will save the church from senile decay, and the world itself from plunging headlong into self-destruction. God has never withdrawn his promise. He still gives the Holy Spirit to those who ask him. The next step is up to us.

Notes

1. John 14:26
2. John 16:8
3. A. E. Taylor, quoted in *The Mark of Cain* by Stuart B. Babbage, Paternoster Press, 1966, p. 73
4. 2 Corinthians 4:2
5. John 3:6f
6. From a sermon in a London church, preached on February 4 1968
7. Romans 8:16f
8. 2 Corinthians 1:22
9. Romans 8:18, 31–39
10. John 16:14
11. 2 Corinthians 3:17f
12. Galatians 5:17, Good News Bible
13. Colossians 1:28
14. Hebrews 5:8
15. Colossians 1:27
16. 2 Corinthians 3:18
17. James 5:16
18. John 4:24, Good News Bible
19. Psalm 103:1f
20. Ephesians 2:18
21. Romans 5:5; 1 John 4:19
22. Psalm 34:3
23. Acts 2:44f; 4:32, 34
24. 2 Corinthians 8:2
25. *Post American*, 1105 W. Lawrence, Chicago, Illinois 60630, USA
26. John 14:17
27. Acts 7:51
28. Acts 5:39
29. 1 Thessalonians 5:12–22
30. 2 Timothy 1:7
31. Ephesians 4:25–32
32. 1 Corinthians 12:1
33. Romans 12:6
34. 1 Corinthians 12:22
35. Published by Mowbrays, Oxford, p. 121f, 1978
36. 1 Corinthians 14:1
37. Luke 11:13
38. Acts 5:32
39. *Thoughts about the Holy Spirit*, p. 62
40. *The British Weekly*
41. James K. Baxter, op. cit., p. 6

CHAPTER SIX

Prayer

Jesus was alone with his disciples. He was deep in prayer, revealing an intimacy with his Father that was unknown to his disciples. They watched him at a distance, intrigued by his total concentration and restful communion with his Father in heaven. 'Lord,' they said, when he had finished and re-joined them, 'teach us to pray . . .'

A quick glance at the Gospel records will show that Jesus constantly taught, exhorted, encouraged and inspired his disciples to pray. Prayer was the breath that he breathed, the driving force of his life, the secret of his astonishing ministry. So it was with the apostles: 'I bow my knees before the Father . . . we have not ceased to pray for you . . . constantly mentioning you in our prayers . . .'[1]

Likewise, prayer has always been a primary mark of the saints of God in every generation of the church. George Whitefield, who retired punctually at 10 pm every night, rose equally promptly at 4 am in order to pray. John Wesley spent two hours daily in prayer, and commonly said that 'God does nothing but in answer to prayer.' Martin Luther commented, 'If I fail to spend two hours in prayer each morning, the devil gets the victory through the day. I have so much business I cannot get on without spending three hours daily in prayer.' The leaders of the Clapham Sect, such as William Wilberforce, who initiated enormous social reforms in England, habitually gave themselves to three hours of prayer each day. They organised Christians throughout the country to unite in special prayer before critical debates in Parliament. They knew, and persistently proved, the power of prayer. William Temple replied to his critics who regarded answered prayer no more than coincidences, 'When I pray coincidences happen; when I don't, they don't.'

With such examples of the heroes of faith, it is hard not to feel a crushing failure! I suspect that most of us are ashamed at the poverty of our prayer life. In western society in particular, we are consumed by activism and have lost the prayerful meditation of our eastern brethren. The prayer of those first disciples, then, is highly relevant for us; 'Lord, teach us to pray . . .'

Why did Jesus pray?

If Jesus was the Son of God, equal with his Father, why did he spend so much time in earnest prayer? Was it really necessary for him? The answer is twofold.

First, he was not only God; he was also man. And man, created in the image of God, is meant to live in complete and constant dependence upon his Creator. The essential nature of sin is independence: I live my own life my own way, doing my own thing. Consequently, God's image in me is sullied and scarred. If I want that image to be restored, I need to turn from my sins, trust Jesus as my Saviour, and live in total dependence upon God – a dependence marked by prayer. 'How much it matters to pray is the measure of what we are expecting from God,' wrote Thomas Smail. The chief end of man is to glorify God and to enjoy him for ever. But we cannot begin to enjoy God until we spend time with him.

Secondly, Jesus was also *the perfect man*. Unless he had remained blameless and sinless, he could never have become our sinbearer. Only as the spotless lamb of God could he take away the sin of the world. We are expressly told that he was in every way tempted as we are, yet without sin.[2] How did he win this constant battle against temptation? It was simply through continuous prayer. 'Pray,' he told his disciples, 'that you may not enter into temptation.'[3]

If Jesus found it absolutely essential to be constant in prayer, how much more should we. 'Prayer – secret, fervent, believing prayer – lies at the root of all personal godliness,' wrote William Carey. Prayer keeps us trusting God for everything, opens the way for the Holy Spirit to transform us into the image of Jesus, and enables God to touch the lives of others whom we meet.

Our approach

God knows that the natural self recoils from prayer. Our fallen nature seeks to hide from the presence of God. 'No one (naturally) seeks for God.'[4] It is precisely at this point that we urgently need the help of the Holy Spirit, and indeed he is given to assist us in prayer: 'The Spirit helps us in our weakness; for we do not know how to pray as we ought, but the Spirit himself intercedes for us with sighs too deep for words.'[5] When we do not know God's will, or when we stumble for the right words, the Holy Spirit is there to help us in our prayers. He knows the mind of God since he is the Spirit of God. He can therefore put within us the longings of God's heart, and interpret our own fumbling prayers so as to make them effective and powerful.

Similar to these 'sighs too deep for words', yet distinct from them, is 'speaking in tongues'. This is a valid form of communication from the human spirit to the Holy Spirit. It is not so much irrational as suprarational. The mind does not always have to articulate in grammatical sentences before there is meaningful communication between two people, especially when they love one another deeply. 'If I pray in a tongue, my spirit prays but my mind is unfruitful.'[6] Is that, then, meaningless prayer? Of course not! He who speaks in a tongue 'edifies himself', 'he utters mysteries in the Spirit', he speaks to God. God, who searches the hearts of men, knows the cries of our hearts, regardless of intelligible speech. But it must be 'in the Spirit'. The apostle Paul knew that the Christian is always engaged in a spiritual battle, not least when we turn to prayer. Here, especially, 'we are not contending against flesh and blood, but against principalities, against the powers . . .' Since these evil powers will do their utmost to make prayer difficult, dreary or impossible, we must 'pray at all times *in the Spirit*'.[7]

To begin with, we must learn *silence* – to be still, until we consciously know that God is God, and that he is with us at this moment, both as a loving Father and as a mighty God. We must train ourselves to listen to him, to be led by his Spirit in prayer, to be sensitive to his guidance, to understand his will, for 'if we ask anything according to his will he hears us.'[8] We should pray specifically that the Holy Spirit will inspire, guide and strengthen us in prayer.

Posture can often help in cultivating this inner silence.

Although varying the posture can be important – and we may pray equally effectively whilst standing, kneeling, walking, or lying down – it is generally found that sitting upright in a chair, both feet on the ground, the arms relaxed on the thighs, is a good posture for releasing muscular and nervous tension. It is then sometimes easier to receive the still, small voice of the Spirit as he draws us gently into a conscious awareness of the presence of God. A few deep breaths, deliberately relaxing any part of the body that may be tense, can all help before a profitable time of meditation and prayer.

Such stillness before God should lead naturally on to worship and adoration. Worship is the opening of my heart to the love of God, it is the coming of a child to his Father, it is drawing near to love and to adore. Passages of scripture, particularly the psalms, may encourage us to worship. So may hymns, songs or choruses. Examples of God's beauty in creation may also stir us into adoration. We should enjoy our freedom in prayer as a true son or daughter of our heavenly father. We can be natural, bold and joyfully confident as we pray. 'For you did not receive the spirit of slavery to fall back into fear, but you have received the spirit of sonship. When we cry "Abba! Father!" it is the Spirit himself bearing witness with our spirit that we are children of God, and if children, then heirs, heirs of God and fellow heirs with Christ.'[9] We have a 'new and living way' into God's presence, and may with confidence draw near to his throne of grace.

God therefore longs for us to enjoy the 'glorious liberty of the children of God.' We may express our worship in word, song, movement, dance, or languages given by the Holy Spirit. 'Bless the Lord, O my soul; and all that is within me, bless his holy name!'[10] The scriptures are full of exhortations to use everything we have in praise to the Lord: 'Let Israel be glad in his Maker, let the sons of Zion rejoice in their King! Let them praise his name with dancing, making melody to him with timbrel and lyre! . . . Clap your hands, all people! Shout to God with loud shouts of joy! . . . Sing praises to God, sing praises! Sing praises to our King, sing praises! . . . I will bless thee as long as I live; I will lift up my hands and call on thy name . . . I will sing with the spirit and I will sing with the mind also . . .'[11]

Thanksgiving, too, is another essential ingredient in prayer.

The practice of prayer becomes dull, if not meaningless, when we lose sight of the glory and greatness of God, or forget his countless benefits. As soon as we take anyone for granted, our relationship with that person begins to crumble. Expressing our appreciation for one another is a very important part of building relationships. 'To say that God wants our praise is to say that he wants us to have the glorious joy of loving him and living in intimate communion with him . . . Love grows and deepens only if it is expressed. Perhaps we have not grown in love and joy because we have failed to express our love and joy in praise. Love and praise call for each other.'[12]

Interestingly, in one place where Jesus burst into spontaneous thanksgiving to his Father, we read that he 'was filled with joy by the Holy Spirit'.[13] As we open our hearts to the Spirit, we shall begin to know the joy of God, or the love and compassion of God, or maybe his grief, when we pray. Prayer will simply be thinking God's thoughts after him, letting him use our bodies as a temple of his Spirit – a temple filled with praise or intercession. When, in obedience to God, we hoist our sails and begin to worship, give thanks and pray, whatever our feelings may be, we shall frequently find the wind of the Spirit filling those limp sails, inspiring us in our fellowship with God.

How should we pray?

When it comes to prayer, there are no experts. We are all children learning from our heavenly Father.

From the example and teaching of Jesus, however, there are a number of important characteristics of effective prayer.

1. *Humility*. There is only one way into the presence of God, and that is through the blood of Jesus. We cannot approach God's throne at all until we have confessed all known sin, and have found God's forgiveness and cleansing through the death of his own Son. Even then, we still need the help and inspiration of the Holy Spirit who gives us 'access to the Father'.[14] In other words, prayer is no more than our humble response to God's initiative. In his great love, he gave us his Son, and sent his Spirit into our hearts crying, 'Abba! Father!' Prayer means saying Yes to God. It means submitting our lives to his will, bowing to his sovereignty, discovering and enjoying the Father's love.

If we believe that God's way is perfect and that in everything he works for good with those who love him, we shall not conceive of prayer as trying to twist God's stern arm, attempting to persuade a reluctant God to do what he does not want to do. Apart from the futility of that, it betrays an utterly false image of God. He is far more willing to bless than we are to pray. He longs that we and others should know his inexhaustible love. But we can frustrate God's will for our lives by rebelling against him, and by insisting on our way, not his. When Jesus told us to pray 'Thy will be done on earth as it is in heaven', he was not asking us to resign ourselves to some terrible fate! Such a thought is like the man in the parable of the talents who said to his lord, 'Master, I knew you to be a hard man'. . .[15] If we have any understanding that God is an infinitely gracious, gentle, tender, loving Father – strong, pure, holy, yes, but essentially loving – and if we have any concept of being his children, then to submit to his perfect will for our lives is the best and greatest thing we could ever do.

We need, then, humility and simplicity when we pray. When the disciples tried to protect Jesus from being troubled by little children, he rebuked them. 'Let the children come to me,' he said, 'and do not hinder them; for to such belongs the kingdom of God. Truly, I say to you, whoever does not receive the kingdom of God like a child shall not enter it.[16] The kingdom of God is full of children and the child-like. We are not to remain childish. In our thinking and living we are to become mature; but we are to stay as children, delighting in the Father's love.

> You must surrender yourself to me.
> You must realise that you are neither big enough nor
>   strong enough.
> You must let yourself be guided like a child.
> My little child.
> Come, give me your hand, and do not fear.
> If there is mud, I will carry you in my arms.
> But you must be very, very little,
> For the Father carries only little children.[17]

There are many times when we shall have to teach our heart to say, 'I do not know.' If I could understand all God's ways and

workings, he would be no bigger than my mind and not worth
believing in – he certainly would not be God. Sometimes in our
talking, or even in our prayers, we speak as though God were
on trial, having to justify his existence to us, having to explain
his actions. When the psalmist was baffled by the age-old
question of the prosperity of the wicked and the sufferings of
the righteous, he sought to work it all out in his mind. It was 'a
wearisome task', he complained, *until* he went into 'the
sanctuary (or presence) of God'. Then it was to him clear that
he had become bitter towards God. Therefore he went on,
humbly and wisely, to say:

> When my soul was embittered, when I was pricked in
>   heart,
> I was stupid and ignorant, I was like a beast toward
>   thee.
> Nevertheless I am continually with thee; thou dost hold
>   my right hand.
> Thou dost guide me with thy counsel, and afterward thou
>   wilt receive me to glory.
> Whom have I in heaven but thee? And there is nothing
>   upon earth that I desire besides thee . . .[18]

When we do not understand, but still submit ourselves to the
Father's will, we shall be profoundly aware of his love and know
his peace and strength flooding into our lives again.

2. *Reality.* The glorious fact about prayer is that we do not
have to pretend to God. He knows all about us anyway. He
simply wants us to share every part of our lives with him, and
that includes our fears and failings, our moods and emotions,
our thoughts and anxieties – everything, even those things of
which we are deeply ashamed. Read the psalms, and see the
total honesty of the psalmist: 'How long, O Lord? Wilt thou
forget me for ever? How long wilt thou hide thy face from me?
How long must I bear pain in my soul . . .?'[19] Constantly he
told God all about his doubts and difficulties, his anger and
despair, his confusion, pain and joy. He kept nothing back from
God. All masks were off. His prayer was real.

So it was with Jesus. We see no stoicism in the Garden of
Gethsemane: 'Father, if thou art willing, remove this cup from

me . . .' Three times he prayed the same prayer, with his sweat like great drops of blood falling on the ground. He shrank from the appalling ordeal of the cross, even though he submitted himself perfectly to his Father's will. Again, look at the transparent honesty of the apostle Paul. In his letters he wrote specifically about his own weaknesses no less than twenty-two times. He admitted that at Corinth he was 'nervous and shaking with fear'. At times he even despaired of life itself. His whole life, including his prayer life, had this refreshing touch of reality about it.

Do not be afraid of bringing your most secret thoughts and desires to God: all he looks for in us is honesty. As soon as we are open with him, he will work gently in our lives to mould us more into the likeness of Christ.

3. *Sympathy.* We may sometimes think that our failure in prayer is due to 'lack of faith'. Often that may be true. But perhaps more often we fail through lack of sympathy or compassion. Jesus was repeatedly 'moved with compassion' when he saw the enormous needs of sinful, suffering men and women. Such compassion naturally led to prayer and practical help. 'If we have God-given compassion and concern for others, our faith will grow for them far more as we pray. In fact, if we genuinely love people, we desire for them far more than it is within our power to give, and that will cause us to pray.'[20]

Compassion means 'suffering with' someone – trying to enter into their pains and problems: 'Remember those in prison, as though in prison with them.'[21] Anne Townsend has written, 'If I can imagine what it must be like to be the one for whom I am praying, then I find I can begin to intercede for that person. My imagination leads me on to want to be more deeply involved with him in his own life. This involvement leads to caring; caring to love; and love to intercession. I may never meet the one for whom I pray; but I may come to love him enough to offer him one of the most precious gifts one person can offer another – that of intercession, "love on its knees".'[22] Prayer is the greatest expression of love we may have to offer – a totally unselfish expression – as the individual who is blessed by God may seldom, if ever, know that we are praying for him.

Compassionate praying will also be positive praying. It is never helpful to pray about all the problems in detail. If we do,

at the end of our prayer we are conscious mainly of the
problems! Instead, we should focus our mind on the Lord,
perhaps thinking of those aspects of his nature, or particular
promises that he has given, which are relevant to those
problems: 'Lord, thank you that you supply our needs . . .,
thank you that your grace is always sufficient . . ., thank you
that your steadfast love never ceases . . ., thank you that you
are sovereign in all things . . .' Negative thoughts, filled as they
often are with fear, unbelief, anxiety, anger or bitterness, may
considerably hinder God's working in our lives. We need
therefore to 'bring every thought captive to obey Christ' when
we pray.[23] In Acts 4, when the disciples were commanded
threateningly not to teach any more about Christ, they came
together for prayer. They said nothing about the considerable
danger they were in, apart from 'Lord, look upon their threats',
but they rejoiced confidently in the Lord's sovereign control
over everything.

Positive prayer, sensitively used, is also the prayer of the
evangelist or healer. The recipient is encouraged to believe that
God is doing something *now* in answer to the prayer of faith.
Such prayer will also help us to believe, when we are praying
secretly on our own. Even the psalmist in depression came
through to the point where he could say, 'Hope in God; for I
shall again praise him, my help and my God.'[24] Many of the
prayers in the psalms struggle through to this point of faith,
when the psalmist looks forward expectantly to a time of
deliverance and blessing.

Compassionate praying will also have breadth in its dimen-
sion. We shall not want to stop with *our* circle of friends, our
church activities or our evangelistic programmes. We shall be
prayerfully concerned about social injustice and needs: un-
employment, poverty, racial discrimination, the plight of the
homeless and oppressed, the sick in mind or body, the broken-
hearted, the lonely, the helpless and hopeless – the list is never-
ending. It is not hard to see why the Clapham Sect, for
example, with their deep spirituality coupled with compassionate concern for people, had to spend three hours each day in
prayer. The trouble of much of the church today is that we have
largely polarised different emphases. Those engaged in social
action often have little time for prayer; those committed to

serious prayer are often detached from social needs. No wonder the church has largely lost its prophetic voice to the nation.

4. *Expectancy*. When we ask for something in prayer, we should start looking for the answer and expect God to work. When the early Christians gave themselves in prayer after the arrest of Simon Peter, they could not believe it when Peter came to them! They did not expect an answer to their prayers. God 'is able to do far more abundantly than all that we ask or think.'[25] At the same time he wants us to pray believing that he is going to answer our prayers.

The English word 'believe' has often a weak connotation. We believe in theory that something *can* happen, but we may not be at all sure that it will. The word 'believe', however, comes from two Saxon words: *be*, meaning 'to be' or 'to exist', and *liefan*, meaning 'as if it were done'. Thus, 'to believe' means 'to accept something as though it were already done, already true, already accomplished.' Jesus once said, 'Whatever you ask in prayer, believe that *you have received it*, and it will be yours.'[26]

The scriptures are full of illustrations of expectant faith. When the Virgin Mary was promised the gift of a son, she began to praise God that it was now true: 'The Lord has done great things for me.'[27] When Jesus was about to raise Lazarus from the dead, he 'lifted up his eyes and said, "Father, I thank thee that thou hast heard me . . ."'[28] When Paul described the nature of the faith that saved he quoted the example of Abraham: 'No distrust made him waver concerning the promise of God, but he grew strong in his faith as he gave glory to God, fully convinced that God was able to do what he had promised.'[29]

Knowing and claiming the promises of God in the scriptures can help us to pray with expectant faith. It is through these promises that we know the will of God, at least in general terms. And, 'if we ask anything according to his will he hears us,' wrote the apostle John.[30]

5. *Persistency*. There is possibly no area of our lives where we can be so careless and lazy as in the matter of prayer. We may neglect it altogether. We may give lip-service to it by trotting off a few familiar phrases, but our heart and mind may wander in many directions. Certainly God works in our lives by grace and, thankfully, not by what we deserve. He may therefore answer even our casual prayers; but normally he waits

until our whole being is concentrated on him. 'Bless the Lord, O my soul; and all that is within me, bless his holy name!'[31] 'These things I remember as I pour out my soul.'[32] 'I will give thanks to the Lord with my whole heart.'[33] The scriptures are full of examples of men and women who gave themselves unreservedly to the Lord in prayer.

In contrast, Jesus rebuked the Pharisees for honouring God only with their lips, when their hearts were far from him.[34]

Jesus also told his disciples that 'they ought always to pray and not lose heart.'[35] He underlined this principle with his stories of the importunate widow and the friend at midnight. God wants us to rely on him for everything (only then shall we enjoy his love), and thus in his wisdom he sometimes delays in answering our prayers to see how much we really want something for his praise and glory alone.

The first disciples knew the absolute importance of persistence in prayer. After the ascension of Jesus into heaven, when they knew they could not witness to him in their own strength, they all 'with one accord devoted themselves to prayer.'[36] Several times in Acts Luke uses this word 'devoted' in connexion with their prayer life; it means a refusal to give up or get discouraged; they determinedly stuck to it; they knew it was essential. When the church in Jerusalem was growing by leaps and bounds, the apostles checked on their priorities. They appointed others to attend to the increasing pastoral and administrative demands, 'but we will devote ourselves to prayer and to the ministry of the word.'[37] That is why God's Spirit was so free to move in power.

6. *Unity*. Jonathan Edwards used to say that every significant spiritual awakening in the church has always been preceded by a concert of unusual, united and persistent prayer. Every lessening of prayer has led, sooner or later, to a depressing sterility: the glory of the Lord rapidly departs. It is a lesson which the church has had to learn painfully time and again. The flesh rebels against prayer, and the devil will seize the opportunity for suggesting endless reasons for not praying. Only the Spirit of God can help us to 'keep alert with all perseverance'.[38]

It is partly for this reason that united prayer is strongly encouraged in the New Testament, as well as personal prayer. Jesus promised that he would be present in special power

whenever two or three of his disciples met for prayer.[39] The
early church were always praying together, 'devoting' themselves to prayer. In this way we encourage one another,
stimulate faith, identify ourselves as members of the body of
Christ, and bring spiritual gifts to build each other up in him.

Corporate prayer often needs good leadership by those who
are sensitive to the Spirit. It may be helpful to start with a time
of worship, consciously lifting our minds and hearts from
ourselves to the Lord. Too many prayers are earthbound. We
are to 'set our minds on things that are above', encouraging one
another to know that the Lord is with us. We need to raise the
level of corporate faith and expectancy. Short bursts of praise
and prayer from as many as possible are far better than the long
prayers of the 'professionals'. Such perorations might impress
some like-minded saints, but they will kill most prayer meetings. Encourage sensitivity both to the Spirit and to one
another. It helps when one theme at a time is 'prayed through',
rather than jumping randomly from one topic to another.
1 Corinthians 14:26 is the New Testament model for such
gatherings: everyone should have some contribution, each
bringing different gifts to glorify Christ and to strengthen his
body.

7. *Forgiveness*. This, too, is crucial for effective prayer. We
must first know God's forgiveness by confessing every known
sin to him, repenting of it, and asking for his cleansing. Here we
must distinguish between the Spirit's conviction and the devil's
nagging. The devil is the accuser of the brethren, who accuses
God's people day and night.[40] The symptoms of his nagging will
be a *general* sense of guilt, or a lack of peace, but no specific
reason for this. When the Holy Spirit convicts, however, we
shall nearly always be 95 per cent certain what it is all about. He
will place his finger on some particular area of our life which is
not pleasing to God. We must ask the Spirit to search our
hearts, and not allow the devil to rob us of God's peace.

We must also forgive one another. 'Whenever you stand
praying, forgive, if you have anything against anyone; so that
your Father also who is in heaven may forgive you your
trespasses.'[41] Repeatedly this note about forgiveness comes in
the teaching of Jesus. Nothing can so quickly and so easily spoil
our relationship with God and with one another than an

unforgiving spirit. Immediately it hinders prayer. As soon as I hold on to sin in my heart, the Lord will not listen.[42] Because he wants us to enjoy continuous fellowship with him, he withholds answering our prayers until we have repented of all known sin and come back to him with our whole heart. That is why Paul urged the Ephesian Christians not to let the sun go down on their anger. If they failed to forgive, they were cutting themselves off from the grace of God, forfeiting his protection, and thereby giving 'opportunity to the devil'.[43]

Jesus once promised: 'If two of you agree on earth about anything they ask, it will be done for them by my Father in heaven.'[44] The word 'agree' means literally to be 'in symphony with' or 'in harmony with'. It is much more than a common mental assent concerning the object of prayer. It is a promise for those whose lives are in love and harmony with one another; and, significantly, this promise is set in the context of the sorting out of relationships, even if this means forgiving someone 'seventy times seven'. It is only when we forgive others that God can forgive us – and it is only when God forgives us that we can pray at all.

When should we pray?
The example of Jesus is once again our perfect pattern. Although his whole life was one continual life of prayer, there were certain times and seasons of prayer which are particularly instructive for all true disciples.

1. *Every morning.* If we take the first chapter of Mark's Gospel as depicting a typical day in the ministry of Jesus, we see the force of verse 35: 'And in the morning, a great while before day, he rose and went into a lonely place, and there he prayed.' Although there may be a few people whose metabolism makes this virtually impossible, there is no doubt that the most important time of prayer for the vast majority of Christians is first thing in the morning, if possible before breakfast and the rest of the day starts. It helps us to tune in to God from the start, thus enabling us both to commit the entire day in prayer to God, and to help us turn to him much more readily at various times throughout the day. In any war, communications are vital. Every day begins with a careful check on these communications, so that throughout the day orders can be passed

on immediately and calls for help can be instantly heard. Without this, any army would be in total disarray. Exactly the same applies within the army of Jesus Christ.

Before we think that we are one of those whose metabolism makes all this impossible, however, let me say that I have personally never found it easy getting up in the morning to pray! Virtually every day is a real battle; but because I believe it to be a battle worth winning, I have taken active and practical steps to 'pommel my body and subdue it'! For many years I have used two alarms to wake me up, since I sometimes find that one on its own may fail to wake me. In the early days after my conversion, I used to have one alarm clock by my bed, then another cheap but very noisy alarm outside my door set to go off ten minutes after the first. Because the second alarm would wake the whole household (and make me thoroughly unpopular), I had some motivation to get out of bed as soon as the first alarm had sounded. This scheme never failed! In many ways, I am ashamed to have to resort to such methods when rising to pray means rising to enjoy the Great Lover; nevertheless I am grateful to those who helped me to see that this is an important daily battle to take seriously and win!

2. *Before making important decisions.* The entire future of the Christian church rested on the choice of those first disciples. Although Jesus probably knew in advance that one would betray him, another would deny him, and all would fail in many ways time and time again, it was crucial that he should get this choice right. Therefore 'he went out to the mountain to pray; and all night he continued in prayer to God. And when it was day, he called his disciples, and chose from them twelve, whom he named apostles.'[45] Humanly speaking, it was an amazing choice: uneducated fishermen, patriotic freedom-fighters, a traitor (tax-collector), a traitor-to-be, ambitious men, impulsive men, pessimistic men, fallible men. Jesus could hardly have chosen a more mixed bunch if he had tried. Yet these were the God-given disciples who were to be the leaders of the Christian church, when instructed in the faith, and equipped by the power of the Spirit. No wonder Jesus spent all night in prayer.

'If any of you lacks wisdom, let him ask God,' wrote James.[46] 'But let him ask in faith, with no doubting . . .' Humble and earnest prayer before God is essential if we are to know the wisdom which 'comes from above'. Major decisions will nearly always call for special times of prayer.

3. *When very busy.* In the midst of an enormously busy ministry, when 'great multitudes gathered to hear (Jesus) and to be healed of their infirmities', we read that 'he withdrew to the wilderness and prayed'.[47] Most Christian work is tiring and draining. On top of the usual physical and mental demands there rages a spiritual battle. When ministering to others, Jesus sometimes knew that power had gone out from him.[48] He felt sapped of his strength. He needed, therefore, constant renewing of body, mind and spirit. For this reason he would regularly escape from people, both to relax and to pray. Without this, he would soon have nothing to offer. He would literally have 'dried up'.

God once rebuked his people through the prophet Jeremiah in this way: 'My people have committed two evils: they have forsaken me, the fountain of living waters, and hewed out cisterns for themselves, broken cisterns, that can hold no water.'[49] Very easily that can be the tragic picture of the Christian worker or the Christian church. All the right words and actions may be there, but the vital life-giving water of the Holy Spirit has dried up. Only the Spirit gives life. We need his living presence continuously flowing through us if we are to meet the spiritual thirst in others. 'Beware of the barrenness of a busy life,' used to be a constant warning of Bishop Taylor Smith, and it is highly relevant in the feverish activism of our western society.

4. *When concerned about others.* 'Simon, Simon,' said Jesus tenderly on one occasion. 'Satan demanded to have you, that he might sift you like wheat, but I have prayed for you that your faith may not fail; and when you have turned again, strengthen your brethren.'[50] If we turned our concern for other Christians more readily into prayer, we should be far more effective as a church against all the forces of the kingdom of darkness. Instead, we so often criticize one another, or slander, attack, judge. A friend of mine said that the army of Christ must be the only army in the world where its soldiers constantly fight with one another. In this way, we are doing the devil's work for him. But when we turn criticism into prayer, we lift up the shield of faith on behalf of the one being attacked, we release the Holy

Spirit's power to encourage or convict (as the need may be), and we keep the love of God flowing between us when the devil is out to divide us.

5. *When tempted.* 'Pray,' said Jesus to his disciples when they were about to be severely tested, 'that you may not enter into temptation.'[51] They were very tired and sleepy, admittedly; but with three of them together they could have encouraged one another in prayer. Sadly they were soon overtaken by fear. When Jesus was arrested, they struck out in panic, and then fled for their lives. Out of fear Peter denied Jesus. Later they all huddled behind locked doors 'for fear of the Jews'.

In contrast, it was only through fasting and prayer that Jesus withstood the tempter's deceit in the wilderness, and later in the garden. We cannot resist temptation in our own strength. Many times I have had to say to God, 'Lord, I cannot do this thing by myself. I've tried, and failed. Please be my strength and shield in the midst of temptation.' Repeatedly I have found that, when there is this expressed dependence on him, God's grace is sufficient in time of need. We might prefer a fully automatic security system to protect us from the evil one, but God wants us willingly to abide in his love, where alone we are safe from the ravages of sin.

6. *When in pain.* 'Father, forgive them,' prayed Jesus as the fierce nails were driven through his hands and feet; 'they know not what they do.' Consciously turning our thoughts towards God, and especially praying for other people, can wonderfully relieve pain. During times of extreme discomfort, when seriously ill, I used to spend much of the night in active prayer. It was the only thing that kept me sane, and it made me profoundly aware of God's never-failing presence and love in the midst of what seemed like a prolonged nightmare. I have also seen the incredible spiritual beauty in the lives of those who, racked with constant pain, had every reason to become bitter and sour, but who deliberately gave themselves to sacrificial, unselfish prayer. No one in his right mind will ask for seasons of pain, but God can use them to transform us more into the likeness of Jesus, providing we accept prayerfully his sovereign will for our lives.

7. *At the moment of death.* 'Father, into thy hands I commit my spirit!' Death has been described as the old family servant

who opens the door to welcome the children home. Sometimes, of course, death takes people suddenly and by complete surprise. But if we know that we are being welcomed home, how good it is to enter that door talking with the one whom we are about to see face to face. If we cling too tightly to this present world, we may find that difficult. But if we hold loosely what we possess now, it makes sense to look forward eagerly to sharing the glory of God.

Ideally, of course, our whole life should become a life of prayer. When we wake, eat, walk, work, rest, chat or retire for the night, we should cultivate enjoying the Father's presence: rejoicing in him, praising him, thanking him, talking to him, listening to him, saying sorry, keeping silent. As we share our life with him, so we allow him to share his life with us.

To prevent laziness or carelessness, intercessory prayer cards or calendars may be helpful; but let them be servants, not masters. It is good, whatever system we may have, to learn to be spontaneous in prayer as well. I frequently pray for people as I meet them in a street or in a home; I usually pray before answering the telephone or going to the front door. When I remember to do this, my attitude to that person can be much more positive and sensitive as a result. If all of us, as Christian disciples, could seriously pray – however briefly – for all those we meet each day, the cumulative impact of the love of God on society could be staggering.

The power of praise

A cursory glance at the psalms will indicate that the prayers of the saints are shot through with praise and adoration. Even in times of pain, depression, loneliness or fear, the psalmist turns his mind to some aspect of God's faithfulness, mercy or justice for which to worship him. 'Great is the Lord and greatly to be praised' – not because we happen to feel great, but because he is eternally great, and therefore eternally to be praised. Moreover, whenever we honour God by giving him a sacrifice of praise, always he honours us.

It was often in response to praise that God's people experienced his presence in powerful and unmistakable ways. 'When the song was raised, with trumpets and cymbals and other musical instruments, in praise to the Lord . . ., the glory of the Lord filled the house of God.'[52] Of course, praise by itself will not automatically produce the required results. In 1 Chronicles 13, David was bringing the ark of God back to Jerusalem, but he and those with him had been careless about the precise instructions given for carrying the ark. Therefore, although 'David and all Israel were making merry before God with all their might, with songs and lyres and harps and tambourines and cymbals and trumpets', the anger of God broke out on Uzzah when he touched the ark, and he died there. Repeatedly God had to show his people, sometimes in dramatic and tragic ways, that he requires obedience, not the mere performance of religious duties; without that obedience, all our praise, however fervent, is vain worship and empty words.

Nevertheless, I have known numerous occasions when God's presence has been manifest through the worship and praise of his people. I was present at an international Anglican conference for spiritual renewal, held at Canterbury in July 1978. There were 350 leaders present from all over the world, including thirty bishops and a good number from the Third World. The final Communion Service, held in the Choir of Canterbury Cathedral, was profoundly moving. There was a magnificent spirit of praise, yet at the same time God warned us through the preached and prophetic word that there would be suffering, even martyrdom, for some of those present. At the time of the 'peace' we were encouraged to greet one another, and I turned to the person on my right. I discovered that he was an American tourist who was drawn into the Cathedral by the sound of singing and praise. I asked him what he thought of the service. 'I have never been anywhere that is so alive,' he replied. I gently enquired if he really knew the One who makes us alive, Jesus Christ, or was he not sure about it. He told me he was not at all sure; so we slipped round the back of the Choir, and as the praise started up again I had to shout the gospel to him. Suddenly he grabbed me by the wrists: 'Can we pray?' he asked. So I led him in a simple prayer by which he could give his life to Christ. I shouted it at him phrase by phrase, and he shouted it back. In that priceless way he became a true Christian, and a few minutes later received the tokens of God's forgiveness and acceptance in the bread and the wine. He even

met his own Bishop of Colorado immediately after the service!
God has broken into that young man's life in a marvellous way;
and it all began with the power of praise. His only hesitation
was that he hoped he was not one of those who might soon be
martyred!

We also see in the Bible God's victory experienced in answer
to praise. The classic example of this is in 2 Chronicles 20, when
Jehoshaphat and the people of Israel were faced with a
seemingly impossible battle. They gave themselves to humble
prayer and fasting, and God directed them through a word of
prophecy. They were to stand still and see the victory of the
Lord on their behalf. They worshipped God for this promise of
his help, and they sent the singers ahead of the army to praise
the Lord: 'Give thanks to the Lord, for his steadfast love
endures for ever.' Then we read these significant words: 'And
when they began to sing and praise, the Lord set an ambush
against the enemy' – and they enjoyed an astonishing victory.
Paul wrote, 'always and for everything' give thanks to God.[53]
Again, 'give thanks in all circumstances'.[54] It is by praise that
we declare our trust in the Lord who saves, lift up the shield of
faith to quench every fiery dart of the evil one, turn our
negatives into positives, and allow the Lord to demonstrate his
power.

Closely connected with this, praise also releases the Spirit of
God in our lives. After the ascension of Jesus, the disciples met
together constantly for prayer, and were, in particular, 'continually blessing God'.[55] It was in this context that the Spirit of
God was poured out upon them at Pentecost; and when he filled
their lives, they worshipped in languages given to them by the
Holy Spirit 'telling . . . the mighty works of God'. Indeed, they
continued day by day praising God; and with such a worshipping, sharing and loving fellowship, it is scarcely surprising
that 'the Lord added to their number day by day those who
were being saved'.[56] Moreover, when they met their first strong
and dangerous opposition, they immediately resorted to prayer
– which was almost entirely praise – and the result was that
'they were all filled with the Holy Spirit and spoke the word of
God with boldness.'[57]

Paul later urged the Ephesian Christians to be continuously
filled with the Spirit, 'addressing one another in psalms and

hymns and spiritual songs, singing and making melody to the Lord with all your heart . . .'[58] Praise often precedes a fresh move of the Spirit of God, and afterwards is the first sure sign of the Spirit's renewed presence. In the words of Pope Paul VI, 'The fresh breath of the Spirit has come to awaken latent energies within the Church, to stir up dormant charisms, and to infuse a sense of vitality and joy. It is this sense of vitality and joy which makes the Church youthful and relevant in every age, and prompts her to proclaim joyously her eternal message to each new epoch.'[59]

Praise also contributes greatly to the unity of all true Christians. When we fly in an aeroplane, the walls and hedges which seem big at ground level at once lose their significance; and when the Spirit of God lifts us through praise more consciously into the glory and beauty of God, the barriers at ground level become meaningless. When there were tensions within the church at Colossae, Paul urged them above everything to put on love 'which binds everything together in perfect harmony'. Three times in one paragraph he exhorted them to be thankful.[60] Here is one of the great secrets of maintaining the unity of the Spirit in the bond of peace. Praise helps to fix our minds upon the Lord, opens our ears to hear his word, and prepares the way for God to pour his love into our hearts. A truly praising church will be a loving church.

Praise, in other words, is (or should be) a foretaste of heaven. There, 'day and night they never cease to sing' praises to God. 'And I heard every creature in heaven and on earth and under the earth and in the sea, and all therein, saying "To him who sits upon the throne and to the Lamb be blessing and honour and glory and might for ever and ever!"'[61] Praise is the language of heaven, and therefore can bring a breath of heaven into our midst here and now. More often than not we shall have to break through the barriers of moods and feelings before we enter the realm of Spirit-inspired praise. When praise is the authentic expression of love and obedience, there is nothing which so glorifies Jesus Christ, and thus nothing which will be so opposed by the devil. To begin with, it is seldom easy. The Bible significantly talks about a 'sacrifice of praise'. But Dr Leon Morris has rightly commented that 'worship that costs us nothing is worth precisely what it costs'.

In his most helpful book, *Praise a Way of Life*, Paul Hinnebusch gives some vivid illustrations of the power of praise. A Christian businessman describes his time in Saudi Arabia whilst on business: 'I felt very depressed by the difficulty of our negotiations there, the silence of the hotel I was staying at, and the oppressiveness of the city I was in, where every man's mind and heart seemed totally opposed to Jesus Christ and to those who profess him as Lord. I got on my knees and began praying quietly to the Lord in "private prayer", but was soon led to pray in tongues, in the Spirit. Soon I raised my arms and started singing in tongues and then switched to singing some of our prayer meeting songs. I stood up and praised the Lord in a loud voice, rejoicing in the name of "Jesus" uttered aloud in that place. Praise and worship of the Lord and the joy of his Holy Spirit filled my heart and being, and within the space of a few minutes my depression was replaced by that exultant joy. This joy increased to higher and higher levels for about an hour and a half. Praise God! I have never been so upborne.'[61]

Similar experiences of the intense reality and glory of God have frequently been experienced by Christians as they have praised their Creator and Redeemer. When Richard Wurmbrand was in communist prisons for fourteen years, three of them in solitary confinement thirty feet below ground level, he learnt to praise God as an act of sheer obedience. As he continued to do so, he discovered a beauty in Christ he had never known before. He also experienced visions of heaven, and those visions helped to sustain his life in the most extreme circumstances.

Today there is a good and growing concern for the spiritual renewal of the church. Ever since the outpouring of the Spirit at Pentecost, God has responded when prayer has been the priority in the hearts of God's people. Charles Finney was right when he said that 'every minister ought to know that if the prayer meetings are neglected, all his labours are in vain.'

Prayer and praise are the greatest spiritual weapons God has given us in our constant battle against the powers of darkness. Nothing – absolutely nothing – can be a substitute for that. 'The Kingdom of God does not consist in talk but in power'[63] – and that power is released only through prayer.

Notes

1. Ephesians 1:14; Philippians 1:4; Colossians 1:9; 1 Thessalonians 1:2
2. Hebrews 4:15
3. Luke 22:40
4. Romans 3:11
5. Romans 8:26
6. 1 Corinthians 14:14
7. Ephesians 6:12, 18
8. 1 John 5:14f
9. Romans 8:15–17
10. Psalm 103:1
11. Psalm 149:2f; 47:1, 6; 63:4; 1 Cor. 14:15
12. *Praise, a Way of Life*, by Paul Hinnebusch, Word of Life, pp. 2–3
13. Luke 10:21, *Good News Bible*
14. Ephesians 2:18
15. Matt. 25:14–30
16. Luke 18:15–17
17. *Prayers of Life* by Michael Quoist, Gill 1963, p. 102
18. Psalm 73
19. Psalm 13:1f
20. *Celebration of Discipline* by Richard J. Foster, Hodder & Stoughton, p. 35
21. Hebrews 13:3
22. *Prayer Without Pretending*, Scripture Union 1973, p. 93f
23. 2 Cor. 10:5
24. Psalm 42:5
25. Ephesians 3:20
26. Mark 11:24
27. Luke 1:30–49
28. John 11:41
29. Romans 4:20f
30. 1 John 5:14
31. Psalm 103:1
32. Psalm 42:4
33. Psalm 9:1
34. Mark 7:6
35. Luke 18:1
36. Acts 1:14
37. Acts 6:4
38. Ephesians 6:18
39. Matthew 18:20
40. Revelation 12:10
41. Mark 11:25
42. Psalm 66:18
43. Ephesians 4:26f
44. Matthew 18:19
45. Luke 6:12f
46. James 1:5f

47. Luke 5:15f
48. Luke 8:46
49. Jeremiah 2:13
50. Luke 22:31f
51. Luke 22:40
52. 2 Chronicles 5:13f
53. Ephesians 5:20
54. 1 Thessalonians 5:18
55. Luke 24:53
56. Acts 2:11, 46f
57. Acts 4:24–31
58. Ephesians 5:18f
59. Quoted by Cardinal Suenens in *A New Pentecost?*, Darton, Longman & Todd, 1975, p. 89
60. Colossians 3:12–17
61. Revelation 5:13
62. Op. cit., p. 222f
63. 1 Corinthians 4:20

CHAPTER SEVEN

The Word of God

The wilderness by the Dead Sea in Palestine is as desolate and hostile as anywhere I know on the face of this earth: craggy, arid and dusty, an abrasive and aggressive challenge to anyone at any time. Put a man there, on his own, without food for six long weeks whilst wrestling with the most profound questions affecting the entire history of mankind, and you will make him vulnerable to any temptation. Add to that the fact that this man is the Son of God with power to turn even stones into bread, and we begin to see the force of this totally reasonable suggestion from the devil: 'If you are God's Son, order these stones to turn into bread.' Why not? It would have satisfied an obvious personal need. In view of his physical weakness and hunger, Jesus' reply to this is startling: 'The scripture says: "Man cannot live on bread alone, but needs every word that God speaks."'[1] More important than all our other needs and wants, more important than even physical life itself, is God's word to man. Exactly what this word is, how it comes to us, how we understand it and respond to it, are questions that we shall try to examine in this chapter. In brief, however, the 'word of God' refers to God's total revelation of himself, God speaking to man in words or ways that make sense.

The church today, at least in many parts of the West, is in a serious spiritual decline, fighting for survival. One reason for this has been a serious neglect of God's word, a loss of nerve in the Christian gospel, and a failure to proclaim the Good News of Jesus Christ with authority. In the imagery of Amos there is a famine, not of bread, but of hearing the words of the Lord.[2] God, however, seems to be creating within our society again a genuine spiritual hunger. 'Human hearts are crying, as never before, "Is there any word from the Lord?" . . . They don't want our views, opinions, advice or arguments. Is there any

word from the Lord? Tell us," they demand.'[3] In the chaotic
uncertainty of modern life, if there is a God who ultimately
rules in this world and reigns in our lives, what is he saying to
us?

Since this question is of supreme importance, we should be
alert to every hindrance which makes it harder for us to hear or
receive God's word.

Hindrances to God's Word

1. *Materialism*. Jesus specifically warned us about 'the cares of
this world, and the delight in riches, and the desire for other
things' that would so easily choke God's word in our lives. On
all sides today we are being bombarded by the false seduction of
material things. These steal our hearts from Jesus, close our
ears to his voice, and turn our feet from his path. Much of the
Christian religion in the affluent West is disturbingly worldly
beneath a thin veneer of pious language. Why do we not listen
to the radical teaching of Jesus? Why do we not present a
genuinely alternative lifestyle, God's new society on earth?
Why have we lost our prophetic voice? Why have we little
relevance to the poor and the oppressed? Why does the
institutional church make it hard for people to believe in Jesus?
We have embraced much of the covetous spirit of this age, and
ignored the truth that we cannot serve God and mammon.

The subtle pressures of the world are so massive that we can
resist them only if we are continuously being renewed in our
minds through the scriptures. We need every word that God
speaks. The devil once showed Jesus all the kingdoms of the
world and the glory of them, and he said, 'All these I will give to
you, if you will fall down and worship me.'[4] It was only through
the scriptures that Jesus was able to resist him. How much more
do we need to 'hide God's word in our hearts'.

2. *Activism*. In his excellent book *Celebration of Discipline*,
Richard J. Foster comments: 'In contemporary society our
Adversary majors in three things: noise, hurry and crowds. If
he can keep us engaged in "muchness" and "manyness", he will
rest satisfied. Psychiatrist C. G. Jung once remarked, "Hurry is
not *of* the devil; it *is* the devil." '[5] Perhaps our lack of hope
about tomorrow has made us frantic about today. We have
become obsessive with time, having lost sight of eternity.

Sometimes, too, we try to shield ourselves from personal pain, frustration or insecurity by frenetic busy-ness. Jesus once had gently to rebuke Martha for 'fretting and fussing about so many things', and encouraged her to be like Mary who was listening to him, absorbing every word that he was speaking.

In our constant rush we think that we have no time for God, forgetting that God himself is the giver of all our time. It is a sad rebuke to the spiritual drynes of activist Christians that increasing numbers of their contemporaries are turning instead to yoga and transcendental meditation. They claim that 'the study and practice of yoga purifies the body, improves the health, and strengthens the mind; above all, it intensifies spiritual growth.' Such practices, however, seek to unite the individual with the impersonal and universal consciousness, which is very different from the true and living God as revealed to us by Jesus Christ. Even if TM and yoga may be psychologically helpful, they are spiritually misleading. The Christian disciple should instead be challenged to take seriously the many instructions in the scriptures to be still before God and to meditate upon his word.

3. *Humanism.* Jesus once rebuked Simon Peter by saying, 'Get behind me, Satan! You think as men think, not as God thinks.'[6] This is the classic description of humanism: with ideas starting from man, not from God, everything is seen from man's point of view, not from God's. Man's thoughts about God are made more important than God's thoughts about man. It is all part of the independent spirit of this secular age, which resists external authority. It is the spirit of anarchy or lawlessness. I do what I want, not what God or anyone else wants. I accept what is meaningful to me, and reject the rest.

The doctrinal and moral implications of secular humanism are both obvious and devastating, and the considerable confusion in today's church is a direct consequence of this. Many do not listen to God, and reject the authority of scripture; instead they shape their beliefs and behaviour by human reasons or by social trends. They reduce their concept of God to what is fashionably acceptable. If, however, they start from man, they are left with man. The God they want is not worth believing in. Paul rightly commented about those who suppressed the truth of God that could be known: 'They became futile in their thinking and their senseless minds were darkened.

Claiming to be wise, they became fools.' As a result, 'God gave them up' to the way of life they had chosen for themselves, with all the destructive alienation of that choice.[7]

4. *Textualism*. A. W. Tozer described textualism as 'orthodoxy without the Holy Ghost'. Speaking of some fundamental churches that are textually sound but spiritually hard and dry, Tozer went on to say: 'Everywhere among conservatives we find persons who are Bible-taught but not Spirit-taught . . . Truth that is not experienced is no better than error, and may be fully as dangerous. The scribes who sat in Moses' seat were not the victims of error; they were the victims of their failure to experience the truth they taught.'[8] Until the Holy Spirit illumines our dull minds and warms our cold hearts, we do not receive God's revealed truth, no matter how accurately we know the right words and teach them to others. Many of the divisions within the church are caused by heated debates about the letter of the law, without understanding the Spirit behind it.

'Man needs every word that God speaks.' The word 'speaks' (*ekporeuomenō*) means 'is continually coming out of' the mouth of God. Since God is the living God, he is constantly trying to speak to us, and we in turn need to listen to him. He speaks, of course, in a wide variety of ways, and we shall look briefly at some of these later in the chapter. The vital response on our part is to train ourselves to ask the question, 'What is God saying to me through this passage, this person, or this event in my life?' It is not enough to know the text. What is God specifically saying to me – perhaps through the text – at this particular moment? If we are to keep spiritually alive and alert, we need every word that God is continually speaking.

Richard Wurmbrand once pointed out that in communist prisons he found Christians who knew Bible verses such as 'My grace is sufficient for you', but they found little comfort in these verses alone. It is God's grace that is sufficient for us, not the verse about it. 'You could have beautiful love-letters from a girl and pictures, and still not have the girl. The question here is having God himself.'

5. *Literalism*. This is an extension of textualism, and an inevitable reaction to the secular humanism of today. In our zeal to avoid the sceptical cutting away of all that is distinctively

Christian, we may fall into the simplistic trap of blind belief: 'It must be true because the Bible says so.' To some this will seem to be obscurantist dogmatism; reasoned debate becomes impossible. It leads easily to a legalistic Christianity, which denies the glorious liberty that should be our inheritance in Christ.[9] At worst, it degenerates into a spirit of bigotry, which is totally convinced of the rightness of its own position, and will not consider the possibility of being mistaken. It also refuses to listen to what other people are saying, and worse, to what God himself may be saying through those people.

This is the attitude particularly of most of the cults, but also of those sections of the true Christian church that could become a cult. A cult is 'a devotion to a particular person or thing as paid by a body of professed adherents.' A cult nearly always follows a particular person and a rigid set of rules and teachings. It is a closed system, in that it does not allow any deviation, any alternative interpretation of a given text. The science of interpretation, hermeneutics, is an exacting science. We need always to ask ourselves, what was the historical, cultural, linguistic and religious context of this particular verse in scripture? What was the original intention of this passage? What was it really saying; and, in the light of this, what was it *not* saying? We shall consider one or two examples later, but we must be wary of those who hold rigorously to some of the *words* of scripture, but have not become truly *biblical* in their thinking. It is dangerously true that you can prove almost anything from the Bible if you ignore the precise principles of biblical exegesis. The literalist narrows his mind and life to the unthinking 'letter of the law', instead of enjoying the liberating effect of the spirit of it. 'The written code kills, but the Spirit gives life.'[10]

6. *Intellectualism*. Jesus came essentially to bring us life. We need every word that God speaks in order that we might *live*. We may have to think and argue about the word of God, but if we stop there, we miss the whole point of it. 'You search the scriptures, because you think that in them you have eternal life; and it is they that bear witness to me; yet you refuse to come to me that you may have life.'[11] An intellectual grasp of the Bible does not in itself bring spiritual life. 'Understanding is a creative act, even a creative art, which involves the whole personality of the reader. If he is not open to the subject matter, indeed if he

is not open to God, a knowledge of certain rules is no substitute.'[12]

In the West we have often embraced the Greek concepts of truth and knowledge to the exclusion of the Hebrew concepts. The Greeks saw truth in terms of propositions, statements and words; whereas in Hebrew thought, truth was seen in terms of deep personal relationships. When Jesus talked about eternal life as 'knowing God', the word translated as knowing (*ginóskein*) is sometimes used for a husband knowing his wife, an intimate personal relationship. Thus if we claim to 'know the truth', when such knowledge causes our attitude towards others to be critical and unloving, it may be open to question how far we know the One who is the Truth, Jesus Christ. Sound doctrine enables us to know the God of love and life.

A purely intellectual knowledge of the scriptures may feed the mind; but if it aggravates a divisive, contentious and quarrelsome spirit, it can hardly be called 'sound' – a word which means healthy or life-giving. Aggressive Protestantism, for example, may teach all the right Bible words, but once again, it is only the Spirit who gives life. The Christian preacher is called, not primarily to impart theological information, but to preach God's word, and that word is 'living and active'.[13] It is always powerful, a dynamic expression of the life and power of the living God. Repeatedly in Genesis 1 we find the refrain, 'God said . . . And it was so.' In Revelation also we find various references to 'the sword of his mouth', referring to the powerful thrust of God's word. That is what it should be like. For the disciple of Jesus, the study of the Bible should never be just an academic exercise. 'To say that the Bible is our authority means both that we let our theological thinking be tested by it and that we let our lives be moulded by it. It shapes our thoughts, emotions, attitudes, desires and wills.'[14] All prayerful study of the scriptures should become literally a life-transforming experience.

7. *Anti-intellectualism*. This is more often the spirit of this age, rather than a surfeit of intellectualism. It is one reason for the popularity of eastern mysticism today, where there can be a dangerous stress of experience and a rejection of mind. 'Guru Maharaj Ji (The Divine Light) comes down and he pours down that Grace and Knowledge with it. That Grace is *satsang*. Then

when that *satsang* hits the mind machine, the very first thing it
does is disconnect it . . . What we have to fight today is mind.'

Some of the more extreme expressions of the charismatic
movement have fallen into this danger. The endless repetition
of simple choruses *can* become little more than a *mantra* or
incantation; we need to beware of an unhealthy interest in the
spectacular, the sensational and the demonic; and must be
cautious about too much dependence on prophecies and visions
in matters of guidance, rather than understanding biblical
principles and prayerfully applying them to the matter in
question. John Stott, in his helpful booklet *Your Mind Matters*,[15]
warns us about the 'misery and menace of mindless Christianity', and positively pleads for 'a warm devotion set on fire
by truth'.

No one can read the New Testament without seeing that
those first Christians had a rich experience of God – sometimes
profoundly mystical. The apostle Paul, however, was extremely
diffident about such experiences, and urged his readers to 'set
their minds on the things of the Spirit', 'to live by the Spirit . . .
(and) walk by the Spirit'.[16] This has nothing to do with
expecting one mystical experience after another; rather it has
everything to do with living out each day a Christ-like life which
demonstrates the fruit of the Spirit.

Hearing the Word of God

If every word that God speaks is vital for us, how does God
speak to us today? How can we both hear and understand his
word rightly?

Christianity is essentially a revealed religion. It is not man
searching in the dark for God. It is God revealing himself to
man in a way so personal that it demands a response. 'In many
and various ways God spoke of old to our fathers by the
prophets; but in these last days he has spoken to us by a
Son . . .'[17] Jesus is God's supreme revelation of himself to man,
and is something that every man of every age and culture can
understand.

It is important to distinguish three main forms of the word of
God.

1. *The personal Word*. The Word of God became a human
being and dwelt amongst us. Above all, God is personal. If we

have seen Jesus, we have seen the Father.[19] If we want to come to God, we must come to the Son. To know God is to know the Son. 'He reflects the glory of God and bears the very stamp of his nature.'[19] He is the image of the invisible God, and in him all the fulness of God was pleased to dwell.[20]

2. *The written Word*, as given to us in the scriptures. Although God is by definition our ultimate authority, the Bible is our final court of appeal for what God has said. Here is the God-given objective test for our belief and behaviour.

Not all theologians would agree with this. Although every true theist would accept the supreme authority of God's word, there have been three main views concerning our understanding of God's word.

First, there is *God's word as interpreted by tradition*: what the church says, God says. The difficulties, however, become obvious when the question is asked, But what does the church say? While many traditions are good and stabilizing, tradition-alism can be devastating. Jesus clearly corrected the religious traditionalists of his day when he said to the Pharisees: 'You have a fine way of rejecting the commandment of God, in order to keep your tradition . . . (You make) void the word of God through your tradition . . .'[21] Time and again Jesus brought back his religious opponents to the authority of the scripture.

Second, there is *God's word as interpreted by reason*: what reason can accept, God says. That is why many professing Christians reject the virgin birth of Christ, his miracles, his bodily resurrection and his personal return. When the ration-alists of Jesus' day, the Sadducee party, found that they could not rationally accept the idea of resurrection, Jesus brought them swiftly back to the truth of the scripture. He reminded them that God had revealed himself in the scriptures as the God of Abraham, the God of Isaac, and the God of Jacob. But, he said, God is the God of the living, not of the dead; and it follows from this that Abraham, Isaac and Jacob are still living even though physically dead. 'You know neither the scriptures nor the power of God.'[22] Their rationalism had become an arrogant stumbling-block to a knowledge of God.

Third, there is *God's word as interpreted by the scriptures*: what scripture says, God says. Jesus certainly endorsed scripture as the word of God: he knew it, taught it, lived by it, fulfilled it.

There is no doubt as to his own understanding of the scriptures as the inspired word of God; and since this was 'Christ's *textbook*', as Dr J. I. Packer has put it, 'Loyalty to Christ, our risen Saviour and enthroned Lord, calls for total submission to Scripture, and anyone, or any church, declining to believe and do what is written there, or failing in practice to be faithful to it, is to that extent a rebel against Christ.'[23] Strong words, but accepting Christ as Lord includes accepting his teaching, in every part, as having divine authority in our lives.

The various New Testament writers also claimed that what they were writing had been given to them by God. 'If anyone does not recognise this, he is not recognised (i.e. by God).'[24] The argument is sometimes raised that since the scriptures were written by sinful men, they must be fallible. This does not follow. If the scriptures are *God-breathed* (*theopneustos*, 2 Timothy 3:16) as was Paul's claim, God is well able to speak by his Spirit through sinful men, accurately and infallibly, just as the Holy Spirit through Mary gave birth to God's perfect Son. God will not use those sinful men as dictating machines for his word; rather, by the breath of his Spirit, he breathes through their backgrounds, personalities, experiences and understandings which have been shaped by the culture of their day. It is still God's inspired word brought to us through human beings.

Moreover, the biblical claim for its own authority is not invalidated by being a 'circular agreement', as some have maintained. If such a claim had first to be authenticated by some external authority, that authority would then have to be superior. 'To prove an "ultimate" authority by appealing to a higher authority would be a contradiction in terms.'[25] The Bible's own claim for divine authority can be tested only by its own consistency, reliability, and by the personal experience of all those who seek to live by it. Therefore, from the self-authenticating testimony of Jesus and the apostles, we must accept the scriptures as the inspired word of God, *as originally given*. Certainly we are not to despise good biblical scholarship as we try to determine both the original text and the cultural and historical context of that text. But having questioned the text, we must then allow the text to question us. Our conscience must become captive to the word of God.

3. *The spoken word*, as given through preaching, teaching,

witnessing or prophesying. Although God often speaks to us through the silent eloquence of creation, through pricks of conscience or peace of mind, through the daily and varied events in our lives, we shall also hear God's word when the scriptures are expounded, when a prophetic word is given (in whatever form), or when a brother or sister is talking with us. God did not finish speaking to us when the scriptures were completed. Although we are not to expect any further revelation of doctrine the spoken word, to be authentic, must be in accordance with the written word, and glorify the personal Word. God is the living God, the God of today; and every day he wants us to enjoy a living relationship with him, involving a two-way conversation.

The prophetic word
Since the apostle Paul exhorts us 'earnestly to desire the spiritual gifts, especially that you may prophesy', and since there has been an upsurge of prophetic gifts and ministries in many parts of the church, together with numerous spurious gifts which have given rise to the cults and sects that proliferate today, some teaching about prophecy is necessary.

Although the foundational gift of prophecy was given once-for-all through the apostles for the completion of the New Testament canon, even in the early church different levels of prophecy were clearly experienced. Paul envisaged this gift as a natural and healthy expression of the local church 'when you come together' (see 1 Corinthians 14). The vast majority of prophetic utterances, even in New Testament times, were not of the 'foundational' variety, but a normal part of the upbuilding of the body of Christ in any place; this gift was clearly distinguished from that of teaching or preaching. Whilst the written word is God's truth for all people at all times, the prophetic word is a particular word, inspired by God, given to a particular person or group of persons, at a particular moment for a particular purpose. We should not be surprised if the prophetic utterance is in the speaker's own words and thought-forms, reflecting his or her own burdens, since God uses us as human beings, with all our human outlooks and experiences, to convey his word. Nor should we be suspicious if the prophecy is steeped in scriptural phrases, since more than half of the Revelation of

St John the Divine comes to us in that way. Nor should we dismiss prophecy if the word is simple – maybe even 'trivial' in the eyes of some. In the Old Testament we read this: 'Then Haggai, the messenger of the Lord, spoke to the people with the Lord's message, "I am with you, says the Lord," '[26] That was all! Not another word came to God's people for a whole month. It was not the most profound or weighty word they had ever heard, but it was the word of the Lord.

God may give prophetic gifts for many purposes. It could be guidance concerning future needs, as when Agabus 'foretold by the Spirit that there would be a great famine over all the world'.[27] It could be directions for the church's ministry, as when the Spirit told the leaders at Antioch to set aside Barnabas and Saul for the first great missionary exploit of the church.[28] But mostly, it is for 'upbuilding and encouragement and consolation'.[29]

Since prophecy is God speaking through a member of the body of Christ, it must be carefully weighed and tested before it is received as the word of God. Speaking of the Montanists in the second century, Michael Green stresses dangers both of abuse and of the over-reaction to abuse: 'When they claimed that they personally embodied the Holy Spirit; when they wrote off other Christians as carnal and proclaimed themselves alone as "Spirit-filled"; when they refused to have their teaching tested by the scriptures but regarded it as every bit as authoritative as the New Testament records, then the church had to take action. That action was to reject the Montanists emphatically, and at the same time, to quench the prophetic spirit in the church. How much better it would have been for the church at large if the Montanists had determined to submit to the authority of scripture, and to resist the temptation to be exclusive and write off other Christians. How much better if the Catholics had stressed tests for the genuineness of prophecy rather than writing off the whole movement, good and bad together.'[30] That is a lesson highly relevant for the church of today.

What are the tests for prophecy, or for any other spiritual gift, especially that which purports to bring the word of God? These should be some of the questions to ask:

(a) Does it glorify Christ? The prophecy might not mention

Christ by name, but is the whole message honouring and glorifying to him? This is always the Spirit's primary work. (John 16:14; 1 Corinthians 12:1–4)

(b) Does it edify the body of Christ? No less than seven times in 1 Corinthians 14 Paul emphasises this point when discussing spiritual gifts, especially tongues and prophecy.

(c) Is it in accordance with the written word of God in the scriptures? If we twist the scriptures, we do so to our own destruction. (2 Peter 3:16)

(d) Is the word given in the spirit of love? This is the hallmark of the Spirit's presence, even when the word is correcting or rebuking.

(e) Is Jesus Lord of the speaker's life? The false prophet will be known by the fruits of his or her life, said Jesus. (Matthew 7:15–20)

(f) Does the speaker submit to the leaders of the church? Strong personalities with independent spirits caused splits and divisions in the New Testament church, and do so today. Paul warned the Ephesian elders about those 'from among your own selves' who would draw away disciples after them, and so cause divisions within the church of God. (Acts 20:19–31)

(g) Does the speaker allow others to judge or weigh what he has said? This must always happen, and troubles arise when such weighing is rejected. (1 Corinthians 14:29)

(h) Is the speaker in control of himself when speaking? It is the mark of an evil spirit's presence that the speaker is 'taken over' by that spirit. But that is never the mark of the Spirit of God. (1 Corinthians 12:2f, contrast 'moved' and 'speaking'; also 14:32)

(i) Is the prophecy fulfilled, if it speaks about some future event? Most prophecy is forth-telling, not foretelling. A Christian prophesying will normally 'tell forth', or speak out, God's word as a means of encouragement or exhortation for the whole congregation, only on much more rare occasions will prophecy predict some future event. When it does, the biblical test is in the fulfilment, or otherwise, of that prophecy. (Deuteronomy 18:22)

Logos and rhema

In recent years, some popular but questionable teaching has arisen which attempts to draw a distinction between *logos* and *rhēma*. Different teachers may express it in different ways. In general terms, *logos* is taken to refer to the whole teaching of the objective word of God in the scriptures that is always true, whereas *rhēma* is much more the particular word that God is now speaking, whether to an individual, to a local fellowship, or to a church as a whole. The distinction that some make between these two words has subtle but far-reaching ramifications.

First, although the *logos* of God is eternally true and important, the claim is that it is the *rhēma* of God that we need especially to hear and obey. The *rhēma* of God is said to be God's word to us for this particular moment in time; it is the sword of the Spirit,[31] the word that acts. It is not mere information, but a dynamic event. It is the word that changes people's lives, gives the church its sense of direction, and wins the spiritual battle. What we need, so the argument goes, is not so much the general exposition of the scriptures as the prophetic word of the Lord for today. In so far as we are obedient to the *rhēma* of God, we shall see him powerfully at work in our midst.

Second, although there may be areas of agreement about the *logos* of God, Christian unity depends in practice, it is claimed, on our response to the *rhēma* of God. If the Lord speaks his *rhēma* to us (perhaps through prophetic utterance), the only thing that matters is that we should obey it, even if it means withdrawing from other Christians in the process. This is how one leader wrote to me: 'Unity is not built on a relationship to my brother, but on a response to the word of God. Thus you may have as much unity as you have agreement on the *rhēma* of Jesus Christ.' If there is not this agreement 'in terms of the *rhēma* of the Spirit', it is virtually impossible, in practice, maintaining any working fellowship. Thus on these grounds, separation from other Christians is necessary.

From biblical, theological and philological perspectives, however, the distinction is impossible to maintain. According to *Kittel's Theological Dictionary of the New Testament*, there seems to be no basic difference in usage between *logos* and *rhēma*. Since *logos* occurs 331 times in the New Testament (in all the writings except Philemon and Jude), and *rhēma* occurs 67 times (32 by Luke and 12 by John), large areas of overlap are inevitable. *The New International Dictionary of the New Testament*[32] accepts that 'Whereas *logos* can often designate the Christian proclamation as a whole in the NT, *rhēma* usually relates to individual words and utterance', but it then immediately illustrates these individual utterances (*rhēma*) like this: 'Man has to render account for every unjust word (Matthew 12:36); Jesus answered Pilate without a single word (Matthew 27:14); the heavenly ones speak unutterable words (2 Corinthians 12:4).' In no New Testament dictionary or Greek lexicon of any substance can the claimed distinction be found.

William Barclay, in his study on *logos* and referring to Jesus as the *logos* of God, wrote: 'By calling Jesus the *logos*, John said two things about Jesus. (a) Jesus *is* the creating power of God come to me. He does not only *speak* the word of *knowledge*; he is the word of *power*. He did not come so much to *say* things to us, as to *do* things for us. (b) Jesus is the incarnate mind of God. We might well translate John's words, "The mind of God became a man." A word is always "the expression of a thought" and Jesus is the perfect expression of God's thought for men.'[33]

In J. J. von Allmen's *Vocabulary of the Bible*, the article on 'Word', referring specifically to *logos*, makes the same point: 'The Word does not point to a reality of which it is only the intellectual expression. It is that reality itself. It is an event. It is not rationality, but a deed . . . The preaching of the Word is not confined to utterance, however appropriate it may be for the faithful transmission of biblical "thought'. Revelation is above all a *deed*, and it is this deed as a whole which is the Word. The Word of God is more than an utterance of God. It is an act of God. For God acts by his Word and he speaks by his action.'[34]

The massive weight of evidence shows that there is no clear distinction to be made between *logos* and *rhēma* in the scriptures, and therefore the two far-reaching inferences mentioned above are based on a false premise. First, God has already given us his written word in the scriptures; and as we read it, preach it or hear it, it may at any time be the power of the Spirit become God's living word for us today – a word that works powerfully in our lives. Although prophecy is one of the gifts of the Spirit, it is wrong to exalt the prophetic word above the written word. Since *logos* and *rhēma* are virtually synonymous, what is required is not a false distinction between the two Greek words, but plain obedience to God's word.

Second, Christian unity is always based upon our relationship with Christ. Although our response to God's word is always important, it does not determine the boundaries of our unity. A true Christian is a man or a woman 'in Christ': if you and I are in Christ, you are my brother and sister, and I am your brother, no matter what response there may be to a certain *logos* or *rhēma* of God. If we separate from one another, we sin against Christ and against his body, since we are all one in him. The only theological grounds on which the Bible permits us to divide concern the divinity of Christ, his death for our sins and his resurrection from the dead. If a person denies any or all of these principal doctrines, a break in fellowship is not only possible, it is inevitable, for our unity is entirely in Christ. If, however, we separate on the grounds of differing responses to some other *rhēma* of God, this has no biblical justification whatsoever. Indeed, the confused teaching by some about *logos* and *rhēma* is a reminder that a little 'knowledge' can often be a dangerous thing.

Understanding God's word

Once we see the different forms of God's word, the authority of the written word and the tests for the spoken word, the questions of interpretation are of the utmost importance. Jesus constantly rebuked his religious hearers for their wrong interpretation of the scriptures. In the Sermon on the Mount he said repeatedly, 'You have heard that it was said . . . But I say to you . . .' In all the examples, Jesus never once changed the word of God as given in the scriptures; he simply corrected the false interpretation of that word, and brought it back to its original meaning and purpose. As disciples of Jesus we must learn rightly to handle the word of truth.[35]

Clearly much depends on the Spirit of truth, the Holy Spirit. It was by his operation that the personal word, Jesus, was conceived in his mother's womb. It was by his inspiration that the written word in the scriptures came into being, and that any true prophetic word will be spoken today. Thus the Spirit who inspired the word must also be the Spirit who interprets the word. 'No prophecy of scripture is a matter of one's own interpretation, because no prophecy ever came by the impulse of man, but men moved by the Holy Spirit spoke from God.'[36] We need the illumination of the Spirit before we can ever discern God's truth. 'No one comprehends the thoughts of God except the Spirit of God,' and he is given to us 'that we might understand the gifts bestowed on us by God'.[37] Constantly Paul prayed for the Christian churches that God would 'give you the Spirit, who will make you wise and reveal God to you, so that you will know him. I ask that your minds may be opened to see his light . . .'[38] Or again, writing to the church at Colosse, Paul said, 'We ask God to fill you with the knowledge of his will, with all the wisdom and understanding that his Spirit gives. Then you will be able to live as the Lord wants . . .'[39] Without the Spirit's direct help, we should all be spiritually blind.

Together with the understanding given by the Spirit, however, our minds need to follow some basic principles of interpretation. Two questions need to be asked. Firstly, what did the text mean to the original hearer? We need to 'distance' ourselves from the text, so that we do not bring to it our own preconceived ideas, or read into it our own pet doctrines, or draw out from it what is meaningful to us in our situation now, *before* we understand what it meant to the original hearers in their situation, which was possibly vastly different. Only then can we ask the second question: What does the text mean for us today? And we must learn correctly to apply for ourselves the true meaning of God's word discovered in answer to the first question.

In particular, we need to examine carefully the words, the context, the literary form and the cultural setting of the text.

(a) *The words.* A good translation is not a transliteration, and therefore some interpretation or paraphrase of the original is always likely in any version used for study. The New English Bible, for example, translates 1 Corinthians 14:13 as '. . . the man who falls into ecstatic utterance . . .', whereas the strict translation from the Greek is 'the one who speaks in a tongue'. To describe speaking in tongues as falling into ecstatic utterance is both a wild and somewhat alarming guess as to the precise nature of the experience. It would certainly confirm some people's worst fears about 'tongues'; but it is inaccurate as a translation and misleading as a paraphrase. The many millions of Christians who speak in tongues as a normal part of the daily devotional life certainly do not fall into ecstatic utterance, except possibly on the most rare occasions. Wherever possible we need to get back to the original text, and inquire carefully as to what the word meant to those first hearers.

Beware, too, of assuming that the same word means the same thing in different places. For example, Paul says that a man is not justified by works, while James says that he is! A contradiction? Not at all. Paul is talking about the means of justification, which is certainly *not* good works; James is talking about the fruit of justification, which certainly *is* good works, for 'faith apart from works is dead'.[40]

Extreme care must also be taken when it comes to an allegorical interpretation of any passage. I have heard many intriguing theories about the 'gold, silver, precious stones, wood, hay, straw' in 1 Corinthians 3, but I am often more impressed by the ingenuity of the speaker than by the accuracy of the exposition! Another preacher, giving a series of Bible studies on the relationships between Saul, David and Jonathan, made the point that Saul was 'head and shoulders' above every other man. So far so good. But when he went on to say that 'head' referred to human wisdom and 'shoulders' to human strength, I began to be suspicious. And when he later identified Saul as representing the established church, and David as the anointed church, making the point that Jonathan died because he stayed with Saul instead of going with David, I felt that a course in hermaneutics might be helpful for that preacher!

(b) *The context*. This must be looked at carefully in two ways. First, any verse or passage must be understood in the light of the whole section of scripture surrounding it. Verses used to support a favourite doctrine, idea or line of action are often verses lifted right out of their contexts, and a fuller examination of the whole section may reveal that the verse is saying something very different from what is claimed. For example, the ten or more verses *either side* of Paul's reference to 'gold, silver, precious stones, etc' are all about the tragedy of divisions in a local church and the importance of unity. In that context, the materials that will stand the test of fire almost certainly refer to the work of those who strengthen the temple of the Spirit by maintaining the unity of God's people.

Second, we must try to grasp the historical context of any passage. That is particularly striking when it comes to the Letters to the Seven Churches in Revelation 2 and 3. Some knowledge of the history, geography and commerce of each city is virtually essential before the imagery can be understood. The historical setting of each of the epistles is also of considerable importance if wrong conclusions are not to be drawn.

(c) *Literary form*. The Bible is a library of books: 66 of them, drawn from numerous sources, written by at least 40 different writers over a period of at least 1600 years. Not all the books, nor passages in each book, are of the same category. The vital issue is to determine what each passage is claiming and saying. 'So history must be treated as history, poetry as poetry, hyperbole and metaphor as hyperbole and metaphor, generalisation and approximation as what they are, and so forth. Differences between literary conventions in Bible times and in ours must also be observed: since, for instance, non-chronological narrative and imprecise citation were conventional and acceptable and violated no expectations in those days, we must not regard these things as faults when we find them in Bible writers . . . Scripture is inerrant, not in the sense of being absolutely precise by modern standards, but in the sense of making good its claims and achieving that measure of focused truth at which its authors aimed.'[41]

(d) *Culture*. This is the most complex consideration of all. We are not to be conformed to this world, and in the right sense the gospel stands in judgement on the culture of every generation. Far too often has the church accepted the existing culture without discernment, and there has failed in its prophetic role to the world. At the same time, the application of its gospel must vary with every cultural setting, or else we shall fail to communicate the timeless truths of the eternal God to the rapidly changing society in which we live. What are the truly biblical constants, and what are the practical variables of those God-given constants? What are the divine imperatives that should be applied to every culture, and what are the New Testament examples of the first-century cultural application of those imperatives, which may be quite different in other cultural settings? These are the crucial questions behind such issues as divorce, homosexuality, apartheid, the ordination of women, the use of creative arts in worship and evangelism, methods of communication, contraception, capital punishment, pacificism, lifestyle, and a host of other major issues.

To illustrate the complexity of all this, Eugene Nida gives a priceless example of cultural variations. He records an argument between western missionaries and African church leaders as to whether Christian women should go naked to the waist as did their non-Christian contemporaries. The missionaries stressed the biblical requirements for modesty in dress; but the African elders replied that they were not having their Christian women looking like prostitutes, who were the only ones in that culture who could afford the colourful extra clothing![42] What is modesty in one culture may be entirely different in another.

A similar issue, but one nearer to our western culture, is Paul's teaching in 1 Corinthians 11 that a woman should have her head covered when praying in public. Some would argue that, if the Bible says so, women must wear hats in church, whatever the cultural norm might be. The first question to ask, however, is this: *why* was Paul stressing the need for women to be so covered, writing as he was to the Corinthian church in that first century? Without going into a detailed exposition of that passage, every respectable woman in those days had her head, and probably her whole body, veiled – as many eastern women do today. It was, and is, a sign of being under the headship of either her father or her husband. Any woman in Corinth who was not so veiled was literally a 'loose woman', a prostitute. Some of the Christian women, however, were so rejoicing in their new-found liberty in Christ that they were discarding their veils, thus causing unnecessary offence for the gospel of Christ. The hostile, pagan world was only too ready to find fault in order to oppose the Christian faith; and therefore, in that setting, unveiled Christian women would be a scandal. Is that true in most western countries today? If not, we miss the biblical point if we require our women to wear hats in church when the majority of their respectable contemporaries outside the church do not.

Questions about sexuality and morality are often of a different nature. We are still in the body; and we cannot say that the New Testament strictures against fornication, adultery and homosexuality were reflections of the strict moral principles of those days. Far from it! They went right against the climate of the times, into which the young church was born. Of the first fifteen Roman Emperors, for example, fourteen were practising homosexuals. Divorce, too, was all the rage. In that first century we read of one woman marrying her twenty-third husband, she being his twenty-first wife! Christian standards were no more easy to keep than they are now, especially when, in the Gentile churches, most of the converts came from precisely this background. So Paul writes to the Corinthians: 'Do not be deceived; neither the immoral, nor idolaters, nor adulterers, nor homosexual perverts, nor thieves, nor the greedy, nor drunkards, nor revilers, nor robbers will inherit the kingdom of God. And such were some of you. But you were washed you were sanctified, you were justified in the name of the Lord Jesus Christ and in the Spirit of our God.'[43] It was instead the mark of the false prophet to relax those moral standards and to teach the 'liberated' promiscuity of the time.

Basic Christian doctrines, too, have nothing to do with what is culturally acceptable. In New Testament days, the Sadducees strenuously denied the resurrection; the Jews were offended by the preaching of the cross. The church, however, did not cease to proclaim Christ crucified and risen again, 'a stumbling block to Jews and folly to Gentiles'.[44] It was also God's message and power for salvation.

Asking careful questions about the cultural setting of New Testament teaching is not, therefore, a slippery slope down which any or every Christian truth might disappear. Most of the issues about doctrine and practice apply to every age and to every culture. But some were clearly specific issues for certain places at that moment in history. I suspect that the apostles would be horrified if they knew that their detailed instructions for Christians in their own world would impose rules and regulations upon all Christians for all time. When the result robs us of some of the glorious liberty of God's children, impoverishes the life of the body of Christ, and hinders the communication of the gospel in relevant terms for today, basic questions about interpretation need to be pressed.

Let me summarise. Throughout any study of the scriptures we must remain in total dependence on the Holy Spirit of God. He who inspired the writers of the original text must also illuminate our minds before we can receive the word of God. God, however, has also given us minds, and he wants us to use them to ask two basic questions: What did the text mean to the original hearers, bearing in mind the written words, their context, the literary form of the passage and the cultural setting? And then, what does the text mean for us today, probably in a very different setting? It is at this point that we must bow to the word of God, let him speak to us, and allow our hearts to be examined and shaped by that word. 'You do not interpret the text, it interprets you.' Our difficulty in hearing God today is that most of us hear only what we expect to hear. We come with our pre-conceived ideas and it is with these same ideas that we go away. Many of us need that divine rebuke which came to Simon Peter when he was prattling away on the Mount of Transfiguration: 'And a voice came out of the cloud, saying, "This is my Son, my chosen; *listen to him!*" '[45]

Lessons for spiritual life
Following on from what we have seen, let me mention three primary lessons.

1. *Listen to God's word.* God's people in Bible times expected to hear God's voice. 'I wait for the Lord, my soul waits, and in his word I hope.'[46] 'Speak, Lord, for thy servant hears.'[47] In the New Testament, we see God speaking to Philip, Saul, Ananias, Peter, Cornelius, the teachers and prophets at Antioch, indeed to anyone within the Christian community. Paul implied that any member of a local church might receive a revelation from God.[48] Today, the majority of Christians find it extremely hard – almost impossibly so – to hear the voice of God. The problem is that we have forgotten how to be still before him, and we give little time (if any) for Christian meditation.[49]

We need to use God's word to bring us consciously into God's presence. Let God's word speak to us, drawing us to the Father and glorifying the Son. By letting our whole mind and being dwell on one of the names of God or on one aspect of his character, the Spirit will help us to 'see God'. Words, phrases or even whole passages of scripture are invaluable for this fresh encounter with God. For some, praying or praising in tongues may also be extremely refreshing. The purpose is not to empty the mind of everything, but to detach the mind from worldly cares in order to attach them to Jesus and his word. 'This aspect is often neglected because in many circles it is assumed that the most important thing about the Bible is its "teaching". However, much of its poetry, its psalms, its parables, its humour and irony, is lost when it is reduced conceptually to "teaching". It confronts us not just with information, but with verdicts. In one direction the evangelical approach may be criticised for being too cerebral. The question: "What can I learn from all this?" is not always the right one to ask. Some parts of Scripture serve not to speak about joy, but to give joy; some serve not to instruct us about reconciliation but to reconcile us. The Bible not only tells us about Christ, but also brings Christ to us.'[50] To begin with, start with five or ten minutes in silent meditation. As you continue, you will be able slowly to increase the length of time, and, more important, you will begin to hear God speak to you through his written word or by his Spirit in your heart. Soon you will be able to enjoy an increasing sense of the presence of the living God, and better able to hear him as he speaks to you each day.

Dietrich Bonhoeffer writes: 'Silence is the simple stillness of the individual under the Word of God . . . But everybody knows that this is something that needs to be practised and learned, in these days when talkativeness prevails. Real silence, real stillness, really holding one's tongue comes only as the sober consequence of spiritual stillness . . . The silence of the Christian is listening silence, humble stillness . . . Silence before the Word leads to right hearing and thus also to right speaking of the Word of God at the right time . . .'[51]

2. *Study God's word.* 'Do your best to present yourself to God as one approved, a workman who has no need to be ashamed, rightly handling the word of truth.'[52] From the very beginning of Christian discipleship there is a need to study carefully the written word of God, and to let the word of Christ dwell in us richly.[53] When those at Beroea heard the gospel, 'they received the word with all eagerness, examining the scriptures daily to see if these things were so.'[54] Today a

growing number of Christians are spiritually alive and enthusiastic but alarmingly ignorant of scriptural truth beyond the purely superficial. How then can we study the word of God to its best advantage?

(a) *Equipment*. In the West we have almost an embarrassment of riches, so the culpability of ignorance is even greater. Nevertheless, biblical scholarship is one of the gifts of the Spirit for the benefit of the whole body of Christ, and is not to be neglected nor despised. It is helpful to have more than one translation, if possible, perhaps one that is known for its accuracy of translation and another that is more of a stimulating paraphrase. Also use a good concordance, in order to follow through a word in different parts of scripture. Several valuable handbooks and dictionaries are available today, too, and a Bible atlas can provide useful background information.

Commentaries, too, can be immensely helpful as we try to grapple with the meaning of the original text. These commentaries vary so much in style, scholarship and content, that it would be impossible to say more than 'get good advice' before you buy. However, use all this equipment to *supplement* your own study of the Bible and to check your understanding of certain words and phrases. If I rely too heavily on commentaries, for example, I may be fascinated by the thoughts of another writer, but I may not hear what the Lord is saying to me. In other words, first do your own study, with prayer and dependence on the Spirit of truth; and only then draw from the other resources at hand.

(b) *Methods*. Variety is the key-word. Any one method can be a useful servant, but none should become master. To begin with, use a systematic form of Bible reading aid – the Scripture Union, for example, has excellent material for almost all ages and educational backgrounds: notes, cassettes, soundstrips, booklets. Other Bible societies also produce valuable help, so look for yourself and choose one that is best for you.

I have also found the following methods stimulating:
Rapid reading: Often I read four or more chapters a day, following either one of the Anglican Lectionaries, or an old system by Robert Murray McCheyne. This helps to give a broad sweep of the scriptures, without being trapped by favourite passages.

Verse by verse: This is particularly valuable as a method for studying one of the epistles or a chapter in one of the Gospels. Try to read the whole epistle several times through first, in order to get the main thrust of the writer's approach; and only then begin a much more detailed study. It is here, of course, that commentaries, lexicons and concordances become especially handy. If preachers learnt how to 'unfold' a passage, so that congregations could be allowed to see the great riches God has for us in his word, the standard of preaching would improve immeasurably, and so probably would the spiritual health of our churches.

Book: Read through the book, if possible several times and with different translations. Then jot down on paper the main themes in the book. Next, take one theme at a time and see how the writer develops this. Use commentaries for passages that need further clarification, and look out for key words that are worth special study on their own. Try to spend time discovering the background to any book, otherwise you will miss the significance of much of its contents.

Topical: This may be either a word-study (looking up the verses on 'forgiveness', for example); or thematic (following through the references say to the healing ministry of Jesus, where no one word will be sufficient to grasp the breadth of the theme). The danger of concordance work must be noted, however. The same Greek word in the New Testament may have several different English translations; and the same English word may cover several different Greek words. Also, there is no guarantee that the same word or phrase (in both Greek and English) will always mean exactly the same thing; when it comes in different passages it may well have quite different purposes.

Character: The Bible is refreshingly honest about all the characters. All the men and women in the scriptures are seen as they really were, warts and all. David was a man after God's own heart: yes, but also a murderer and adulterer. Simon Peter was the rock-like leader of the early church: yes, but impetuous, self-confident and weak. To begin with, study carefully one of the minor characters ('minor' because of the little detail known), such as Epaphroditus, Ananias or Philip. Such studies will nearly always be immensely fruitful.

Bible study is valuable both privately and corporately. Read

Psalm 119: see the personal benefit drawn from much private
meditation on the word of God. Then look at the way Jesus
taught his disciples together, a practice they continued in the
early church.[55] Both approaches are important, although in
certain situations the stress may have to be on one rather than
the other. Coming straight from Cambridge University to work
in a dockyard parish, I naively told some of the members of our
youth fellowship to read their Bible in their bedroom quietly on
their own. Some roared with laughter. One lad was one of 13
children living in a small council house. The idea of having a
'quiet time' for Bible reading and prayer was out of the question
from the beginning. Added to that, some could hardly read at
all, and a Bible of some 1,300 pages was a hopeless proposition.
Fortunately there are now cassettes available, as well as other
imaginative Bible material, so that the problem is lessened.
Nevertheless I soon saw that corporate study was the only
realistic way of trying to read the Bible there at all: and even
then some skill was needed to make a group work well.

  3. *Obey God's word*. God speaks to us, not primarily to
impart information, but to guide our feet, to re-direct our lives,
to change us continually into the likeness of Christ. 'Do not
deceive yourselves by just listening to his word; instead, put it
into practice.'[56] As J. Aitken Taylor has expressed it well: 'One
does not pray, "God, help me resolve the seeming contra-
dictions I have found in the Bible." One rather prays, "God,
help me to receive thy word wholly, unquestioningly, obediently. Let me make it indeed and altogether *the* lamp unto my
feet and the light unto my pathway."'[57] We must let God's
word address us, challenge us, transform us.

  Use it to shape your life. If the world is not to squeeze us into
its own mould, we must let God re-mould our minds from
within.[58] God's values are totally different from the world's. If
we are to stand against the steady pressure of the world through
advertising and events of every day, we need to saturate our
minds and hearts in the word of God.

  Use it to overcome temptation. Learn the lesson from Jesus,
who overcame all the attacks of Satan in the wilderness by
driving him away with 'the sword of the Spirit, which is the
word of God'. The three recorded scripture verses that Jesus
used in that temptation all come from Deuteronomy 6 and 8. It

may have been that Jesus was meditating on those passages at that time, so that those relevant verses came quickly to him when facing temptation.[59]

Use it for guidance – not as a 'promise box', picking out texts at random; but aim to know this book so well that increasingly you have 'the mind of Christ', and are able to apply the God-given timeless principles to particular questions.

Use it to help others. I once talked with a lawyer for about two hours about the Christian faith, in general terms. It was mostly my word against his – a stimulating conversation, but little more. Then I opened my Bible, and showed him six or seven verses. With twenty minutes the Spirit of God had spoken powerfully to him and cut right through his intellectual defences. I was a very young Christian at the time, but I never forgot the lesson this taught me. The Bible, when handled rightly and in a spirit of prayer, has the power to change lives.

Use it also when bringing encouragement, comfort, rebuke, instruction or hope. God's word feeds our faith and renews us in God's love. Quoting texts by themselves may be useless. But when a person is able to understand the truth and implications of God's word, it wields authority and power that our own human arguments will never have. 'You have the words of eternal life,' said Peter to Jesus. And he was right.

Notes

1. Matthew 4:3f, GNB
2. Amos 8:11
3. James S. Stewart, *Preaching*, The Teach Yourself Series, Hodder and Stoughton, 1955, p. 20
4. Matthew 4:8f
5. Op. cit., Hodder & Stoughton, 1980, p. 13
6. Mark 8:33, NEB
7. Romans 1:21–32
8. Source unknown
9. Romans 8:15–21
10. 2 Corinthians 3:6
11. John 5:39f
12. Tony Thistleton, essay in *Obeying Christ is a Changing World*, Collins, 1977, p. 99
13. Hebrews 4:12
14. Tony Thistleton, op. cit., p. 116

15. IVP, 1972.
16. Romans 8:5; Galatians 5:25
17. Hebrews 1:1f
18. John 14:9
19. Hebrews 1:3
20. Colossians 1:15, 19
21. Mark 7:8–13
22. Matthew 22:29–32
23. *Under God's Word*, Marshall, Morgan & Scott, 1980, p. 41
24. 1 Corinthians 14:38; cf. Galatians 1:11f; 2 Peter 3:15f; Revelation 1:1f; et al.
25. Tony Thistleton, op. cit., p. 114
26. Haggai 1:13
27. Acts 11:28
28. Acts 13:2–4
29. 1 Corinthians 14:3
30. *I Believe in the Holy Spirit*, Hodder & Stoughton, 1975, p. 173
31. Ephesians 6:17
32. Ed. By Colin Brown, Paternoster, 1976
33. *More New Testament Words*, SCM, 1948, p. 116f
34. Op. cit., p. 460
35. 2 Timothy 2:15
36. 2 Peter 1:20f
37. 1 Corinthians 2:11f
38. Ephesians 1:17f, GNB
39. Colossians 1:9f, GNB
40. James 2:2b
41. From the Chicago Statement on Biblical Inerrancy, 1978, quoted by J. I. Packer, op. cit., p. 58
42. *Customs, Culture and Christianity*, Tyndale, 1963
43. 1 Corinthians 1:9–11
44. 1 Corinthians 1:22–24
45. Luke 9:35
46. Psalm 130:5
47. 1 Samuel 3:9
48. 1 Corinthians 14:26–31
49. See *Celebration of Discipline*, by Richard J. Foster, Hodder & Stoughton, 1980 for a helpful chapter on 'The Discipline of Meditation'.
50. Tony Thistleton, op cit., p. 105f
51. *Life Together*, SCM, 1954, pp. 59f
52. 2 Timothy 2:15
23. Colossians 3:16
54. Acts 17:11
55. Acts 2:42
56. James 1:22, GNB
57. From an article in the *Presbyterian Journal* for April 12, 1978, and quoted by J. I. Packer, op. cit., p. 60f
58. Romans 12:1f, J. B. Phillips
59. Matthew 4:1–11

CHAPTER EIGHT

Spiritual Warfare

Every Christian knows that discipleship is a struggle. On a personal level, why are we so often reluctant to pray? Why do we find it so hard to love and forgive? Why do we often shrink from keeping our hearts wide open to God and to other Christians? Why do we not more readily speak to others about Christ? Why do we continue to be proud, selfish, angry, jealous, covetous? Why are we so easily defeated? Why are relationships falling apart at every level? Why is there such oppression, injustice and frustration? On an international level, why is there so much hatred, violence and war? Why is it easier to fly to the moon than to find peace in Northern Ireland? Why are we destroying ourselves on this earth? The questions are endless.

Two main answers are given in the Bible. First, in our rebellion against God, we have become captive to sin: 'I do not understand my own actions,' wrote Paul. 'For I do not do what I want, but I do the very thing I hate.'[1] Second, we are involved in a spiritual battle, in which Satan seeks constantly to frustrate God's will for our lives.

Today many people find it hard to believe in a personal devil, whilst a few see satanic forces in every direction. C. S. Lewis has warned us of this double danger: 'There are two equal and opposite errors into which our race can fall about the devils. One is to disbelieve in their existence. The other is to believe, and to feel an excessive and unhealthy interest in them. They themselves are equally pleased by both errors and hail a materialist or a magician with the same delight.'[2] Even amongst Christians who do believe in the devil's existence, there is often a marked blindness about the reality of spiritual warfare and the nature of the enemy's tactics. 'Much of the church's warfare today is fought by blindfolded soldiers who cannot see the

forces ranged against them, who are buffeted by invisible
opponents and respond by striking one another.'[3] That is
doubtless the reason for much of the bitterness, misunderstanding and hostility within the Christian church: we are under
spiritual attack, we fail to see the nature of it, so in our
frustration we hit out at more visible targets.

The biblical witness

Those who find the whole concept of Satan's activity difficult to
take seriously, tending to dismiss it as fanciful or medieval,
should note carefully the volume of biblical teaching on this
subject. Leaving on one side the numerous passages in the Old
Testament, it is significant that as soon as Jesus began his public
ministry he 'was led up by the Spirit into the wilderness to be
tempted by the devil.'[4] Later, when Jesus began to concentrate
on his coming sufferings and death, the supreme purpose of his
earthly ministry, the battle against Satan is again explicitly
mentioned. When Simon Peter resisted the teaching of Jesus
that he 'must suffer many things . . . and be killed', at once
Jesus rebuked him: 'Away with you, Satan; you are a stumbling-
block to me. You think as men think, not as God thinks.'[5] Satan
constantly tries to blind our minds to the purpose of God, and
tempts us to see man as the centre and standard of reference.
Then again, when Jesus was facing the ordeal of the cross, he
had another tremendous spiritual battle in the garden of
Gethsemane – a battle won by prayer and obedience to his
Father's will.

Jesus also talked about 'the evil one' snatching away the seed
of God's word;[6] he warned that the enemy who sowed weeds in
the field was the devil;[7] he told the Jewish leaders that 'you are
of your father the devil';[8] and he prayed that his disciples
should be kept from the evil one.[9] Much of his healing ministry
involved the casting out of evil spirits and demons. There was
no doubt about the power and personality of the devil in the
life, teaching and ministry of Jesus.

The apostles, too, gave careful instruction about this spiritual
battle. Paul warned his readers that 'even Satan disguises
himself as an angel of light.'[10] He stressed that he had forgiven
those who had wronged him 'to keep Satan from gaining the
advantage over us; for we are not ignorant of his designs.'[11]

Elsewhere he urged the Christians to put their relationships right 'and (to) give no opportunity to the devil.'[12] He wrote about 'the snare of the devil'[13] and 'the doctrines of demons'.[14] He exhorted the Ephesian church to 'put on the whole armour of God, that you may be able to stand against the wiles of the devil. For we are not contending against flesh and blood, but against the principalities, against the powers, against the world rulers of this present darkness, against the spiritual hosts of wickedness in the heavenly places.'[15] He encouraged the Colossians by saying that, through the cross of Christ, God had 'disarmed the principalities and powers . . . triumphing over them in him.'[17] Peter warned, 'Be sober, be watchful. Your adversary the devil prowls around like a roaring lion, seeking someone to devour. Resist him, firm in your faith.'[18] Many more references like these will be found in the New Testament.

The historical evidence

Throughout the history of the church, Christian leaders have frequently taken the spiritual conflict seriously and taught others how to experience the victory of Christ. Ignatius Loyola (1491–1556) wrote a great manual on spiritual warfare and conquest (a book still used widely in Jesuit retreats), and in this he included the 'Rules for the Discernment of Spirits'. He shows the contrast, for example between conviction of sin by the Holy Spirit and the satanic counterfeit of condemnation leading to despair; also the contrast between the illumination of the Spirit and the false 'enlightenment' of the devil which leads only to further sin and spiritual darkness.

The Reformers largely accepted Loyola's directions as biblical; and although they rejected much of the medieval superstition that had erupted, they took seriously the spiritual conflict. Martin Luther (1483–1546) knew long and painful attacks by the evil one, especially in the realm of depression. Later, prolific works on spiritual warfare were written, including *Christian Armour* by William Gurnall (1616–1679). The priceless full title of this book is this: 'The Christian in Complete Armour, or, A Treatise on The Saints War with the Devil: wherein a Discovery is made of the Policy, Power, Wickedness, and Stratagems made use of by that Enemy of God and His People. A Magazine Opened, from whence the Christian is furnished with Spiritual Arms for the Battle, assisted in buckling on his Armour, and taught the use of his Weapons; together The Happy Issue of the Whole War.' My copy of 1837 has 818 concentrated pages of detailed exposition from Ephesians 6:10–20.

John Bunyan (1628–1688), well-known for *Pilgrim's Progress*, *The Holy War* and *Grace Abounding to the Chief of Sinners*, illustrates the powers of darkness as lions chained on a short tether on either side of the road to the Celestial City. These lions can maul travellers who wander from the middle of the path, but cannot touch those who keep themselves in the centre of God's will. With vivid imagery and biblical accuracy he shows that the forces of evil are held in check by the victory of Christ, and they can do nothing which ultimately destroys God's kingdom and glory.

John Wesley (1703–1791) and George Whitefield (1714–1770) too were under no doubts about the reality of this spiritual struggle, as their writings and sermons indicate. Whitefield's *Journals* refer frequently to this battle in the heavenly places: 'Satan endeavoured to interrupt us . . . Satan is disturbed . . . By and by, I expect Satan and his emissaries will rage horribly. I endeavoured to forewarn my hearers of it. Lord, prepare us against a day of spiritual battle!'

Jonathan Edwards (1703–1758) was especially alert to the counter-attacks of Satan during times of spiritual revival. He saw that Satan's main strategies were those of persecution, accusation, and infiltration. He noticed the attacks on the leaders and subjects of revival along the lines of despair, discouragement and mutual suspicion. If possible, Satan sets Christian against Christian, leader against leader, that he may divide and conquer. Edwards also observed how the devil, if unable to prevent a revival, sought to push those involved to unhealthy extremes: 'If we look back into the history of the church of God in past ages, we may observe that it has been a common device of the Devil to overset a revival of religion, when he finds he can keep men quiet and secure no longer, then to drive them to excesses and extravagances. He holds them back as long as he can, but when he can do it no longer, then he'll push 'em on, run 'em upon their heads.'[19]

In this century, with the confusing counterfeit work of Satan during the great 1904–5 revival, Evan Roberts and Jessie Penn-Lewis wrote *War on the Saints*. And in more recent years, with all the fresh interest in the occult, many serious Christian books have been written with a clear biblical and pastoral perspective.[20] Through the perplexities surrounding this subject, and through the cheap sensationalism of the 'lunatic fringe', some church leaders today are sceptical about any satanic conflict with God. It has little fashionable respectability; but serious teaching about this warfare can be traced throughout the centuries since the days of the early church.

Discerning the spirits

'The ability to distinguish between the spirits' is one of the spiritual gifts given to us by God for the benefit of the whole body of Christ, and undoubtedly this played a considerable part in the ministry of Jesus and the apostles. Jesus knew instantly what he was dealing with, when confronted by those who were tormented or possessed by evil spirits: 'You deaf and dumb spirit, I command you, come out of him, and never enter him again.'[21] The effect was immediate; and the boy, whose affliction had defied the attempted ministry of the disciples, was made whole. Jesus never treated ordinary physical diseases in this way, but he knew at once when faced with his enemy. Peter, too, was able to unmask Simon Magnus who had joined himself with the baptised believers who were converted through Philip's ministry; and Paul set free the girl with the spirit of divination. In each case they had to discern accurately the nature of the conflict. A biblical understanding of spiritual warfare gives insight into the bewildering confusion in the church down the centuries.

'A good deal of the church's history becomes somewhat more intelligible if biblical principles for the discernment of principles are employed. They must be applied with *exquisite caution* (italics mine). But some rather tumultuous periods of renewal, counter-infiltration and counter-attack can only be sensibly interpreted with their use. Otherwise the scene is as confusing as a football game in which half the players are invisible.'[22] John tells us in his First Letter that we are to 'test the spirits to see whether they are of God',[23] and this is particularly important in an age when the cults and sects are proliferating; but this should be done with 'exquisite caution', lest a genuine work of God is written off as spurious, heretical or even demonic. Some have done just that with the whole of the charismatic movement, good and bad together; but they would have been wiser to have exercised the caution of Gamaliel, for 'if it is of God . . . you might even be found opposing God!'[24]

Satan is described as the 'god of this world' who seeks to blind people's minds to the truth of Jesus Christ.[25] He is 'the deceiver of the whole world'[26] who uses a host of evil spirits to persuade men to believe lies about God, to disbelieve God's word, and to indulge in the works of the flesh which bring even greater spiritual darkness and misery. The New Testament mentions the existence of the spirits of error, lust and fear; unclean spirits, seducing spirits, deaf spirits, dumb spirits, lying spirits which deceive men by false guidance and false prophecy; familiar spirits working through occult practices; and a host of others as well. These demonic agents cause a strong aversion to biblical truth, a blindness to its meaning and a rejection of what is understood. They work equally within the institutions of the church and certain academic theological studies. The denial by some church leaders and scholars concerning the deity of Christ, his resurrection from the dead and his glorious re-turn, are examples of the blinding influence of the god of this world.

He is also called 'the prince of the power of the air', who opposes in every way the rule of Christ, and who holds evil structures and unjust political systems in his grasp. His powerful work seems to lie behind the massive and illicit use of drugs, the pornographic industry, the bondage to materialism which so often destroys human dignity, and the senseless obscene violence which increasingly dominates our world. Paul warned Timothy that 'in these last days there will come times of stress. For men will be lovers of self, lovers of money, proud, arrogant, abusive, disobedient to their parents, ungrateful, unholy, inhuman, implacable, slanderers, profligates, fierce haters of good, treacherous, reckless, swollen with conceit, lovers of pleasure rather than lovers of God, holding the form of religion but denying the power of it.'[27] Although the root of all this is to be found in the sinful heart of fallen man, the extent of corruption and evil is sometimes so great that only the adjectives 'satanic' or 'devilish' can describe their insidious influence.

Direct attack

There are a number of well-tried tactics of the evil one that we need to understand. First, Satan seeks to destroy God's work by the direct attack of persecution, or by various assaults on the bodies, minds and spirits of God's people, especially those fully involved in Christian work. When Peter told his readers to watch out for the devil as a 'roaring lion', he went on to say, 'Resist him, firm in your faith, knowing that the same experience of suffering is required of your brotherhood throughout the world.' He had previously been talking about the 'fiery ordeal' which would come upon them, telling them to 'rejoice in so far as you share Christ's sufferings.'[28]

Every active work of God has been contested in this way, from the vicious persecutions against the early church under the Roman Emperors to the tortures and imprisonments of Christians during this century, especially in communist and Islamic countries. It is estimated that there have been more martyrdoms for Christ during the twentieth century than during the rest of the history of the church put together. These attacks have usually been accompanied by false accusations based on gross misunderstandings of Christian faith and work. Right-wing dictatorships, and totalitarian governments of every political wing, have accused Christians of subversive influence, of revolutionary intrigue and of law-breaking activities. Trumped-up charges followed by the mockery of justice have led to untold suffering. The wanton aggression against Christians, whose lives are marked by godly love and radiant faith, is often diabolical in its intensity.

It is notoriously difficult discerning the root causes of physical or mental afflictions, but the timing, significance and ferocity of some indicate the work of the 'roaring lion'. Many Christian workers, for example, have battled over the years with depression. Charles Spurgeon, the great Baptist preacher, knew 'by most painful experience what deep depression of spirit means', especially on Monday mornings after an exhausting time of preaching the day before. Writing of Luther's similar conflicts, Spurgeon said, 'his great spirit was often in the seventh heaven of exultation, and as frequently on the borders of despair . . . He sobbed himself into his last sleep like a great wearied child.' Luther himself, however, could be quite practical about this. His attitude to depression was this: 'Don't argue with the devil. Better to banish the whole subject . . . Seek company or discuss some irrelevant matter, e.g. what is happening in Venice . . . Dine, dance, joke and sing . . . Shun solitude . . . Manual labour is a relief; harness the horses and spread manure on the fields.' An attitude like this can be a healthy response to satanic attacks of dampening depression. We shall often have to discern the interplay of four different sources of affliction: physical factors (sickness, fatigue, malnutrition, hormonal or chemical imbalance); psychological factors (natural dispositions); fallen nature; and demonic attack. The devil may of course take advantage of any area of weakness, but where there is some disorder, various forms of treatment may be appropriate concurrently.

Accusation

Second, Satan aims to disrupt God's work by the indirect attack of accusation. He is the 'accuser of the brethren', who seeks to overwhelm the church with a flood of lies.[30] Opposition to the work of God's Spirit may come from within the church as well as from without. Within the church, there may be a quiet opposition to spiritual renewal when it is politely ignored altogether, especially by the leaders of the church. Or else the whole renewal may be caricatured in exaggerated proportions, reinforced by the aberrations and excesses that inevitably exist, and then vigorously opposed. Devastating criticisms by one group of Christians towards another often reveal extraordinary misunderstandings of the truth of the situation. I have heard good and honest Christian leaders accuse one another of error or misconduct in a way that has left me almost speechless, except for the fact that I have no doubt made similar accusations unwittingly myself. There has been such an extraordinary twisting of the truth that it could only be the 'accuser of the brethren' hard at work.

Inevitably Satan capitalises on the genuine faults and failings of Christians, both to divide the church and to cause the name of God to be 'blasphemed among the Gentiles'.[31] Paul was often concerned that Christians should watch carefully their behaviour, in order that the name and the word of God might not be discredited.[32] The popular image of the church in secular western society is that of a pathetic and useless relic of some bygone days. True, there may be *some* elements of the church's existence that could lead to such an image – it is not wholly false. But it is such a distortion of the real picture that it is effectively a gross lie, sadly a lie that is believed by the majority of the population. Such is the devil's skill. He is the 'slanderer' as well as the 'accuser'.

The work of the accuser also causes great distress in the minds of countless Christians. With frightening accuracy and frequency we are reminded of our sins and weaknesses, and quickly fall into condemnation and despair. Blasphemous or evil thoughts may assail the mind, especially during times of worship or prayer, and many believers consequently feel appalled by their sinful disposition which enables such thoughts to arise. We need to understand clearly that these are no more than the 'flaming darts of the evil one'.[33] However, unless we learn how to lift up the shield of faith by claiming Christ's victory both for ourselves and for one another, we may in time become bound by obsessive guilt and continuing depression.

Exploitation

Third, Satan is out to damage God's work by exploiting the carnality of Christians to pollute the Spirit's activity. God is a God of truth; but Satan can use powerful personalities in the church to turn the truth of God's word into narrow, hard-line bigotry. A Christian becomes so sure that he is right and that others are wrong, that with his tongue or pen he lashes out with biting criticisms at other brothers in Christ.

God is a God of love; but Satan can use the frailty of human flesh to turn a genuine experience of God's love into emotional entanglements, or even into adulterous or homosexual acts. There are immense pressures on Christian marriages today; some of this pressure is natural in the context of the general breakdown of family life in society, but some of it seems devilish in its destruction of outstanding Christian workers and leaders.

God is a God of peace; but Satan can play on our weaknesses

so that we become peace-lovers rather than peace-makers. We avoid conflict; we fail to resolve tensions in relationships; we allow sin to continue within the fellowship without being challenged; we agree with all points of view in a muddy ecumenism instead of clear unity in Christ. Christ the Bridegroom looks for moral and doctrinal purity in his bride, the church. In his word he tells us to 'speak the truth in love' so that we can grow up in every way into him. He knows that we are not perfect: we will all make mistakes, and we do not yet see things clearly. But as we sort out our relationships with honesty, love and forgiveness, so the God of true peace will be with us.

Counterfeits

Fourth, Satan seeks to confuse God's work with counterfeit movements, which not only deceive many, but discredit genuine movements of the Spirit of God. As the 'angel of light' he seduces deeply religious people with 'deceitful spirits and doctrines of demons',[34] bringing them into the bondage or either legalism or licence. He deludes weak Christians by those who are disguised as 'servants of righteousness'[35] and by counterfeit miracles, 'pretended signs and wonders'.[36] He may draw them into a false religion which has all the outward form, but none of the life and power of the Spirit of God.[37] In the experiential mood of today, alongside genuine charismatic experiences have mushroomed a host of occult practices and eastern mysticism. Sects that promise spiritual fulfilment and reality have grown like a wasting disease, encouraged by the spiritual barrenness of much of the orthodox church.

This has been the pattern of church history from the New Testament times onwards. The apostles and church fathers saw gnostic heresies and mystery religions as expressions of deceiving spirits. They were alert to the 'spirit of antichrist' and the 'spirit of error'. They warned other Christians about false prophets 'secretly bringing in destructive heresies';[38] they mentioned by name those who opposed the truth, 'men of corrupt mind and counterfeit faith'.[39] When we see the same confusing influences in both church and society today, it would be foolish to dismiss these apostolic warnings as first-century superstition. More humbly we ought to acknowledge our own limited vision of the spiritual realm, accept the teachings of scripture as God's word, and give due warning about the dangers of counterfeits for our churches today.

Temptation

Fifth, Satan tries continually to defeat God's people with temptation. He is called 'the tempter'. Generally his actions encourage inconsistencies in Christian witness. We are tempted, therefore, to lose our temper, to be slack about our work, to covet what is not ours, to feed our pride and to nurse our hurts. Such temptations are aimed at specific weaknesses in our Christian lives.

What may be harder to detect, but in the long run much more powerful and effective, is the temptation to a lifestyle that is subchristian: worldly materialism, social distinctions, middle-class morality, western affluence – all these covered with a thin veneer of spirituality. The unbeliever, however, sees through this disguise. There is no genuine alternative lifestyle which gives credibility to Christian witness. There is nothing substantial to distinguish the believer from the unbeliever. Why should he be encouraged to join this 'religious club'? It has little to say about real life; only a few religious activities. The temptation to avoid the challenge of true discipleship is both subtle and considerable. It is devastatingly effective, and it keeps the Christian powerless as an ambassador for Christ.

As Christians we are clearly called to live in the world and yet not be conformed to the values of the world. Some understanding of the nature of the world is therefore important. Some Christians think at once of drink, drugs, sex or gambling. All of these can be poor and unhealthy substitutes for the place of Christ in our hearts. But John tells us that 'the whole world is in the power of the evil one.'[40] This would include the world of education, politics, philosophy, economics, industry, entertainment, television, radio, press. It is not that these things are necessarily wrong in themselves; but naturally they belong to the world that is controlled by Satan. Everything that is not directly under the Lordship of Christ belongs to the kingdom of this world and is in opposition to the kingdom of God.

Jesus once said, 'As it was in the days of Noah, so it will be in the days of the Son of man. They ate, they drank, they married, they were given in marriage . . .'[41] Notice carefully those words. Jesus did not say that they lusted, they fornicated, they gambled, they murdered. No! These evils might well have been true, but Jesus refers only to the ordinary, natural things in life which they went on doing 'until the day when Noah entered the ark, and the flood came and destroyed them all'. Why did God's judgement fall? It was because this was their whole world, their entire life. They were preoccupied with everything but God. God was not at the centre of their lives as he always ought to be.

The problem for a Christian, therefore, is not how to avoid eating, drinking, marrying and giving in marriage. Of course not! The question is how to avoid the *power behind* these things, since the whole world is in the power of the evil one. Even the ordinary, harmless, everyday things belong to the world which is in the control of Satan. How, then, can we be free from the strong pull of the world? How can we overcome the desires, ambitions, and attractions which can so easily draw us away from the love of God? The answer is that in Christ and through his cross we have already been crucified to the world, and the world has been crucified to us.[42] As with sin, we no longer belong to that old realm. We have been transferred into the realm where Jesus reigns.

In practice the reality of this truth will be seen only as we keep our hearts open to the love of God, and trust his Spirit within us to control our lives and to change us continuously into the likeness of Jesus. 'Because he cleaves to me in love, I will deliver him . . .'[43] We cannot love God and love the world at the same time. It is, therefore, only as the love of God is poured into our hearts each day by the Holy Spirit that we are able to experience freedom from the pull of the world. It would be foolish to suppose that this is a once-for-all spiritual battle. Certainly we now belong, for all time, to that realm of grace where Jesus reigns. But each day we need to submit every part of our lives to his sovereign rule, and also to be renewed in his love and filled with his Holy Spirit. Only in this way shall we increasingly enter into the 'glorious liberty of the children of God'.[44]

Possession
Sixth, Satan may mock God's work by taking possession of something that was created by God for his glory, usually a

human being. Satan, as the 'murderer' and 'destroyer'[45] desires to destroy God's work, and the destruction of the human personality by the indwelling of evil spirits is a frightening reality. We see it often in the Gospels. The man with the unclean demon was thrown down by it before it came out of him at the command of Jesus.[46] The demons in 'Legion' caused him to break the chains and fetters with which he had been bound, and drove him into the desert; when finally cast out of the man by Jesus, they destroyed a whole herd of swine.[47] The boy with the unclean spirit was tormented and convulsed by the spirit, it 'tore' at him and 'shattered' him; it would 'hardly leave him', until rebuked by Jesus.[48] Indeed Jesus warned that if an unclean spirit went out of a man, he would be 'seeking rest'; if later he found a man's life swept but empty, he would bring seven other spirits more evil than himself' to dwell there, 'and the last state of that man becomes worse than the first'.[49]

I have personally witnessed the destructive power of demonic forces in the lives of several individuals. I have seen mocking, lying and tormenting spirits take hold of the personality of human beings created in God's image, causing them to say and do evil and violent things outside of their control. I have heard demonic voices speak through people. I have witnessed the wretched existence of those who have become manipulated by the powers of darkness – usually through personal involvement in occult practices, although there are other causes, too. I have prayed through hours of terrible conflict when those who are possessed by Satanic forces begin to turn to Jesus for deliverance. I have been frightened by the reality of such evil, and yet experienced the greater power of Jesus Christ. From what I have personally known over the last ten to fifteen years, I could not possibly doubt the existence of the devil, even if I had intellectual difficulties with some of the concepts involved.

Normally, however, the destructive character of Satan is expressed in much less bizarre forms, though still dangerous and real. Satan works through human institutions that humiliate the individual, through social and political systems that oppress the poor and weak, through human avarice that exploits the defenceless for 'filthy lucre', and through sinful lust that indulges every passion of the flesh, and abuses young people as expendable objects of sex. 'The involvement of the forces of darkness in stirring up and shaping these works of destruction against God's creation does not eliminate human responsibility and guilt. It simply explains the fearfully logical strategy often apparent in evil and the blindness and virulent energy present in human beings involved in such genocidal actions as the murder of six million Jews under Hitler.'[50]

If we fail to see the spiritual conflict, we shall be tempted to respond in bitterness and hatred towards *people*. However, the perpetrators of the evil in this world are not our enemies, nor are we to regard them as such. That is why Jesus told us to love our enemies and to pray for those who persecuted us. All men, good or evil, are loved by God, and are to be loved by Christians as well. God loves the sinner, even though he hates the sin. We are to see clearly that we are not contending against flesh and blood. Our real warfare is against the spiritual principalities and powers that rule over the lives of men and over the structure in which we live. In view of the scale, subtlety and intensity of the spiritual conflict, there is great need for God's gift of spiritual discernment. It is as we pray for this specifically that God will increasingly give it to us. Paul prayed that the Colossians would be filled with the knowledge of God's will, and 'with all the wisdom and understanding that his Spirit gives'.[51]

God's freedom fighters

In the New Testament epistles, it is assumed that most readers will be familiar with the spiritual battle, and therefore only occasional explicit exhortations are given to encourage the churches in it. Today we can make no such assumption. Thus a brief summary of some of the main principles of victory and freedom may be helpful.

1. *Know your enemy.*. Speaking of Satan, Paul said, 'We are not ignorant of his designs.'[52] We should be well acquainted with the character and strategy of the evil one, without dwelling on this too much. Never forget, however, his active and destructive work: 'Watch and pray that you may not enter into temptation,' said Jesus to his sleepy disciples;[53] and in the family prayer we say, 'Deliver us from evil' or from the evil one.

2. *Keep yourself in the love of God.* Jude, writing about those in the last days who would scoff, who would set up divisions,

worldly people, devoid of the Spirit, went on to assure his readers that God 'is able to keep you from falling'; but on their part they were to build themselves up on their most holy faith, pray in the Holy Spirit, and keep themselves in the love of God.[54] It is sometimes said that the Christian who sins is a fool; because, if we abide in Christ, there is no need to. In the same way, although we must know about Satan's power, we are not to be frightened of it. If we walk in the light with Christ, there is nothing to fear from the powers of darkness. Paul knew that 'neither death, nor life, nor angels, nor principalities, nor things present, nor things to come, nor powers . . .' absolutely nothing could separate a Christian from the love of God in Jesus Christ. If therefore we keep ourselves in that love, we are perfectly and eternally safe. The evil one will not touch us.[55]

3. *Be strong in Christ*. This was Paul's instruction to the Ephesian church: 'Be strong in the Lord, and in the strength of his might.'[56] Christ is 'far above all rule and authority and power and dominion, and above every name that is named . . .; all things (are) under his feet.'[57] We cannot trust him too much in this struggle, for 'he who is in you is greater than he who is in the world.'[58] In particular, our victory over Satan is to be seen in the cross of Christ, for it was there that God 'disarmed the principalities and powers',[59] and it is 'by the blood of the Lamb' that we are able to conquer the accuser of the brethren.[60]

The power of the cross can be quite dramatic in releasing people from Satanic bondage. On many occasions I have seen that reading verses and passages about the cross have been powerful in spiritual warfare, especially in the most severe expressions of it. Generally speaking, a prayerful and confident trust in God's power over Satan through the cross of Christ is all that is required. We should therefore resist frequent 'deliverance ministries' and indiscriminate exorcisms. Every malaise cannot be ascribed to satanic oppression or possession and to do so yields untold distress and may create serious disorder. To use the much less sensational principles described in this section will be effective in the vast majority of cases. Christ has won the victory for us. We are to stand firm in it, proclaim it and rejoice in it. That is the way to resist Satan. We must beware of instant formulae for deliverance. We are to crucify the flesh and walk in the Spirit; and we can, in nearly every case, do so together in the power of Christ.

4. *Be filled with the Spirit.* Paul, having warned the Ephesians about the 'unfruitful works of darkness' and the days 'that are evil', urged them to go on and on being filled with the Spirit.[61] They would need all the gifts of the Spirit to equip them for effective warfare. He told Timothy to be inspired by the 'prophetic utterances which pointed to you', so that 'by them you may wage the good warfare'.[62] Repeatedly, and perhaps painfully, God will have to remind us of our own utter weakness without him. Pride, seen by self-confidence and self-reliance, so easily dominates our thinking. Like Simon Peter, we think we can do it ourselves: others may fail, but we shall stand firm. If ever we are shocked by the sin of another Christian, we are blind to our own weakness. We need to come to that point, in every area of our lives, where we *have* to depend on the Holy Spirit. Unless we are daily cleansed from our sin by the blood of Jesus, and daily filled with the Spirit, we shall never overcome the evil one.

5. *Be active in Christian witness and service.* In the same context of being filled with the Spirit, Paul urged his readers to 'make the most of the time' and to wake out of sleep. Jude, too, exhorts the Christians to convince those who doubt and to snatch others out of the fire. In other words, in view of the cosmic struggle in which we are engaged, there is not a moment to lose. Every day we need to know what the will of the Lord is, and do it. Isaac Watts was right when he said that 'Satan finds some mischief still for idle hands to do.' There is of course a balance and previously we noted Carl Jung's comment that 'Hurry . . . is the Devil'. In the Gospels we see Jesus maintaining this balance working to the point of exhaustion, yet calm and at peace in his spirit, busy but not rushed, alert but not tense. He perfectly accomplished the work that God had given him to do, and Satan had no foothold in his life.

6. *Be quick to put right your wrong relationships.* Every church is a fellowship of sinners. Inevitably we shall hurt others and get hurt ourselves. Jesus knew the need for persistent teaching on the necessity for forgiveness, seventy times seven, if need be. Paul knew that we would at times be angry, justly or unjustly. Unless, however, we deal with our anger, and with the

problem that prompted it, immediately – before the sun goes down – we would give 'opportunity to the devil'.[63] If we go to bed angry, we may not easily sleep; and in the morning we may well find ourselves both depressed and irritable. If there is any break in fellowship between two Christians, the devil will be quick to exploit it.

We also need to keep our lives constantly open to one another in love. In this way we can help each other in the spiritual battle. But if I don't know what is happening in your life, and you don't know what is happening in my life, we shall be of little use when either is in trouble. If, however, we are genuinely sharing our lives together, when you are down I may be able to lift you up, and when I am down you may do the same for me. 'Two are better than one . . . For if they fall, one will lift up his fellow; but woe to him who is alone when he falls and has not another to lift him up . . . And though a man might prevail against one who is alone, two will withstand him. A threefold cord is not easily broken.'[64] Paul's instructions about the battle were written to a church, not just to individual Christians. They were to stand together, pray together, lift up one another – and they could do this only as they were genuinely united in love.

7. *Put on the whole armour of God.*[65] God gives us all the protection that we need. We must see that there is a 'ring of truth' about our walk with the Lord, that our lives are right ('righteous') with God and with one another, that we seek to make peace wherever we go, that we lift up that shield of faith together to quench all the flaming darts of the evil one, that we protect our mind from fears and anxieties that easily assail, and that we use God's word to good effect in the power of the Spirit. Remember it was by the repeated sword thrusts of God's word that Jesus overcame his adversary in the wilderness.

8. *Be constant in prayer.* 'Pray at all times in the Spirit, with all prayer and supplication. To that end keep alert with all perseverance, making supplication for all the saints.'[66] If, through prayerlessness, we lose our close contact with God, we shall never stand firm in the battle. We need daily his 'marching orders'. We must come to him, wait upon him, renew our strength in him, listen to him, trust in him, and then go out into the world to face the enemy. If Jesus knew the constant need of

this for his own ministry, how much more should we acknowledge our weakness by humble, persistent prayer.

9. *Use the festal shout.* 'Blessed are the people who know the
festal shout', sang the psalmist.[67] Throughout the centuries,
God's people were often encouraged to shout praises to God,
particularly in the context of battle. Joshua told the people to
'Shout; for the Lord has given you the city . . . So the people
shouted, and the trumpets were blown. As soon as the people
heard the sound of the trumpet, the people raised a great shout,
and the wall fell down flat . . ., and they took the city.'[68] When
Jehoshaphat was faced with a powerful enemy, he called God's
people to prayer and fasting. The Lord spoke to them through
prophecy, encouraging them that he would give them victory in
the battle. They fell down to worship, and the singers stood up
to praise the Lord 'in a very loud voice'. As they went into
battle, the singers went ahead of the soldiers, singing praises to
God. And the Lord gave the victory.[69] 'Shout to God with loud
songs of joy!' says the psalmist. 'God has gone up with a
shout.'[70] Further in Acts 4 when they were faced with a powerful
conflict against the rulers who murdered their Master they lifted
or raised their voices together to God and said, 'Sovereign
Lord . . .' and they praised him with a loud voice that he was in
control of everything, asking merely for boldness to speak his
word. No wonder they were filled afresh with the Holy Spirit;
and no wonder the powers of darkness were driven back.

In Festivals of Praise around the world, I have encouraged
many thousands of Christians to give the Festal shout, 'The
Lord reigns!' As large congregations have joined together in
'loud shouts of joy', many have told me afterwards what an
encouragement this simple act has been. We need to strengthen
one another's hand in the Lord. When people all over the world
are stirring up each other with shouts of hatred, shouts of
violence, shouts supporting this political candidate or that
football team, surely we ought to follow this biblical principle
and shout praise to God. It can help to lift us up above the
mountains of difficulty, and strengthen our faith in the living
God. After all, 'if God is for us, who is against us?'[71] We need
to encourage one another in the midst of dangerous and
bewildering days, and proclaim together that Jesus Christ is the
Lord who reigns.

Notes

1. Romans 7:15
2. *Screwtape Letters*, Bles 1942, p. 9
3. Richard Lovelace, *Dynamics of Spiritual Life*, Paternoster Press, 1979, p. 18
4. Matthew 4:1
5. Matthew 16:23, NEB
6. Matthew 13:19
7. Matthew 13:39
8. John 8:44
9. John 17:15
10. 2 Corinthians 11:14
11. 2 Corinthians 2:11
12. Ephesians 4:27
13. 1 Timothy 3:7; 2 Timothy 2:26
14. 1 Timothy 4:1
15. Ephesians 6:11f
16. Colossians 2:15
17. James 4:7
18. 1 Peter 5:8f
19. Edwards, *Thoughts on the Revival*, p. 410
20. Michael Harper, *Spiritual Warfare*, Hodder & Stoughton, 1970. Kurt E. Koch, *Christian Counselling and Occultism, Occult Bondage and Deliverance*. John Nevius, *Demon Possession*. John Richards, *But Deliver us from Evil*. J. Stafford Wright, *Christianity and the Occult*. Michael Green *I Believe in Satan's Downfall*, Hodder & Stoughton, 1981
21. Mark 9:25
22. Richard F. Lovelace, op. cit., p. 256
23. 1 John 4:1
24. Acts 5:39
25. 2 Corinthians 4:4
26. Revelation 12:9
27. 2 Timothy 3:1–5
28. 1 Peter 5:8f; 4:12f
29. *Lectures*, vol. 1, p. 167
30. Revelation 12:1–17
31. Romans 2:24
32. 1 Timothy 6:1; Titus 2:5
33. Ephesians 6:16
34. 1 Timothy 4:1
35. 2 Corinthians 11:15
36. 2 Thessalonians 2:9
37. 2 Timothy 3:5; Revelation 13:13f
38. 2 Peter 2:1
39. 2 Timothy 3:8
40. 1 John 5:19
41. Luke 17:26f

42. Galatians 6:15
43. Psalm 91:14
44. Romans 8:21
45. John 8:44; Revelation 9:11
46. Luke 4:33–36
47. Luke 8:26–33
48. Luke 9:37–43
49. Luke 11:24–26
50. Richard F. Lovelace, op. cit., p. 140
51. Colossians 1:9, GNB
52. 2 Corinthians 2:11.
53. Matthew 26:41
54. Jude 17–25
55. 1 John 5:13
56. Ephesians 6:10
57. Ephesians 1:21f
58. 1 John 4:4
59. Colossians 1:20
60. Revelation 12:10f
61. Ephesians 5:1–18
62. 1 Timothy 1:18
63. Ephesians 4:26f
64. Ecclesiastes 4:9–12
65. Ephesians 6:10–20 I have written more fully about this in *Hidden Warfare*, Send the Light Trust, 1980, chapter 4
66. Ephesians 6:18
67. Psalm 89:15
68. Joshua 6:16, 20
69. 2 Chronicles 20
70. Psalm 47
71. Romans 8:31

CHAPTER NINE

Evangelism

Christ's call to discipleship is not primarily for the benefit of the disciple. His own apostles were slow to realise this, always wondering what they were going to get out of it, and who would be the greatest amongst them. Jesus rebuked them. 'Even the Son of man came not to be served but to serve, and to give his life a ransom for many.'[1] And Jesus laid down his life for one reason: because he had compassion on people in need. 'When he saw the crowds he had compassion for them, because they were harassed and helpless, like sheep without a shepherd.'[2]

What then was his plan of action? He called to him twelve potential leaders, gave them instructions, and sent them out to preach and heal, saying 'The kingdom of heaven is at hand.'[3] A little later seventy others were sent out for much the same purpose, 'to go into every town and place where he himself was about to come'.[4] It would not be easy: some would reject them, others persecute them. They would be involved in a great spiritual battle. In fact, the seventy came back bubbling over with joy; and undoubtedly this mission had been for them a wonderful learning and stimulating experience. As disciples, they were called and sent out; and in going out they grew in their discipleship. Later still, Jesus made it clear that every disciple is called both to be a witness to Jesus and to be committed to the task of evangelism. 'As the Father has sent me, even so I send you . . . You shall be my witnesses . . . to the end of the earth.'[5] If Christ's first call to us is 'Come', his second is 'Go' – 'Go your way . . . Go and preach the gospel . . . Go and make disciples . . .'[6]

Naturally they were not launched into powerful and effective evangelism overnight. Gently Jesus had to help them to lose their fears, to overcome their inertia, to see the urgency of the harvest, and to watch and pray. He had to teach them constantly about the kingdom of God. He had to strip them of pride and self-confidence, and to show them, sometimes in humbling and painful ways, that they could do nothing on their own; only by prayer and fasting could they expect to see the power of God at work. At times he had to test the reality of their love, challenge their commitment, and prepare them for spiritual battle. Often he warned them of hard times ahead, but promised them also the power of his Holy Spirit, by whose inward help they would be able to do the works that he had done, and even greater ones.

When we look at the early church, frail with its human fears and failings but alive in the Spirit, we see everyone gossiping about the gospel. Who first carried the good news of Christ to the great Gentile city of Antioch, and up and down the Phoenician seaboard? It was not the professionals. It was the 'little people', the nameless laity – the *idiotēs*, as they were later called – who went everywhere preaching Christ. No opposition could stop them. It was the whole church, active in witness and bold in evangelism, that dramatically changed the world of their day.

In the church today we need to think carefully how we can encourage the same spirit of evangelism that made such an impact on the first few centuries of the church's history, and is so effective today in south-west Asia, much of Africa and Latin America. How can we overcome the natural reticence, partly cultural, that makes most western Christians like the great Canadian rivers in winter, frozen at the mouth? How can we release our congregations from the natural fear of men and resistance to change? How can evangelism spontaneously flow from our church services and fellowships out into the streets, homes and places of work – where people are?

Breaking the ghetto mentality

Following a mission to Oxford University in which he shared with Cardinal Suenens, Bishop Stephen Neill wrote, 'We are still faced with the problem of the real outsider. In this mission, as in so many others, most of those attending were good Christians, or part-Christians, or "spoiled-Christians". Where do we make contact with the real outsider, and to what kind of message is it likely that he will give an ear? No one seems to know the answer to these questions. The greater part of our so-called evangelism takes place within or on the fringes of the church; we do not seem yet to have found the way to break out of the Christian ghetto into the world.'[7] There is a valid place for Christian missions and festivals, when Christians unite together for evangelism or joyful celebration. Fringe Christians need to become clearly committed to Christ; others need constant encouragement. Spiritual renewal always precedes effective evangelism. For the last few years I have been involved in numerous festivals in different parts of the world, when the gospel is proclaimed in the context of music and praise, dance, drama, colour and joy. Such events have a triple aim: evangelism, renewal and reconciliation between Christians – three inseparable strands of Christian mission.[8] Nevertheless we must be honest and admit that only a few real outsiders find Christ in this way. This is where we see the vital necessity of personal witness leading to effective discipleship. There are other ways of reaching the outsider, but nothing will be a substitute for this personal approach.

In view of this, the church needs to give much more training and support to Christians where they are at home and at work. It is the daily, unspectacular witness of Christians who are alive in Christ, that will most likely break into areas that the church is not otherwise touching at all. 'Men of business, trade, industry come and worship with us, and we tell them to be good husbands and appoint them our treasurers. We do almost nothing to equip them for their daily work, which is where God's kingdom has to come effectively today . . . We need to develop among all God's people, not merely the professionals, the sense of vocation as to where we live and work. What seems to be lacking in a divine strategy now is a mobile task force at God's disposal.'[9]

In many western countries – those in Europe, for example – the church is in a missionary situation. The vast majority of people know little or nothing about the Christian faith, and regard the church as irrelevant. The church needs small groups of deeply committed Christians to move into those areas as Christian trade unionists, teachers, politicians, social workers – every area of life – so that the church can be what Christ has called it to be, the salt of the earth and the light of the world.

The Christian dramatist, Murray Watts, has put it forcefully like this: 'We look at the TV today and say, "How terrible! The violence, the immorality, the pornography – the meat has gone bad!" Of course, it's gone bad, because the salt never got there in the first place.' But others have got there. Various secular, revolutionary and religious groups have infiltrated strategic sections of society with a philosophy that cannot begin to match the gospel of Christ. They have done so successfully for one reason only: they mobilise trained and dedicated disciples who are willing to sacrifice everything to achieve their goal. If we Christians pray that God's kingdom may come, we must be willing to be the answer to our own prayers, with all the imaginative boldness of those first disciples.

Witness and Evangelist

It is important to stress that not every Christian is called to be an evangelist. All are witnesses to Christ, all must be committed to the church's task of evangelism; but only some are evangelists.[10] It is Peter Wagner's belief that only about ten per cent of those in any church have this particular gift.[11] This means that whilst those ten per cent should be trained and encouraged in this gift, the other ninety per cent must resist a nagging sense of guilt that they are not evangelising in the way that some others are. Every gift is necessary to strengthen the body of Christ for the total work of God's mission here on earth.

First then, what are the marks of a *witness*?

(a) A witness must have *a first-hand experience of Christ*. Hearsay is not acceptable in a court of law, nor in the court of this world's opinion. People will listen only to what we have personally seen and heard.

(b) A witness must be *able to express it in words*. Although we may witness through our lives, our work, our relationships, our attitudes, our suffering and even our death, we must still 'be ready at all times to answer anyone who asks you to explain the hope you have in you.'[12] We must do so 'with gentleness and respect', and with the integrity of our lives demonstrating the truth of what we say.

(c) A witness will have *confidence in the power of God*: the power of the gospel, the power of the message of Christ and him crucified, and the power of the Holy Spirit. He knows that

God can break through any defences, and change any heart. This confidence will not be brash, but humble and sensitive, marked by much prayer. He knows that without God he can do nothing, but that with God all things are possible.

(d) A witness will have *compassion for those who are spiritually lost*. He will care for them as individuals who matter deeply to God: made in his image, redeemed by his Son, and to be indwelt by his Spirit.

Second, what are the marks of an *evangelist*? He will of course have, at least potentially, the qualities required for effective Christian witness; and some of these may be more fully developed in his life than in the life of someone who is a witness but not an evangelist. As well as these, he or she should have the potential for three other abilities.

(e) An evangelist will have *a certain clarity* with which he explains the gospel to others. He must be sure about his message, and able to communicate it with simplicity and relevance.

(f) An evangelist will be able to pass from an appeal to the mind to *an appeal to the will*. After some instruction about the facts of the gospel, he is aiming to call people to lay down their arms of rebellion, to turn to Christ in repentance and faith, and to accept him as Lord and Saviour.

(g) An evangelist will have *a God-given faith* that, if the Holy Spirit is truly at work in this situation, there can be a definite response to Christ here and now.

Repeatedly we have stressed the need to spot the 'potential' in people. It is only as we encourage one another to pray and work for this potential that it will be developed in our lives. Also, others may discern God's gifts to us more easily than we can ourselves; this may protect us from selfish ambition which could spoil those gifts. Every gift is to be used for the glory of God and for the benefit of his people.

Motivation

'To revolutionise the world,' said Dom Helder Camara, 'the only thing needed is for us to live and to spread the gospel of Jesus Christ with real conviction.' True. But in many churches today the primary issue is that of motivation. There are more training courses in evangelism than ever before; but even with all the knowledge of what to say and how to say it, the question still faces us, 'How are Christians motivated to do it?'

It is worth taking a look at one of the New Testament disciples, Philip the evangelist. We know little of the background of this man. He is first mentioned in Acts 6 when he and six others were appointed to a practical administrative task in the church. His subsequent impact as an evangelist, however, was considerable. What caused Philip and many others like him in the early church to preach Christ so readily?

1. *He was full of the Spirit.* This is the one outstanding fact we know about the seven, including Philip, who were appointed in Acts 6 to help in the pastoral care of the church at Jerusalem: they were full of faith, wisdom and the Holy Spirit. And the Spirit who filled them is the Spirit who comes to bear witness to Christ. 'The urge to witness is inborn in the church, it is given with her nature, with her very being. She cannot not witness. She has this being because of the Spirit who indwells her. Pentecost made the church a witnessing church, because at Pentecost the witnessing Spirit identified himself with the church and made the Great Commission the law of her life . . . So spontaneous was the response of the church to the Spirit-effected law, that the need of consciously obeying the command of Christ was not felt . . . It formed no part of her motivation.'[13] As the love of Christ was continuously poured by the Spirit into the hearts of those first disciples, it naturally overflowed out to others.

Paul once wrote that 'our gospel came to you not only in word, but also in power and in the Holy Spirit and with full conviction.'[14] The Greek word for 'full conviction', *plerephoria*, suggests a cup so full to the brim that it overflows. When people bump into us, the Spirit filling our hearts 'to the brim' will spontaneously touch their lives with the presence of Christ. If our hearts are not full of the Spirit, we may be reluctant to bear witness, since we have no witness to bear; and if, from a sense of duty, we do speak about Christ, our words may be empty words – they will not convey the reality of Jesus.

A professor of philosophy at Princeton University became a true Christian, having been an agnostic, when he studied very carefully the lives of some of the great saints of God down the centuries. The inescapable fact that really gripped him was the

spiritual radiance of their lives. Often they suffered intensely –
many of them far more than most other human beings, yet
through all their pain their spirits shone with a glorious lustre
that defied extinction. This philosopher became convinced that
some supernatural Being was the source of their extraordinary
joy; and this truth brought him to Christ.

A friend of mine once said that the most important thing about
us is not what we say, not what we do; it is 'our unconscious
influence – impregnated with the fragrance of Jesus'. Jesus
wants us to *be* his witnesses; he wants us to be with him, to
spend time with him, to be in constant communion with him. It
is who we are and what we are that counts. *Being* is more
important in Christian witness than saying or doing. St Ignatius
of Antioch once said, 'It is better to keep silence and to be, than
to talk and not to be.'

The following may not be great poetry, but it states a great
truth:

> Not merely in the words you say
> Not only in your deeds confessed,
> But in the most unconscious way
> Is Christ expressed.
> Is it a calm and peaceful smile?
> A holy light upon your brow?
> Oh no! I felt his presence while
> You laughed just now.
> For me 'twas not the truth you taught,
> To you so clear, to me so dim,
> But when you came to me you brought
> A sense of him.
> And from your eyes he beckons me,
> And from your heart his love is shed,
> Till I lose sight of you, and see
> The Christ instead.[15]

2. *He had seen God at work*. We cannot say precisely what
Philip had seen, but since he was well known in the rapidly
growing church in Jerusalem, he might easily have been present
when the pentecostal Spirit was poured out on those first
disciples. Perhaps he was overwhelmed with the love of God

and with the presence of the risen Christ. Perhaps he worshipped God in a language given by the Holy Spirit, 'lost in
wonder, love and praise'. He might have seen the 'many
wonders and signs' done through the apostles, rejoiced when
the healed cripple came into the temple 'walking and leaping
and praising God'. Maybe he joined in prayer to the Sovereign
Lord as they prayed for boldness to speak God's word in the
face of mounting opposition. Maybe he was there when the
room shook with the power of God as all those present were
filled with the Spirit. Undoubtedly he experienced the loving
care and incredible generosity of that new-born church, resulting in the powerful and effective preaching of Jesus Christ. He
would surely have known of God's dramatic judgement falling
on Ananias and Sapphira when, in a critical time of the church's
life, they both lied to the Holy Spirit. Certainly he witnessed the
astonishing growth of the church, from the 120 on the Day of
Pentecost to many thousands – all in a few weeks. They had
'filled Jerusalem' with their teaching; and even after the
apostles had been warned and beaten, 'every day in the temple
and at home they did not cease teaching and preaching Jesus as
the Christ'.[16]

There is nothing so inspiring as seeing God at work. When
men and women are won for Christ, when lives are changed
(sometimes dramatically so), when Christians give generously
and spontaneously to God's work, when some are healed of
sickness and others delivered from demonic powers, when there
is a glorious sense of God's presence in the praise of his people,
when there is an almost tangible experience of the love of God
within the body of Christ – then you can believe or do almost
anything! 'We cannot but speak of what we have seen and
heard.'[17] That is why spiritual renewal is so vital to evangelism.
If the life of a church is at a low level, it is a battle to believe and
harder to witness with any ring of truth. But when there is a
demonstration of the love and power of God in the lives of his
people, it is natural to explain spontaneously what it is all
about.

3. *He was spurred on by suffering.* Shortly after Philip's
appointment in the church, Stephen, one of the seven, was
arrested and brought to trial. The power of God had been so
strikingly present with him that the rulers had to take action.

Courageously Stephen drew the lesson from the history of
God's people that whenever God did something new amongst
them, his work was opposed and rejected. 'You stiff-necked
people,' concluded Stephen, 'uncircumcised in heart and ears,
you always resist the Holy Spirit. As your fathers did, so do
you.' It was true, and it needed to be said. Stephen was
martyred for his boldness, but his suffering gave courage to the
church. From the resulting wave of persecution that arose
against the church, they were all scattered throughout Judea
and Samaria; and 'those who were scattered went about preaching the word'.[18] No doubt Philip and the others thought deeply
about the content of Stephen's speech. Perhaps the truth of
what he said and the radiance with which he said it spurred
Philip to go to the 'untouchables' in Samaria.

Paul later wrote that it was through his own suffering and
imprisonment that 'most of the brethren have been made
confident in the Lord . . ., and are much more bold to speak the
word of God without fear'.[19] 'The blood of martyrs is the seed
of the church', and in every age the persecution of Christians
has nearly always led to the spread of the gospel. Bonhoeffer
used to say that 'the church is a community of those who are
persecuted and martyred for the gospel's sake', and he too was
one of the countless millions who have laid down their lives for
the sake of Christ.

In his excellent book, *Evangelism – now and then*, Michael
Green writes of three Ugandans, accused of political crimes
against General Amin, who were converted in prison. 'They
grew in the power and love of the Holy Spirit. Then they were
led out to die by public executioner. They urged Bishop Festo
Kivengere, who was allowed there to encourage them, to go
and tell the gospel to the executioners, while they bore witness
joyfully to Christ before the crowd, and continued praising the
God who had forgiven and would soon be receiving them right
up till the moment when the shots rang out from the amazed
firing squad. That story went round the country like wildfire.'[20]

The trouble with much of the church in the West is that it is
too comfortable. In most places it costs little to be a Christian.
The image of the church is too flabby to warrant persecution. It
is not worth opposing its movement since it is on the retreat
anyway. But when the church begins to be God's new society,

an effective counter-culture challenging the covetous spirit of the age, growing in influence, it will certainly be persecuted. When the selfish ambitions of sinful men are threatened by the light and love of Jesus Christ seen in the church, they will strike back. If the church is willing to be renewed by the Holy Spirit, and should persecution result from this, Christians will either have the courage to witness boldly for Christ, or they will drop out altogether. It will be a time of purification for the church. It will be a time of powerful evangelism.

In a telling parable, the Church of England's report on evangelism said this: 'When Jesus said to his disciples "I will make you fishers of men" the picture that he and they had in mind was that they would 'launch out into the deep' of the particularly treacherous lake of Galilee dragging or casting a net over the side of the boat and then trying to bring the net ashore. It was a dangerous occupation in a dangerous milieu, but their livelihood depended on it. It was their full-time occupation. The commonest modern image of a fisherman in England (with apologies to deep-sea trawlermen) is of a man safely sitting alone under an umbrella on a river bank with a baited rod and line occasionally landing a small fish out of the river and into his bucket. He runs no risk and catches very little worth catching. His is a weekend pastime not a daily occupation. His living does not depend on it.'[21] As long we 'play' at evangelism, with no risk to ourselves and no price to pay, we shall make little or no impact on our society. When we see evangelism, not as a gentle Sunday sport, but the serious, costly business of everyday life – the livelihood of the church – we may have to ride out many storms but there will be a fishing harvest for God's glory. In some parts of the world Christians are being urged by church leaders *not* to evangelise because, it is said, the religious and political situation is too sensitive. How would Stephen or Philip have reacted to that?

Message
There was nothing vague, defensive or apologetic about the message of Philip. 'Philip went down to a city of Samaria, and proclaimed to them the Christ' (8:5); 'he preached good news about the kingdom of God and the name of Jesus Christ' (8:12); 'he told him the good news of Jesus' (8:35). God's message

entrusted to us is Jesus Christ. It centres, not on a proposition or on a philosophy, but firmly on the person of Christ.

'Evangelism is the presentation of the claims of Christ in the power of the Spirit to a world in need by a church in love.'[22] The 'claims' of Christ are on the basis of the uniqueness of his person, his death for our sins, his resurrection from the dead, and his coming again to judge the living and the dead. The letter to the Hebrews was written to those who were wavering in their faith because of the struggles of discipleship; and the whole message of the letter is simply this: *There is no one like Jesus!* He is described as God's last word, the Creator of the world, reflecting the glory of God and bearing the very stamp of his nature; he upholds the universe by the word of his power. He has once for all offered himself as a single sacrifice for sins, so that we now have confidence to come into God's presence by the blood of Jesus. There is no one like him.[23]

Without Jesus, therefore, we have nothing of ultimate importance; we have missed the main purpose of our existence. Peter said boldly, facing the Jewish leaders who had recently secured the death of Jesus, 'There is salvation in no one else, for there is no other name under heaven given among men by which we must be saved.'[24] Paul wrote that one day we must all come to terms with him: 'We must all appear before the judgement seat of Christ.'[25] Christ himself taught clearly and repeatedly about the judgement to come, because in his great love for us he had not only told us about our greatest need, he also died to bear our sins and so meet that need. It is now urgent that we turn from our sins, trust him as Lord and Saviour, and receive his Spirit into our hearts. How shall we escape God's righteous judgement if we neglect such a great salvation?[26]

How, too, shall we help others to escape if we are diffident about this gospel, ashamed of it, apologetic about it? How shall we convey the truth and urgency of it all if we re-write the gospel in sophisticated philosophical terms, or so dilute its content that it is not worth the response of any person's life? How shall we help others to believe in Jesus if he is not central in our message and the consuming passion of our lives? How will people believe that 'there is no one like Jesus' if they see his followers quarrelling with one another, unwilling to work together, often pre-occupied with things that are trivial in comparison with Christ? How will men and women be convinced of their need of God if we are not burdened for those who are lost, if we are apathetic about evangelism, and if we are not willing to pay the price of reaching people for Christ? These are questions that many outsiders take seriously, and the church should do so as well.

God has entrusted us with the ministry of reconciliation. We are to call people to be reconciled to God through Jesus Christ, 'God making his appeal through us'.[27] But we need to remember that Christ himself proclaimed the kingdom of God. It is God's declared purpose in Christ to 'unite all things in him',[28] and God intends that the whole world should be reconciled through Christ. Thus evangelism which is solely concerned with personal salvation is not New Testament evangelism. The preaching of Christ affects every area of life – personal, social, political, educational, everything. I talked about this with Dr William Glasser at Fuller Theological Seminary, and he asked me a rhetorical question, 'What is the gospel for South Africa? That Christ died for your sins?' When I led some evangelistic missions in South Africa universities I could not expect a hearing unless I spoke, in part, about some of the burning issues facing those students. What does God say about *apartheid*? What does it mean for a Christian to 'be subject to the governing authorities'? (Romans 13). Certainly I preached about God's answer to man's sin through the death and resurrection of God's Son. But the evangelist must listen to, and take seriously, the questions people are asking; only then will he be relevant.

Professor David J. Bosch from South Africa has put it in this way: 'If we communicate only that part of the gospel which corresponds to people's "felt needs" and "personal problems" ("Are you lonely? Do you feel that you have failed? Do you need a friend? Then come to Jesus!") while remaining silent on their relationship to their fellow men, on racism, exploitation and blatant injustice, we do not proclaim the gospel. This is the quintessence of what Bonhoeffer called "cheap grace".[29] Many today have rejected what they have heard as the Christian gospel and embraced instead, for example, the Marxist philosophy, partly because they do not see as realistic the evangelistic message so often heard: if you change the individual you will change the world. David Bosch has put it neatly like this: 'Christianity which does not begin with the individual, does not begin; but Christianity which ends with the individual, ends.' Certainly God is infinitely concerned with the salvation of the individual; but his purpose is for the healing of creation. Everything is to come under his sovereign rule or Kingdom.

Philip's preaching of the kingdom of God was therefore accompanied by many signs of the kingdom: 'And the multitudes with one accord gave heed to what was said by Philip, when they heard him *and saw the signs which he did*. For unclean spirits came out of many who were possessed, crying with a loud voice; and many who were paralysed or lame were healed. So there was much joy in that city.'[30] Much of our society today is marked by depression, frustration and despair. More than ever we need to proclaim and demonstrate the good news of the kingdom of God. God rules over sin, evil and death. When people see his power to change people's hearts, to restore broken relationships, to break oppression, to enforce justice, to heal emotional hurts and physical diseases, then 'with one accord' they will begin to take notice.

At the very least we need to communicate with joyful enthusiasm the most glorious good news in the world. That is why drama and mime, music and dance, have a real part in the telling of this news to a world that is increasingly word-resistant. 'Today we need overdrawn images, parables, stories, fantasies if you like. Secular Western man is too sad, too dull, suffering from personality malnutrition. It is time to stand up and tell our story with enthusiasm.'[31] With a team gifted in music, dance and drama I have witnessed the joyful surprise of many 'real outsiders' at the vitality and relevance of the gospel of Christ. In prisons, on the streets, in schools and universities, I have seen the freshness in this form of communication cutting through the apathy and antagonism of many towards the church.

One leading terrorist wrote to me from a prison in Northern Ireland after a service in that prison: 'I had been considering for some time becoming a Christian, but after seeing your team I no longer had any doubts, and have now been saved by the blood of Christ.' His letter revealed two interesting facts. First, in spite of a life sold out to violence he was spiritually hungry.

Second, it was the communication of the whole team, not my words, that really got through to him. Why should the devil have all the best forms of communication?

It is worth noting that Philip's evangelistic ministry was not perfect. He lacked spiritual discernment in the case of Simon, the occult magician: 'After being baptised (presumably by Philip) Simon continued with Philip.' It required the apostle Peter to unmask this counterfeit conversion: 'Your heart is not right with God. Repent therefore . . . For I see that you are in the gall of bitterness and in the bond of iniquity.' We all need one another's gifts within the body of Christ. Philip also required the ministry of Peter and John before the believers in Samaria received the Holy Spirit. It has often been argued that before the Samaritans, whose religion had been a corruption of Judaism, could be fully received into the body of Christ there was need of apostolic witness and confirmation. That may be true. It is also possible that Philip's evangelistic message had neglected any direct reference to the Holy Spirit, as was the case with Apollos in Acts 18. When today there is no reference to the person and work of the Holy Spirit at the point of conversion, confusion may later arise. Probably much of the charismatic debate has occurred for this very reason. Peter's instructions on the Day of Pentecost were clear: 'Repent, and be baptised every one of you in the name of Jesus Christ for the forgiveness of your sins; and you shall receive the gift of the Holy Spirit.'[32] The statement called *Gospel and Spirit*, resulting from the charismatic-evangelical dialogue in England, commented: 'We are agreed on the need . . . to present the full range of Christ's salvation and gift for us in all our evangelism and teaching – i.e. to preach a complete, rather than a truncated, gospel.'[33]

Method
The most striking feature of Philip's evangelistic work was this: he was obedient to the Spirit of God. Obediently he crossed the Jewish-Samaritan divide, and the Spirit was manifestly with him. Obediently he left that fruitful ministry and travelled many miles to the desert road between Jerusalem and Gaza, not knowing why he was going there. Obediently he went up to one particular traveller, because the Spirit told him to do so. Later

he obediently left that man and 'preached the gospel to all the towns till he came to Caesarea'. As we focus attention on Philip's personal evangelism with the Ethiopian eunuch, we see that in his obedience Philip went to the right man at the right time with the right words and the right ministry.

1. *The right man.* The "Chancellor of the Exchequer" from Ethiopia was evidently a man in whom the Spirit of God had been working, long before Philip came on to the scene. He had been to Jerusalem to worship and was clearly in search of God. Perhaps the Jewish settlements in Upper Egypt had aroused his curiosity. Frequently I pray this prayer of Bishop Taylor Smith: 'Lord give me eyes to see, and grace to seize, every opportunity for Thee.' Believing that God's Spirit is at work throughout the world, we need to see what the Spirit is doing in people's lives, and then have the sensitivity and boldness to take the opportunities as they come. Ethiopian tradition claims that this statesman became not only the country's first convert, but also their first evangelist. He was certainly the right man.

2. *The right time.* When Philip ran to the Ethiopian's chariot at the Spirit's instruction, he heard the man reading aloud from the scriptures; and not just anywhere in the scriptures, but from Isaiah 53! What perfect timing! There is a time to speak, and a time to keep silence. In my evangelistic experience, there are certain moments in a person's life when God seems especially near and easily found. We are to 'seek the Lord while he may be found, (and) call upon him while he is near.'[34] Although there is urgency with the gospel, and Paul exhorted Timothy to proclaim the gospel 'whether the time is right or not',[35] we should expect God to guide us to people at those times when his Spirit is drawing them to himself, whether they themselves realise this or not. The moment when Jesus met the Samaritan woman at the well is another obvious example of this.

3. *The right words.* He asked a question which immediately related to what the man was doing; 'Do you understand what you are reading?' It drew a positive response, and an invitation to Philip to join him in the chariot to talk further. Several interesting points follow from this.

(a) We need to use words that are relevant to the person concerned. In this case Philip's opening words were not only relevant, they were courteous and led easily to further con-

versation. A great friend of mine, who is an Anglican clergyman, won his dustman for Christ a little time ago. He said to
this man, 'Bill, I want to introduce you to the greatest dustman
in the world. He will empty your rubbish at any time of any day
or any night!' Bill was fascinated by this, and it was immediately
relevant. He soon understood that Jesus had come to take the
rubbish out of his heart, and to clean up his life altogether. In
principle that is exactly how Jesus approached the woman at the
well. She had come to draw water, so he spoke to her of living
water which would quench her every thirst.

(b) Although it is helpful to have a simple framework by which
we can lead a person to Christ, pray also for what could be
called 'prophetic witness'. A woman longed to speak to her
neighbour about Christ, but she was no evangelist and seemed
to find no opportunity. So she prayed one morning, 'Lord, what
can I say to my neighbour that will show her that you love her?'
This Christian woman was not used to hearing direct answers to
prayer like that, so she was startled when she had a strong
impression, almost as though the Lord had spoken to her aloud,
that she was to go to her neighbour and tell her not to be afraid.
Obediently she went. She knocked on the door and asked if she
might come in. Nervously she started, 'I think God is wanting to
say something to you this morning. I think he is saying to you,
"Don't be afraid."' Her neighbour at once burst into tears. She
had heard only that morning that her daughter needed an
operation, and this poor mother was full of fear. The thought
that God could care about her so much that he sent a message
to her personally, broke through all her defences. She was now
longing to know the God who loved her that much.

(c) In evangelism, we must know our Bibles. Philip could at
once pick up the passage that the Ethiopian was reading, and
from that passage he shared with him the good news of Jesus. In
particular, we need to know from the scriptures both the way by
which anyone can find God, and also brief answers to the most
common questions – questions that are asked over and over
again. In my book *Is Anyone There?*[36] I have glanced at some of
the questions or comments that I hear repeatedly:

What about the suffering in the world?
The church is so dead and irrelevant.

What about other religions?
There are too many things I don't understand.
I've tried before, but it didn't work.
I am afraid of getting involved.
How does God guide me?
I could never keep it up.
Can't I keep it to myself?

Other common remarks are:

I don't feel any need of God.
Isn't trying hard or going to church good enough?
I can't accept the Bible.

We are not expected to have a complete answer to these
questions: with many of them, such as suffering, that would be
impossible. Anyway, if we could know all about God and his
ways of working, God would be no bigger than our tiny finite
minds and not worth believing in. But it is helpful to have some
thoughtful and biblical comments about these questions so as to
prevent them, if possible, from becoming excuses or barriers to
belief.

In many cases, those who don't believe don't want to believe.
Often it is a matter of the will:

Convince a man against his will,
He's of the same opinion still.

Also, if a person's faith rests in a clever argument, he will
always be at the mercy of what may seem to him to be a cleverer
argument. Paul was concerned so to preach 'Jesus Christ and
him crucified' in the power of the Spirit that the faith of those
who responded 'might not rest in the wisdom of men but in the
power of God'.[37] When the Samaritan woman raised a theological question as to where God should be worshipped, in
Jerusalem or in Samaria (a question significantly raised when
Jesus was touching very personal areas in her life which called
for repentance), Jesus did not fully answer her but brought her
back to the spiritual issues: 'God is Spirit, and only by the
power of his Spirit can people worship him as he really is.'[38] It is

good, then, to be acquainted with the common problems that
are raised, have some positive remarks to say about each one,
but also seek to turn the problem round in a more personal and
helpful direction.

Leading a person to Christ

If I am lost in some town and I ask someone the way, I want
them to say to me, 'Turn left, turn right, turn left, turn
right – and there you are!' No doubt they could describe it in
much more complicated and accurate terms, but those simple
directions are all I need to hear at that moment. If someone is
lost spiritually and he asks us the way, he too wants simple
directions. Perhaps we could describe it in much more complicated and theological terms, but something clear and simple
is all that he needs to hear at that moment. What simple
directions are there to Christ? I have used many ways of
describing it over the years, but this is one of my favourite,
perhaps because it was through these directions that I found
Christ personally at the age of 21:

Think of it as four steps, A B C D. Each of these four steps I
state, explain, illustrate and apply. This is how I might put it to
someone.

A. *Something to admit.* You must first admit your need of God,
especially that you have sinned and therefore need his forgiveness. Sin means going your way, not God's; doing what you
want, not what God wants. In the Bible Paul says, 'There is no
distinction, since all have sinned and fall short of the glory of
God. (Romans 3:22–23) As far as a good life is concerned, you
could be on the top of Mount Everest; and in comparison with
you, I could be at the bottom of the valley. The point is, there is
really 'no distinction' since neither of us can touch the stars. We
both come miles short of God's perfect standards shown to us in
the Bible, and supremely in the life and teaching of Jesus
Christ. Our sins have separated us from God, and we need his
forgiveness.

B. *Something to believe.* Believe that Christ died for you.
Suppose that this hand (holding up my left hand) represents
yourself, and this object (putting a book on my hand) represents your sin – coming as a 'cloud barrier' between you and
God. That is why God seems unreal and distant. Suppose that

this other hand (holding up my right hand) represents Jesus –
he had no other sin on him at all. Isaiah 53:6, speaking of the
coming sufferings of Jesus on the cross, says this, 'All we like
sheep have gone astray; we have turned every one to his own
way; and the Lord has laid on him (illustrated by transferring
the book from my left hand to my right) the iniquity (or guilt) of
us all.' Now, where is your sin? It was taken by Jesus when he
died on the cross. Simon Peter, who at one time could not
understand why Jesus had to die, put it later like this: 'Christ
died for our sins once for all. He the just suffered for the unjust,
to bring us to God.' (1 Peter 3:18) When Jesus died for you, he
made it possible for you to know the love of God for ever.

C. *Something to consider.* Jesus must come first in your life.
Jesus once said, 'If any man would come after me, let him deny
himself and take up his cross and follow me'. (Mark 8:34) We
must say *No to sin*, being willing to turn away from all that we
know is wrong in our life – with God's help. We must say *No to
self*, being willing for Jesus to be Lord over every part of our
life: home, work, time, money, ambitions, relationships, everything. We must say *No to secrecy*, being willing to be known as a
Christian, even if some may mock and oppose us. But don't be
afraid of opening your life to the one person who loves you and
cares about you more than anyone else in the world, and who
wants only the best for your life. (I sometimes refer to Mark 8:
35–38 to help a person think through the 'profit-and-loss
account'.)

D. *Something to do.* Give your life to Jesus, and, as you do
that, he will give his life to you by his Spirit coming to live
within you. Think of the marriage analogy. When I was married
some years ago, the clergyman who married us said,

'David, will you have this woman?' 'I will.'

'Anne, will you have this man?' 'I will.' At that moment a
new relationship was established. In the same sort of way:

'Saviour, will you have this sinner?' Always he says, 'I will'.

'Sinner, will you have this Saviour?' The moment you say 'I
will', and really mean it, a new relationship will be established.
Other points follow from this analogy.

(a) When I said 'I will' at my wedding, I had to promise to
'forsake all others', or put Anne first. When I said 'I will' to
Jesus, I had to be willing to put Jesus first.

(b) When I said 'I will' at my wedding, I had no feelings at all; it was just an act of will. So it was with Jesus. Relationships do not depend on feelings, but on commitment and trust.

(c) When I said 'I will' at my wedding, it was only the beginning of a new relationship. We had to work hard at it, and it hasn't always been easy. When I said 'I will' to Jesus, it was only the beginning of a new relationship, and it hasn't been plain sailing ever since. There have been moments of doubt, disobedience, rebellion, and so on. But when you work through the difficulties in any relationship, so it matures and develops.

Putting the directions like this on paper may seem stiff and stereotyped. Every person is different, and every conversation will flow differently. We must make sure that each step is understood before proceeding to the next, and this may involve asking a few questions and adding more explanations and illustrations. The key to it all is prayer, sensitivity to the Spirit and genuine love for the individual concerned. J. I. Packer once expressed our dependence on the Spirit of God in evangelism in this way: 'However clear and cogent we may be in presenting the gospel, we have no hope of convincing or converting anyone. Can you or I by our earnest talking break the power of Satan over a man's life? No. Can you or I give life to the spiritually dead? No. Can we hope to convince sinners of the truth of the gospel by patient explanation? No. Can we hope to move men to obey the gospel by any words of entreaty that we may utter? No. Our approach to evangelism is not realistic till we have faced this shattering fact, and let it make its proper impact on us.'[39] It is only through much prayer, humbly acknowledging our complete helplessness and seeking for the guidance and illumination of the Spirit, that the scales may fall from a person's eyes to enable him to see the light of the gospel of the glory of Christ.[40]

Once a person appears to understand the steps to Christ, it is good to offer some practical action. 'If you like,' I often suggest, 'I will lead you in a simple personal prayer, which you could echo phrase by phrase in your own heart, either silently or aloud as you prefer; or I can give you some literature to help you understand more fully the step you are taking.' Gently I may encourage a prayer of commitment to Christ there and then as often I have seen the parable of the sower enacted, in that after the seed has been sown the devil is quick to snatch it away before it has time to take root in the soil of a person's heart. If he is willing to pray, I sometimes go quickly through the prayer I intend to pray, to see if he is happy to echo it for himself. Then I pray slowly, a few words at a time – something like this:

> Lord Jesus Christ,
> I know that I am a sinner,
> and I need your forgiveness.
> Thank you for dying on the cross for me,
> to take away my sin.
> I am willing to turn from all that is wrong in my life.
> I am willing for you to be first in my life.
> And now I come to you;
> I say "I will".
> I give my life to you, my Lord and my Saviour.
> Please give your life to me by your Spirit,
> and come to live with me for ever.
> Thank you, Lord Jesus.
> Amen.

The person may follow me in prayer, aloud or silently, and then I will pray another short prayer of encouragement, thanking Jesus for hearing our prayer, and asking that this person might be filled with the Spirit, discover God's purpose for his life, grow in his relationship with Jesus (with the help of other Christians), and share the love and truth of Jesus in this needy world.

After that I may point out one more promise of Jesus to help him stand firm against any doubts which may later come to him; and then fix up another time in a day or two when we can talk further together. Nearly always I give some suitable literature before we part, so that he has something to read that will help him to grasp the basic steps that he has taken.[41] The young Christian will then need careful follow-up, either through personal sessions with him or through a 'beginners' group', when subjects such as these need to be looked at over the course of several weeks: assurance, growth, prayer, the Bible, foundational truths of the faith (God, Christ, the Holy Spirit, the cross and resurrection, the church, spiritual gifts, etc.); also we need to look at witness, guidance, giving, and a lot of other issues as they arise.[42]

Remember that winning the person for Christ is only the beginning. With the love of God and the sensitivity of his Spirit, we are to serve that person until he or she becomes a true disciple of Christ. When we see that person winning someone else for Christ, or at least taking a full part in the body of Christ, we can rejoice that in the Lord our labour is not in vain. As we have seen from the rest of this book, the task of discipling one another never finishes. It demands everything we have, but offers immense rewards. William Barclay once said, 'There is no joy in all the world like the joy of bringing one soul to Christ.' That is the privilege and responsibility of every disciple.

Notes

1. Matthew 20:28
2. Matthew 9:35f
3. See Matthew 10
4. Luke 10:1–20
5. John 20:21; Acts 1:8
6. Luke 10:3; Mark 16:15; Matthew 28:19
7. Quoted by Bishop John Taylor in *The Winchester Churchman*, July 1979
8. I have written more extensively about this in *I Believe in Evangelism*, Hodder and Stoughton, 1976
9. John Poulton, The Monthly Letter for May/June 1979 of the WCC Commission on World Mission and Evangelism
10. Ephesians 4:11
11. C. Peter Wagner, *Your Church Can Grow*, Glendale, California, USA: Regal, 1976, p. 72–76
12. 1 Peter 3:15, GNB
13. H. Boer, *Pentecost and Missions*, Lutterworth, pp. 122, 128
14. 1 Thess. 1:5
15. Source unknown
16. Acts 5:28, 42
17. Acts 4:20
18. Acts 7:8:1–5
19. Philippians 1:14
20. Op. cit., IVP, 1979, p. 26
21. *Evangelism in England Today*, a Report by the Church of England's Board for Mission and Unity, Church House Bookshop, Great Smith Street, London SW1P 3BN

22. *A New Canterbury Tale*, published by Grove Books, Bramcote, Notts, England
23. Hebrews 1:1–3; 10:10–20; et al.
24. Acts 4:12
25. 2 Corinthians 5:10
26. Hebrews 2:3
27. 2 Corinthians 5:20
28. Ephesians 1:9f
29. *Witness to the World*, Marshall, Morgan & Scott, 1980, p. 206
30. Acts 8:6f
31. John Poulton, op. cit.
32. Acts 2:38
33. Available from The Evangelical Alliance, 19 Draycott Place, London SW3 2SJ
34. Isaiah 55:6
35. 2 Timothy 4:2, GNB
36. Hodder & Stoughton, 1979, Chapter 6
37. 1 Corinthians 2:1–5
38. John 4:1–26
39. *Evangelism and the Sovereignty of God*, IVP, 1961, p. 108
40. 2 Corinthians 4:3f
41. I normally use my booklet *A New Start in Life*, Kingsway, or my book *Live a New Life*, IVP, 1975. Other suitable material is also available.
42. I have written more fully about follow-up in *I Believe in Evangelism*, Hodder & Stoughton, 1976, chapter 7. See also Appendix B (pp. 269f) for further suggestions of a basic teaching course.

CHAPTER TEN

Discipleship and Simple Lifestyle

Two sharply contrasting illustrations will indicate the present-day scandal of economic inequality within the world-wide family of God.

In *Time Magazine*[1] there was a fascinating article about American evangelists who run weekly television shows. Searching questions could be asked of some of them concerning the content of their gospel and the style of their presentation. For all my personal misgivings, I hope I have the generous spirit of the apostle Paul who wrote that if 'Christ is proclaimed . . . in that I rejoice'.[2] I am sure that some, at least, will experience God's love, peace and healing through these programmes. What disturbs me much more is the lifestyle of these and other preachers. One evangelist, according to the article, received gifts from listeners amounting to $51 million each year, a fiftieth of which he keeps for his own personal income. He already owns a luxurious house, a fleet of cars and numerous other material advantages. The journalist from *Time* was understandably critical.

One month after reading that article I was present at the International Consultation on Simple Lifestyle, held in England under the joint chairmanship of Ronald Sider and John Stott. On the opening evening an evangelist from Columbia spoke through an interpreter. He told us of an utterly exhausting day's preaching in one village, and feeling tired and very hungry returned to the pastor's house where he was staying. The pastor, his wife and five children were there, but the table was set with only one plate on it – clearly for the visiting evangelist. He sat down, and on the plate the pastor's wife put one egg and one small potato. 'Is that all?' he thought to himself. 'But I am so hungry!' Nevertheless he bowed his head to give thanks to God for the food before him. As he was about to start, he asked if the rest of them had already eaten. Hastily the pastor's wife replied that she would fix them up with something later. Since it was already 10.30 in the evening, the evangelist made further enquiries. He discovered that they had no money and no food in the house apart from this one egg and one small potato. He asked the wife to put seven other plates on the table. He divided his already tiny meal into eight minuscule portions, invited them all to sit with him at the table, bowed his head again, and gave thanks.

Such examples could be multiplied many times over, indicating the staggering difference in lifestyle between members of the same family of God. Is this what God intends for his children on this earth? How far does the lifestyle of the western church, in particular, help or hinder the task of mission and evangelism in the world? For many of us, on both personal and corporate levels, there is an urgent need for a new image altogether, a radical discipleship modelled on the simplicity of Jesus, if we are to demonstrate with credibility the values of the kingdom of God and thus speak with authority about the God who so loved the world that he gave the inexpressible gift of his own Son.

The Christian dramatist, Murray Watts, once told me this true story. A man born deaf, and raised in a good middle-class Christian home, was brought to a living faith in Christ through an incident on a train in India. He found himself in the same carriage as a beggar who was praising God with his whole heart. This beggar was materially destitute, but overflowing with thanksgiving and praise. It was the amazing sight of this that broke through to the deaf man and allowed the love of God, which had always surrounded him, to flow into his heart.

This true incident is by way of a parable. The world is increasingly deaf to a church that has sold out to materialism. It is only when the world is confronted with a church that is wholly dependent on God, perhaps because it has voluntarily or involuntarily accepted material poverty for the sake of the countless poor that God is trying to reach, that any impact will be made. Affluence and spiritual complacency often go together, just as material bankruptcy can often accompany spiritual wealth. It is when others see that we have 'nothing but God' – and therefore have everything to praise and thank him for – that the reality of his living presence amongst us will be seen by those who doubt his existence.

Today there is no shortage of pious words, affirmations of faith, discussions about hunger, or expressions of spirituality. But the world is still waiting for the demonstration, in hard, costly and practical terms, of what we proclaim with our lips. 'I was hungry, and you formed a committee to investigate my hunger . . . I was homeless, and you filed a report on my plight . . . I was sick, and you held a seminar on the situation of the underprivileged . . . You have investigated all aspects of my plight. And yet I am still hungry, homeless and sick.'

'The life of Jesus and his disciples,' writes John Taylor, 'was not only eucharistic but also defiant. He knew it was not enough to say these things; the world is waiting for concrete examples and realisations. So in our day it is not enough to point out the contrast between our idolatry of growth and the Bible's theology of enough; we have to opt out of the drift and help one another to live in cheerful protest against it . . .'[3]

It was surely for this reason that Jesus not only taught and challenged his disciples on the whole issue of money and possessions but shared his whole life with them. Unless their obedience was demonstrably true, he knew that he would be building a castle in the air instead of his church on the rock, against which neither the gates of hell nor any other gates could prevail. How then can the vital ingredients of effective discipleship be proved and developed?

Obedience

From the very beginning Jesus sought to teach his followers the absolute necessity of total obedience to him as Lord of their lives. He had come to usher in the kingdom of God, which involved his reign or rule over every area of their lives, whether they understood or not – whether they agreed or not. In Luke 5, when Jesus, the carpenter's son from Nazareth, told Simon, the experienced Galilean fisherman, to throw his nets into the sea in broad daylight, we can understand the professional protest: 'Master, we toiled all night and took nothing!' Yet such was the commanding presence of Jesus in his boat that Simon went on, 'But at your word I will let down the nets.' The catch was staggering. Here was the first and foremost lesson for

Simon to learn if he was later to be 'catching men': one minute's obedience to Christ is worth infinitely more than striving, even to the point of exhaustion, in the wisdom and energy of the flesh.

Throughout the short period of discipleship this lesson had to be taught again and again, but we can see in the astonishing growth of the early church how effective it became. An efficient army will always be marked by instant obedience to the word of command. Both conventional armies, specialist units and terrorist organisations know the absolute importance of this. Without unquestioning obedience, the effectiveness of any group will be seriously diminished. To obtain this quality of response, numerous hours of training on seemingly minor matters are essential.

Especially we need to learn obedience when it comes to material possessions. Juan Carlos Ortiz has often remarked about the way we tend to select those Bible verses which are comforting but ignore those that we find disturbing. We happily respond to the reassuring words of Jesus: 'Fear not, little flock, for it is your Father's good pleasure to give you the kingdom'; but we may easily ignore the very next verse, 'Sell your possessions and give alms.'[4] Yet this sacrificial act of obedience may well be a vital part of the way in which God will give us the kingdom. When we fail to take the challenge of Jesus seriously, we may wonder why the kingdom of God is not coming in the power that Jesus apparently promised. It is because we have embraced the independent spirit of the world which says 'Yes, but . . .' and however hard we try to rationalise it, saying 'Yes, but' to Jesus is none other than disobedience. That is why there is not a greater demonstration of the power of the Spirit: God's Spirit is given only to those who obey him.[5]

In Matthew 6:19–24 Jesus puts the issue in a series of sharp contrasts. We must make our choice between two treasures (earthly or heavenly), two conditions (light or darkness), and two Masters (God or Mammon). In other words, we have to face up to the searching question, Who or what comes first in our life? And nowhere is this question more clearly answered than in our whole attitude to possessions.

It is important to stress that Jesus is not forbidding the ownership of private property. Even when the sharing amongst

Christians was at its best and most generous, Peter said to
Ananias about the sale of his land, 'While it remained unsold,
did it not remain your own? And after it was sold, was it not at
your disposal?'[6] Several of the disciples had possessions of their
own, as is implied by the statement that they went on continuously (Greek imperfect tense) selling what they had to
provide for those that had not.[7] Further, Jesus is not against
some wise provision for the future. As Paul later wrote: 'If any
one does not provide for his relatives, and especially for his own
family, he has disowned the faith and is worse than an unbeliever.' (1 Timothy 5:8) Nor certainly is Jesus encouraging us
to ignore or despise the numerous good gifts of God's creation.
Matter is not intrinsically evil, as the gnostics wrongly taught.
'Everything created by God is good, and nothing is to be
rejected if it is received with thanksgiving.' (1 Timothy 4:1–5)
Paul knew 'how to be abased, and how to abound', and he
found the Lord's peace in facing either plenty or hunger, either
abundance or want. (Philippians 4:12)

What Jesus spoke strongly against was hoarding up treasures
'*for yourselves*'. This is not only foolish, for all these earthly
treasures will sooner or later decay or disappear; it is selfish in
the light of the vast needs of men, women and children
throughout the world – a straight denial of the love of God;
and, worst of all, it is idolatrous, 'for where your treasure is,
there will your heart be also.'

'Worldly possessions tend to turn the hearts of the disciples
away from Jesus. What are we really devoted to? That is the
question. Are our hearts set on earthly goods? Do we try to
combine devotion to them with loyalty to Christ? Or are we
devoted exclusively to him? . . . Where our treasure is, there is
our trust, our security, our consolation and our God. Hoarding
is idolatry . . . Everything which hinders us from loving God
above all things . . . is our treasure, and the place where our
heart is . . . If our hearts are entirely given to God, it is clear
that we *cannot* serve two masters; it is simply impossible . . .
Our hearts have room only for one all-embracing devotion, and
we can only cleave to one Lord . . .'[8]

'The eye is the lamp of the body,' said Jesus. In other words,
without the clear vision of the eye my whole body has to walk
and move in darkness. It cannot see what it is doing or where it is

going. It is only as our 'eye' (a biblical synonym for 'heart') is set wholly on the light of Christ that my whole life can have clear direction. But if my eye or heart serves another master – for it cannot serve two – then my whole life is left in deep darkness. 'The love of money is the root of all evils'; every day reveals the inescapable and ugly truth of that statement.

In calling or selecting his disciples, Jesus allowed therefore no compromise at all. Even with the lovable, talented, promising, seeking, rich young ruler, Jesus still told him, 'Sell all that you have and distribute to the poor, and you will have treasure in heaven.' The man went away sad. But Jesus could strike no bargain, for no man can serve two masters.

However, in this well-known incident there are various details that are instructive. First, as Ron Sider comments, 'When Jesus asked the rich young man to sell his goods and give to the poor, he did not say, "Become destitute and friendless". Rather he said, "Come follow me". In other words, he invited him to join a community of sharing and love, where his security would not be based on individual property holdings, but on openness to the Spirit and on the loving care of new-found brothers and sisters.'[9] Second, what Jesus looks for first and foremost is not poverty but obedience. Obedience could lead to poverty, if that is what Jesus requires of us; but choosing poverty in itself could be choosing my own way of life, or some religious ideal, which is not at the command of Jesus. Third, having made that point, and being aware of the dangers of legalism over this matter of lifestyle, many of us are so skilled at spotting the loopholes and saying 'Yes, but . . .' that Ron Sider is quite right when he states that 'what 99 per cent of all western Christians need to hear 99 per cent of the time is "Give to everyone who begs from you", and "sell your possessions".' Fourth, we must never minimise the seductive danger of riches. (1 Timothy 6:9–10; James 4:1–2; etc.) Covetousness is perhaps the most serious sin in the West (or North) today, and no covetous person will inherit the kingdom of God. The strictures against all forms of covetousness in the scriptures are powerful. Always we come back to this basic issue: Who or what comes first in our life? Only when the Lordship of Christ is clearly recognised – and our attitude to possessions will test this as nothing else can – can we truly be his disciples. While we must equally be wary of such attitudes as Pharisaism or legalism, on this matter of lifestyle, God still requires of us a true biblical radicalism which refuses to be conformed to this world.

Faith

This too is crucial if we are to see the power of God at work. It is 'he who believes in me' who 'will also do the works that I do', as Jesus promised his disciples during his last discourse with them. (John 14:12) 'Whatever you ask in my name, I will do it, that the Father may be glorified in the Son.'

When Jesus tells us in Matthew 6:25–34 'do not be anxious', he is asking us another crucial and penetrating question: Whom or what do you really trust? What is the clear object of your faith? Again the logic is compelling, for we have to face up to this alternative: *either* we are trusting our heavenly Father – for everything; *or* we are ultimately trusting in some form of worldly securities. Material possessions often create anxiety. We worry about having enough money to buy what we want; then, when we get it, we worry about keeping it safe or in good condition. We worry about whether we have sufficient to give us security for the future. We worry about changing values of both currency and possessions, about economic instability, inflation, slumps and recessions. Jesus warned us about the spiritual damage that comes from such anxiety: the seed of God's word can easily become 'choked by the cares and riches and pleasures of life'.[10] If we have faith in the faithfulness of our heavenly Father, we shall live a day at a time: 'Don't worry at all then about tomorrow. Tomorrow can take care of itself! One day's trouble is enough for one day.'[11]

All this could sound a little naive and irresponsible, until we realise that Jesus is calling us out of the kingdom of this world into the kingdom of God – a kingdom demonstrated by the loving care and generous sharing of the people of God. It is, in fact, especially in this quality of our shared life together that we experience the reality of God's love, and this in turn casts out our fear and enables us to develop true faith in him.

Certainly this was the lifestyle that Jesus adopted for himself, and instructed his disciples to do the same. Indeed, it could almost be said that the power and effectiveness of their ministry depended on their willingness to trust God for everything. Remember his commission to the twelve: 'Preach as you go, saying, "The kingdom of heaven is at hand." Heal the sick, raise the dead, cleanse lepers, cast out demons. You received without paying, give without pay. Take no gold, nor silver, nor copper in your belts, no bag for your journey, nor two tunics, nor sandals, nor a staff . . .' (Matthew 10:7–10) Most of us will readily understand that their faith was at times unable to rise to such levels. How could the 5,000 be fed? What about the time when they were hungry themselves? Jesus simply and gently rebuked them, 'O men of little faith!'[12] However much we might sympathise with them, it was their little faith over these material matters that meant little faith in spiritual ministry. When the disciples a little later asked why they could not cast out a demon from a boy, Jesus replied, 'Because of your little faith.'[13] That is why he constantly tested and stretched their faith over the ordinary, everyday matters of lifestyle; only as their faith developed there would they be able to believe for the much more vital work of the kingdom of God.

Exactly the same testing was given when the seventy were sent out: 'Carry no purse, no bag, no sandals . . . Wherever you enter a town and they receive you, eat what is set before you; heal the sick in it and say to them, "The Kingdom of God has come near to you" . . .' Off they went, inexperienced, untaught, but with simple faith; and 'they returned with joy, saying, "Lord, even the demons are subject to us in your name!"' And Jesus too rejoiced, 'I thank thee, Father . . . that thou hast hidden these things from the wise and understanding and revealed them to babes' – that is to those who exercised an unwavering faith in the reality and faithfulness of their heavenly Father. (Luke 10:1–21)

Most of us would like to arrive at a happy compromise. Of course we want to seek first the kingdom of God; but earthly treasures continue to attract, tug away at the heart, cause anxiety, and lessen our faith. We may not want to be extravagantly wealthy providing we have clear financial security. However, in wanting the best of both worlds we lose the transforming power of the kingdom of God. Again we must stress that Jesus is not forbidding personal property; but when we in any way start 'craving' for these things we may well wander away from the faith and pierce our hears with many pangs. (1 Timothy 6:10)

'It is want of faith that makes us opt for earthly rather than heavenly treasure. If we really believed in celestial treasures, who among us would be so stupid as to buy gold? We just do not believe. Heaven is a dream, a religious fantasy which we affirm because we are orthodox. If people believed in heaven, they would spend their time preparing for permanent residence there. But nobody does. We just like the assurance that something nice awaits us when the real life is over.'[14]

This is important. We may glory in the fact that a man is justified by faith. But how real is that faith before we can know that we are justified? John White puts it in this way: 'We must be suspicious of any faith about personal justification that is not substantiated by faith in God's power over material things in our everyday life. Faith about pie in the sky when I die cannot be demonstrated. Faith that God can supply my need today *can* be demonstrated.'[15]

That is precisely the challenge to the rich young ruler. Having told him to sell what he had and to give to the poor, Jesus promised him that he would have 'treasure in heaven'. 'Come,' said Jesus, 'follow me.' But at that critical point, the young man, with all his good living and religious enthusiasm, did not have true faith in Jesus. He did not believe him; or, if he did, he would not obey him. Jesus admitted to his startled disciples that it is not easy for a rich man to enter the kingdom of heaven. But, he promised those who felt that they had now left everything for his sake, 'every one who has left houses or brothers or sisters or father or mother or children or lands, for my name's sake, will receive a hundredfold, and inherit eternal life.'[16] In some measure the disciples experienced immediately the greater riches that God has in store for us when we put our whole life into his hands. They discovered a depth of relationships in their apostolic band that they had never known before. They shared a common life. They lived together, worked together, prayed together, learnt together. They had given up everything, and, as a result, had gained so much more.

So the question is, when it comes to the financial crunch, who or what do we really believe? Do we have faith – true faith – in Jesus? It is by faith that we are justified, and it is by faith that we shall see the power of God in our ministry. It is God's rebuke to us affluent Christians, as we hedge ourselves around with earthly treasures and securities, that God's power is today much more obviously demonstrated amongst those who have little or nothing of this world's goods. But they are rich in faith.

Integrity

Because of the constant danger of false prophets, whose work was (and is today) marked by deceit and corruption, Paul and the others leaders in the early church repeatedly stressed their own complete integrity in all their evangelistic, teaching and pastoral work: 'We are not, like so many, peddlers of God's word; but as men of sincerity, as commissioned by God, in the sight of God we speak in Christ . . . We have renounced disgraceful, underhanded ways; we refuse to practise cunning or to tamper with God's word, but by the open statement of the truth we would commend ourselves to every man's conscience in the sight of God . . . We put no obstacle in any one's way, so that no fault may be found with our ministry, but as servants of God we commend ourselves in every way . . . Open your hearts to us: we have wronged no one, we have corrupted no one, we have taken advantage of no one . . .'[17] Without any hint of hypocrisy or pride, Paul could say, in his open, disarming fashion, 'You yourselves know how I lived among you all the time from the first day that I set foot in Asia, serving the Lord with all humility . . . You know what kind of men we proved to be among you for your sake . . . You remember our labour and toil, brethren.'[18] So we could multiply examples.

The integrity of the messenger is vital for the authority and converting power of the message. Jesus could throw out the challenge to his critics, 'Which of you convicts me of sin?' (John 8:46) Although Jesus came from a reasonably secure family business, his family was far from wealthy, and he himself willingly became poor for us that we through his poverty might become truly rich. Possibly because of the deceitfulness of riches, Jesus saw that a marked simplicity of lifestyle was a vital part of the credibility of his whole ministry. That is why he insisted that his disciples should live the same way. They shared a common purse; they gave regularly to the poor (as is suggested by John 13:29, et al.). They denied themselves some of the

material possessions and comforts that most of them had been
used to. And later they taught others to live in the same way: 'If
we have food and clothing, with these we shall be content. But
those who desire to be rich fall into temptation, into a snare,
into many senseless and hurtful desires that plunge men into
ruin and destruction . . .' (1 Timothy 6:8–9); 'Keep your life
free from the love of money, and be content with what you
have.' (Hebrews 13:5)

It was one of the marks of the false prophet that his heart was
'trained in greed' (2 Peter 2:14); he would flatter people 'to gain
advantage' (Jude 16). It was for this reason that any prospective
leader in the church must be 'no lover of money' (1 Timothy
3:3) and 'not greedy for gain' (1 Timothy 3:8; Titus 1:7).

'The poverty of Christ's messengers is the proof of their
freedom . . . As they go forth to be the plenipotentiaries of his
word, Jesus enjoins strict poverty upon them . . . They are not
to go about like beggars and call attention to themselves, nor
are they to burden other people like parasites. They are to go
forth in the battle-dress of poverty, taking as little with them as
a traveller who knows he will get board and lodging with friends
at the end of the day. This shall be an expression of their faith,
not in men, but in their heavenly father who sent them and will
care for them. *It is this that will make their gospel credible.*'[19]
(italics mine).

In the commercial and advertising world of today many
people are understandably suspicious of anything that may
appear to be sales talk or a promotion act. How genuine is it?
What is the catch? Is it all that it seems to be? If in any way the
'salesman' is personally benefitting, financially or materially,
from what he is trying to 'sell', we are doubly cautious. It is
therefore imperative that, as Christ's messengers speaking of
the free gift of God, we do not make a personal and financial
profit from the work God has called us to do. Unless we
renounce worldly values, and adopt a much simpler lifestyle,
our ministry will lack credibility in the eyes of an unbelieving
and cynical world.

Today, some literature from quite a well-known evangelist
came in my mail. After an impassioned statement about the
needs of 'this hour', there was a strong appeal to me to 'yield
yourself to the Holy Spirit and ask for His guidance in your

special thanksgiving gift – for his goodness to you!' And, in case I had missed the point, there was a postage-paid envelope for my 'reply', together with a slip for me to complete, entitled 'MY GIFT TO REVERSE THE TREND!' I was encouraged to sign this slip, which says, 'Dear Brother (name of evangelist), I am thankful to God for His goodness, His love in choosing me, in challenging me to rise up and become one of His Partners in prophecy for the Healing of the Nations . . . I have felt led of the Holy Spirit to send £_____ as my November gift to overtake the Heathen . . .' At the end of the form I was reminded that 'this is God's Hour!' No doubt many vulnerable Christians will respond financially to the challenge. Several widows in my own church have responded generously to similar pressures. No doubt this evangelist will continue to enjoy 'success'. Since he seems to preach Christ, it may be that God will bless his efforts in one way or another. But the whole approach tragically lacks the credibility of the Master.

When I am interviewed by secular journalists or broadcasters concerning my work as an evangelist, one inevitable question is, 'What do you get out of it?' They are asking not about job-satisfaction, but about financial reward. To be able to speak truthfully in answer to this question is a vital part of my integrity when it comes to anything else I may want to say. When covetousness is one of the most common and gross sins, it is more important than ever that the church should guard itself against the strong and subtle pressures of this temptation.

These snares are possibly greater for those with an independent ministry that is not firmly rooted in the discipline of a local church. Certainly within a local congregation, explicit biblical teaching must be given regularly about the Christian responsibility to give generously to the Lord and to his work. However, the main aim of this teaching is both that God may be glorified through the joyful offering of our possessions, and that Christians may be blessed through such giving. With fund-raising techniques, on the other hand, the main aim is obviously the raising of funds. Thus instead of being primarily concerned with the worship of God and the freedom of God's people, the focus shifts on to the economic prosperity of some religious project. It is at this point that the integrity of those involved must come under question.

Identification

Just as the ingredients of obedience, faith and integrity were, of
course, perfectly exemplified in the life and ministry of Jesus, so
the model of identification is found in its most sublime form in
his incarnation. Here the word of God became a human being
and dwelt amongst us. In Martin Luther's simple words about
Jesus: 'He ate, drank, slept, waked; was weary, sorrowful,
rejoicing; he wept and he laughed; he knew hunger and thirst
and sweat; he talked, he toiled, he prayed . . . so there was no
difference between him and other men, save only this that he
was God and had no sin.'

Although the primary theological debate today rages over the
divinity of Jesus, many less academic and orthodox Christians
have more difficulty coming to terms with the genuine humanity
of Jesus. It is possibly because we tend to think of him as being
intrinsically different and separate from ordinary men that the
church, as a whole, has often retreated to its own religious
ghetto, and thus failed to be God's agent in the healing of the
whole of God's creation. We have wrongly divided the sacred
and the secular. In trying to keep ourselves 'unstained from the
world', we have sometimes kept ourselves from the world
altogether. How then can we begin to carry out our God-given
ministry of reconciliation? Paul rejected such religious detachment. 'I have made myself a slave to all, that I might win the
more . . . I have become all things to all men, that I might by all
means save some. I do it all for the sake of the gospel, that I
may share in its blessings.'[20] Here is this vital incarnational
principle applied in the realm of effective evangelism and
compassionate service.

Throughout the scriptures God is clearly seen to be on the
side of the poor. Although he is no respecter of persons, and is
rich to all who call upon him, he is a God of justice. Therefore,
since by greed or neglect, the rich oppress the poor and
inevitably add to their weight of suffering, God must be on the
side of the poor. Moreover, he identifies with the poor. When
we are kind to the poor, we lend to the Lord. (Proverbs 19:17)
When we offer practical help to those who are hungry, thirsty,
lonely, naked, sick or in prison, we are doing it as to Jesus.
(Matthew 25:34–40) The reason why Jesus was loved and
welcomed by ordinary and often poor people was partly

because he consciously identified himself with them. He had come 'to preach good news to the poor', and he could do so because he had 'nowhere to lay his head'. On the cross he was literally stripped of everything. No one could be more destitute than a naked man fastened to a cross. Yet the apostle Paul repeatedly refers to 'the power of the cross' – materially nothing, spiritually everything.

The early church continued the same pattern. Peter and John had neither silver nor gold to offer to the crippled beggar at the Gate Beautiful, but they did have the power of the Spirit of Christ: 'In the name of Jesus Christ of Nazareth, walk.' When we see in this young church the extraordinary quality of their sharing and the generosity of their giving, it is not surprising that God was able to work through them with 'many wonders and signs'. It was because God found them faithful in handling the lesser material riches, that he was able to trust them with his much greater spiritual riches. Their willingness to live by the principle of 'enough', so that any abundance might be given to every good work, was plain proof of the grace of God amongst them; and that grace clearly manifested itself in many different ways. It is small wonder that the word of God increased so rapidly, not least amongst the poor and needy of that day.

The church of the West today, however, appeals largely to the affluent middle class. Is this because we have frequently erected cultural barriers which make it very difficult for many to hear 'good news to the poor'? Our church buildings, our vicarages or manses, our styles of dress, language and music – all these can become highly selective factors, determining which sections of the community we are likely to reach for Jesus Christ. It is not that we should aim for damp and draughty buildings instead (some of us have these anyway!); but as soon as we become materially ambitious for our buildings we stand in great danger of shutting the door of the gospel on those who need the Saviour so much. It is sobering to remember that the fastest period of growth in the entire history of the church was almost certainly during the first three centuries when there were no church buildings or material assets at all.

On a recent visit to the United States of America, I went to several churches of different traditions that were all, in their way, immensely impressive. I was immediately struck by the numerous facilities of their buildings, the efficiency of their organisations, the quality of their printed service sheets for every Sunday, the colourful information and welcome cards in every seat, the precise timing of each service, the musical quality of organist and choir, together with the bright colours of their robes, and, not least, the size of the congregations. My general impression was that of quality performance backed up with obvious business efficiency. Those churches made our little efforts in England look shabby and amateurish in comparison, and I felt that we had much to learn. After all, administration is one of the gifts of the Spirit. At the same time, I had to struggle to sense God's presence and to hear his voice. There was little freedom in worship, and I wondered how many genuine conversions took place amongst those right outside the social and cultural ethos of those churches. I feared that the genuinely 'un-churched' members of society would have felt uncomfortable and conspicuous in the distinctive middle-class conformity of those congregations.

In contrast I went to another church[21] which had no building of its own, but used a huge school gymnasium for its Sunday services. Every week an enthusiastic team of men rolled out the carpets, set up 2000 chairs, erected a stage, and organised some effective PA equipment. The contrast between the more conventional churches and this one was staggering. With an almost total absence of structure and organisation, the services were relaxed, the worship sensitive and intimate, and within the gentle control of the main pastor there were opportunities for many to bring spiritual gifts to edify the whole body of Christ. The congregation had grown from nothing to 2000 in four years, and the vast majority of these were genuine conversions, many amongst those who had become disillusioned by the conventional formality of the more established churches. There was no mistaking the manifest presence of the living God in that gymnasium. His love, joy, life and generosity tangibly expressed amongst that fellowship were overwhelming. Conversions, healings, deliverance and blessings of many kinds happened every week. Anyone searching for spiritual reality would have found the whole activity utterly meaningful. In terms of material facilities they had very little; in terms of spiritual power, surely God was in that place. Here was the incarnate body of Christ. In that setting, it was the ordinary sinners who heard the gospel gladly.

Love

This is the supreme quality of all, without which all our eloquent preaching would be as a noisy gong or a clanging cymbal. It was, above all, the love of Christ that controlled and compelled that persecuted early church. 'So being affectionately desirous of you, we were ready to share with you not only the gospel of God but also our own selves, because you had become very dear to us.' It was their infectious love that drew people to them, and to the Lord, like a magnet; the poor and the outcast, the sick and the lame, Jew and Gentile, slave and free, male and female, even a few who were rich and influential – they all came, apart from those whose hearts were inflamed with jealousy or hardened towards God. In so far as those Christians loved one another, others could see both that they were manifestly the disciples of Jesus and that God was evidently abiding in their midst. Love is always the greatest thing in the world, and it never fails to be the most powerful evidence of the God of love.

Christian love, however, is always marked by sacrificial giving: 'God so loved the world that he gave his only Son.' There was nothing sentimental about this greatest expression of love of all time. In the same way the evidence and demonstration of love must be much more than the eloquent words of an evangelist. No one can read the first few chapters of Acts without noticing that the amazing sharing of their lives and possessions so demonstrated the love of God amongst them that others were drawn to Jesus Christ almost irresistibly.

'All who believed were together, and had all things in common; and they sold their possessions and goods and distributed them to all, as any had need . . . And the Lord added to their number day by day those who were being saved.' (Acts 2:44–45, 47)

'Now the company of those who believed were of one heart and soul, and no one said that any of the things which he possessed was his own, but they had everything in common. And with great power the apostles gave their testimony to the resurrection of the Lord Jesus, and great grace was upon them all. There was not a needy person among them, for as many as were possessors of lands or houses sold them, and brought the proceeds of what was sold and laid it at the apostles' feet; and distribution was made to each as any had need.' (Acts 4:32–35) Note that the remark about powerful evangelism is sandwiched between the comments about their shared life. In other words, it was precisely in the context of this loving, sacrificial care of one another that the good news of Jesus Christ made such an impact.

In Acts 6 we see the same pattern repeated again. The needs of some Greek widows were not being met. When, however, the apostles took active steps to attend to their material needs by setting aside seven men 'full of faith and of the Holy Spirit', we read that 'the word of God increased; and the number of disciples multiplied greatly in Jerusalem . . .'

There was no compulsion to sell property or to give money. Nor was there any pressure brought to give up the right of private ownership. It is clear that many Christians kept at least some of their possessions and lands, even though a number of them went on selling what they had as the needs continued. But such was the love of God amongst this new community in Christ that they longed to express this love towards their brothers and sisters according to the obvious needs that arose. 'If any one has the world's goods and sees his brother in need, yet closes his heart against him, how does God's love abide in him?' (1 John 3:17). Even when there was a prophecy of a famine, the newly formed Gentile church at Antioch responded at once in love towards their Jewish brethren in Judea by sending such money as they could 'every one according to his ability'. (Acts 11:27–30)

When attempting to teach the biblical values about lifestyle in western churches, I have usually encountered strong and determined opposition, except perhaps from students. Most Christians will readily agree with teaching about faith, love, hope, service, mission. But touch the area of money, possessions and a simple lifestyle, and you will touch a very sensitive spot indeed. I have often wondered why this is. The reason is, I think, partly that our security is often ultimately in these things, however much we may consciously deny this; partly because the god of mammon exercises a much more powerful influence in our lives

than many of us realise; and partly because most of us in-
stinctively know that we cannot withstand the pressures of the
world and live by biblical standards on our own. The trouble is
that very few western churches know anything of the degree of
the sharing of lives and possessions that was certainly the norm
in New Testament times, and is best exemplified today in
churches in the Third World or where there is active persecution. For countless Christians in the West 'discipleship'
means little more than going to church regularly, giving a
proportion of one's income – usually at best one tenth, and
often far below that figure – and getting involved in a limited
number of church activities.

Consequently, the lifestyle of most western Christians and
churches has no prophetic challenge at all to the affluent society
all around. In fact it is scarcely distinguishable from it. We
have, quite unconsciously, adopted the values and standards of
the world; and as the standard of living has risen considerably
over the last thirty years, so we Christians, along with our
neighbours, spend that much more on our cars and carpets, TV
sets and washing-machines, furniture and hi-fi equipment, until
we regard most of these things as necessities for 'modern life'.
Where is there any serious attempt to live on 'enough', to be
'content with food and clothing', and to give the rest away for
every good work? Where is there that commitment to one
another in love, so that we really share our possessions, reduce
our standard of living – despite inflation – and express the love
of Christ in costly, tangible, sacrificial terms?

Ron Sider has expressed it like this: 'In the New Testament
we see Jesus calling together a new community of people who
began to live a whole new life-style. The early church was a new
society. It was one new body where all relationships were being
transformed . . . If anything is clear in the New Testament it is
that they were sharing financially in a massive way . . .
Extremes of wealth and poverty are simply not what God wills
among his people . . . Now, if the one world-wide body of
believers today would dare to implement that vision so that
something like economic equality existed within the universal
body of Christ . . . it would probably be the single most
powerful evangelistic step we could take. When the church in
Jerusalem shared dramatically they found the work of God

increased. The evangelistic impact of the first Christians'
financial sharing was just astounding. Unfortunately, the
radical character of New Testament *koinonia* is largely missing
from the contemporary western church.'[22]

I make no greater claims than having just begun to learn the
first lesson in all this. I am being challenged all the time, and
expect to be much more so in the coming years. But I do know
that some steps towards a simpler lifestyle have been encouraged partly through living in an extended household for
eight years, where together we seriously committed ourselves to
this end, and so were free 'to stir up one another to love and
good works'. All I can say is that, although our progress has
been shamefully slow and small, we have begun to discover the
riches of Christ and the depths of Christian fellowship as never
before; and, together with these, we have found at least a
degree of liberation from some of the snares of this world. We
are far from being able to say, with Paul, 'as poor, yet making
many rich; as having nothing, and yet possessing everything';[23]
but I think we know a little bit more of what the apostle meant.
In this way we were also able to release both money and man-
power for the kingdom of God.

Money talks

I was recently asked by a leading Anglican bishop if I thought it
right to try to reproduce a New Testament church in this highly
complex, technological twentieth century. My reply was that I
believed the New Testament principles to be timeless, but that
the outworkings of them must always be contemporary to be
relevant to this particular generation. We are not to follow the
exact pattern of the early church slavishly. At the same time,
when the evangelistic impact of the western churches is mostly
very weak, when the needs of this present day are increasing all
the time, and when the crisis of the church today is primarily in
its lack of spiritual power and life and love, it is imperative that
we examine closely those basic principles that both made the
church so effective 2000 years ago and that make the church so
effective in some areas today, especially in the Third World.

Undoubtedly one great area concerns the Person and work of
the Holy Spirit. We desperately need individual Christians and
churches continuously filled with the Spirit. Nothing can be a

substitute for that. But if the life and love of Jesus are to be clearly manifest – and without this all our gospel words will be empty words – the church must learn again what it means to be the body of Christ on earth. It needs to demonstrate God's new society, marked by love and seen in the costly, practical sharing of lives and possessions together. Money talks – not least in this covetous generation. When others see that our faith really means something, in practical and material ways, then the good news of Jesus Christ will be very much more than religious words.

James K. Baxter once wrote: 'The first Christians did not start to share their goods in a free and full manner till after the bomb of the Spirit exploded in their souls at Pentecost. Before then, they would be morally incapable of this free and joyful sharing. The acquisitive habit is one of the deepest rooted habits of the human race. To say, "this is yours, not mine" and to carry the words into effect, is as much a miracle of God as raising of the dead.'[24] It is by such miracles of God's grace that others may catch a glimpse of the realities that we proclaim so loudly with our lips. But without such tangible evidence of the love of God amongst us, we shall have to accept E. M. Forster's rebuke when he referred to 'poor, talkative, little Christianity'.

'Little children, let us not love in word or speech but in deed and in truth.'[25]

(The substance of this chapter was given as a keynote address at the *International Conference on Simple Life-style*, held in England, March 1980.)

Notes

1. 4th February 1980.
2. Philippians 1:18
3. *Enough is Enough*, SCM, p. 62, 1975
4. Luke 12:32f
5. Acts 5:32
6. Acts 5:4
7. Acts 4:34
8. Dietrich Bonhoeffer, *The Cost of Discipleship*, SCM, 1959, pp. 154–157

9. Quoted in *Rich Christians in An Age of Hunger*, Hodder & Stoughton, 1977, p. 87
10. Luke 8:14
11. Matthew 6:34, J. B. Phillips
12. Matthew 16:7f
13. Matthew 17:14–21
14. John White, *The Golden Cow*, Marshall, Morgan and Scott, 1979 p. 39
15. Op. cit., p. 41–42
16. Matthew 19:29
17. 2 Corinthians 2:17; 4:2; 6:3; 7:2
18. Acts 20:18; 1 Thessalonians 1:5; 2:9
19. Bonhoeffer, op. cit., pp. 186f
20. 1 Corinthians 9:19–23
21. Calvary Chapel, Yorba Linda, Placentia, California
22. From an interview in *Third Way*, 13 January 1977
23. 2 Cor. 6:10
24. 'Thoughts about the Holy Spirit', p. 11
25. 1 John 3:18. For a sensitive and balanced statement on this whole subject see *An Evangelical Commitment to Simple Lifestyle*, Appendix A (pp. 261ff)

CHAPTER ELEVEN

The Cost of Discipleship

Jesus never promised an easy life to those who followed him. It is true he came to meet the deepest needs of every one of us. Only in him can we find forgiveness for the past, a new life for the present, and a glorious hope for the future.

At the same time Jesus came to build his church. Far from being a comfortable club existing entirely for the benefits of its members, the church is to be God's agent for the healing of the whole of creation, existing mainly for the benefits of its non-members. Church-membership therefore necessarily involves discipleship, and that means accepting the full demands that Jesus clearly made. Jesus was, in fact, so honest about the cost of discipleship that many of the enthusiastic crowds who flocked after him turned back and no longer went with him. There were only 120 of them waiting for the promise of the Holy Spirit in that upper room; and, although more than 500 saw the risen Christ, those 120 presumably represented most of those who were willing to accept his call. In sheer numbers his three years of ministry had not been exceptionally fruitful. And it is not hard to see the reason why. Although he healed the sick and relieved the oppressed without any conditions attached at all, to those whom he called and to those who wanted to join his number, he spelt out the cost of discipleship in clear and forthright terms.

When one man said to him, 'I will follow you wherever you go', Jesus replied, 'Foxes have holes, and the birds of the air have nests; but the Son of man has nowhere to lay his head.'[1] Here Jesus was warning this would-be disciple where the obedience of faith would lead. In worldly terms it means a life of constant uncertainty and insecurity; but in spiritual terms it means a life of continuous certainty in things not seen,[2] and of total security in the love of God. Jesus calls people to put their

whole trust in God, and not in the uncertain riches of this
world. Faith is the essence of all true discipleship, for without
faith it is impossible to please God. In order to test the reality of
faith the disciple must therefore expect to find himself frequently in situations where he has to trust in God. Like their
Master, those first disciples often did not know where their next
meal was coming from, or where they would sleep for the night.
In following the call of Jesus, they had left their homes and their
jobs, their money and their possessions, and were trusting
wholly in him. Although he never failed them and promised
them that their Father in heaven would meet every need they
had, their faith often faltered when it came to the test. 'O you of
little faith! Why did you doubt? Have you no faith?' were his
humbling rebukes. Constantly he sought to encourage his
disciples, to teach them, guide and strengthen them; but until
they learnt, sometimes the hard way, to trust him and obey him,
Jesus knew that all his training would be in vain.

The path of obedience

From the earliest days of Christ's ministry people were repeatedly astonished at the authority of his person. 'The people
were astounded at his teaching; unlike their own teachers he
taught with a note of authority.'[3] Sometimes they asked in
amazement amongst themselves, 'Who then is this, that even
wind and sea obey him?'[4] But what many did not appreciate
was that all authority in heaven and earth had been given to
him.[5] Jesus was not just a wonder-worker with unusual
authority; he was the Lord of glory with all authority. At the
name of Jesus every knee must bow and every tongue confess
that he is Lord. There can be no half measures with Christ. If
we want to be his disciples, we must take his supreme authority
as Lord over every part of our life, without any exception. If we
are not willing for him to be Lord, he cannot be our Saviour.
With Jesus it is all, or nothing. To be in the kingdom of God is
to accept Jesus as King; and if Jesus is King, his word has
authority and must be obeyed.

The first disciples understood this clearly. In Acts 4, when
Peter and John were 'charged not to speak or teach at all in the
name of Jesus', they replied, 'Whether it is right in the sight of
God to listen to you rather than to God, you must judge; for we

cannot but speak of what we have seen and heard. Later, they prayed again for boldness to speak the word of God. Again in Acts 5, after further serious threats, Peter and the apostles answered, 'We must obey God rather than men. The God of our fathers raised Jesus whom you killed by hanging him on a tree . . .' It is no wonder that their opponents 'were enraged and wanted to kill them'; and it is no wonder that the word of God spread like wildfire through that ancient world. Those first Christians learnt obedience, whatever the cost in terms of personal sacrifice. For many, it meant literally laying down their lives for the gospel of Christ. That is why God was so powerfully working through him. He gives his Spirit to those who obey him.[6]

In the words of J. B. Phillips: 'Perhaps because of their very simplicity, perhaps because of the readiness to believe, to obey, to give, to suffer, and if need be to die, the Spirit of God found what he must always be seeking – a fellowship of men and women so united in faith and love that he can work in them and through them with the minimum of hindrance.'[7]

This call of Jesus to his disciples was also, however, a call of love. Their obedience to his word meant trusting in his love. It is because Jesus loves us and has laid down his life for us that he looks for a total response of love on our part, a love that is seen for its reality in obeying his commandments. Do we really want to be his disciples? Do we genuinely want God's best and perfect will for our lives? Are we honestly willing to trust ourselves to a God who demands all, but who loves us more than anyone could ever love us and who longs only for our highest good?

The test must be unquestioning obedience to his word. If we reject his word, we question his wisdom and doubt his love, and so cannot be his disciples.

That is the important truth behind some of the words of Jesus that may seem to us, as they seemed to the crowds in his day, such 'a hard saying'. 'If any one comes to me and does not hate his own father and mother and wife and children and brothers and sisters, yes, and even his own life, he cannot be my disciple.'[8] This was an idiomatic way of saying that our love for Jesus must be so unhesitatingly first that our love for those who are nearest and dearest to us is as hatred in comparison. The Lordship of Jesus means that no one can have equal claims with him to our loyalty and allegiance. There can be no compromise. There is no conditional surrender. 'Whoever does not bear his own cross and come after me, cannot be my disciple . . . Whoever of you does not renounce all that he has cannot be my disciple.'[9]

With such a call to a life of total and uncompromising obedience, we should not be surprised if we are strongly tempted to qualify Christ's call, to modify its stringent demands by taking a more 'reasonable' line in the light of modern culture, which, we tell ourselves, is 'so different from that of the first century'. With our intellectual and theological approach we may try to hold a 'more balanced' view which softens the zeal of those New Testament enthusiasts, or so interpret the teaching of Jesus that we skilfully avoid its direct and disturbing challenge. It is important, we say, not to take things too literally. We must not become legalistic. We must not ignore the vital principles of hermeneutics. Jesus may have *said*, 'Love your enemies'; but what he *meant* was, 'Do not take active revenge against someone who has wronged you.' If Jesus *said*, 'I am the way . . ., no one comes to the Father, but by me', what he clearly *meant* was, 'I am one way by which you may come to God, but of course there are many others.' When Jesus *said*, 'Seek first the kingdom of God,' what he really *meant* was, 'Although there will be many other things you must seek first in order to exist and have a normal life, make sure that you do not leave God's kingdom out of your life altogether.' In these ways we can try to evade the clear call of Jesus to absolute obedience. The tragedy is that, if we do this, our whole attitude to him is wrong. We do not believe that he loves us and longs only for what is best for us. And in our unbelief and disobedience we cannot truly be his disciples.

The necessity of faith

We have already seen that the aim of Jesus in testing our obedience is to bring us to the point of genuine faith in him. Everything ultimately depends on God's grace – his undeserved love as he takes the initiative in reaching out to us when we are lost and helpless. But although all God's gifts to us are given 'by grace', they are received through faith. Faith is indispensable. Faith is the open hand by which we take what God is offering us in his grace. We are therefore justified by faith. We have access into God's presence by faith. We receive the Spirit by faith. Christ dwells in our hearts by faith. Those upon whom the Spirit fell at Pentecost and on other occasions were sometimes described as 'full of faith and of the Holy Spirit'; and it was 'by faith in his name' that God was able to work with unusual power amongst them. We see Philip, later termed the evangelist, acting by faith in the unusual promptings of the Spirit of God in Acts 8, which brought new life to the Samaritans and then to the Ethiopian eunuch. See the faith of Ananias as he went nervously to the feared Saul of Tarsus, arch-enemy of the Christian church; note the faith of Simon Peter (even if a reluctant faith) as he crossed the great divide into the house of Cornelius, the Gentile. The whole story of the early church is one continuous demonstration of active faith in the risen Christ. Their evangelistic enterprise makes a magnificent 'volume 2' to the epic stories of the great heroes of faith recorded in Hebrews chapter 11.

In all these examples, however, we see that the faith which is able to receive God's grace will be proved by obedience to God's word. Without obedience, there is no faith. 'By faith Abraham *obeyed* when he was called to go out to a place which he was to receive as an inheritance; and he went out . . .'[10] To quote Bonhoeffer: 'Only he who believes is obedient, and only he who is obedient believes . . . When people complain that they find it hard to believe, it is a sign of deliberate or unconscious disobedience . . . Only the devil has an answer for our moral difficulties, and he says, "Keep on posing problems (of faith) and you will escape the necessity of obedience."'[11]

It is significant that John suggests in his Gospel that the opposite to believing in Jesus is disobeying him: 'He who *believes* in the Son has eternal life; he who *does not obey* the Son shall not see life, but the wrath of God abides on him.'[12] Paul also makes it clear that, whilst we are saved through believing in Jesus, God's righteous judgement will one day come 'upon those who do not know God and upon those who *do not obey* the gospel of our Lord Jesus.'[13] Just as faith and obedience go hand in hand, so unbelief and disobedience are two sides of the same coin. It is no good calling Jesus 'Lord' unless we do what he says.

Calvin once said, 'While it is faith alone that justifies, the faith that justifies is never alone.' Always it is accompanied by good works, since faith without works is dead. And the basis of the good works that James is talking about in his epistle is obedience to the word of God: 'Be doers of the word, and not hearers only, deceiving yourselves.'[14]

'The issue at point is crucial – the one that matters most. We do need more "decisions" in evangelism, more effective church management and organisation, more money to run churches, and sometimes we may even need better buildings and facilities. But woe be to us as Christians if we do not see that the greatest need of the hour is to help Christians clearly understand and obey the teachings of Christ . . . Praying a prayer to invite Christ into one's heart, having an emotional experience, testifying for Christ, sharing the "plan of salvation", entering into the fulness of the Holy Spirit, teaching the Bible, and many other Christian acts are valid and good. But they mean nothing, *absolutely nothing* . . . if Jesus is not obeyed in our private lives.'[15]

The disciple of Jesus is the follower of Jesus. He has committed himself to go the way that Jesus goes. He has pledged himself to a life of absolute obedience. When he fails to obey he must repent and ask for Christ's forgiveness at once, for sin breaks the discipleship and spoils the relationship. Without obedience there is no faith; and without faith there is no discipleship.

The way of the cross

Jesus repeatedly taught his disciples that there was only one way that he could go: 'the Son of man must suffer many things, and be rejected by the elders . . .'[16] It is important to notice the clear distinction between suffering and rejection. If Jesus had only suffered he might have drawn immense sympathy from all his Jewish contemporaries. His passion would have been marked with great dignity and honour. But it was not to be like that. The agony and irony of it all was that, although he loved and welcomed all men, he himself was 'despised and rejected by men'. Humanly speaking his passion was totally without honour: 'as one from whom men hide their faces he was despised, and we esteemed him not.'[17] He bore the excruciating pain and shame of the cross. He was mocked by the soldiers, tortured by the scourging, thorns and nails, jeered at by the crowd, sworn at by one of the thieves, forsaken by almost all his friends. There was no dignity about the cross. Klausner, the Jewish historian, wrote that 'crucifixion is the most terrible and cruel death which man has ever devised for taking vengeance on his fellow men.' Cicero called it 'the most cruel and the most horrible torture'.

Yet this was the way that Jesus had to go; and he saw any attempt to dissuade him from it as the work of the devil, even if the suggestion came from one of his closest disciples. Christ could never have been Christ without the cross. That was the crucial lesson that Peter had to learn immediately after his great confession. It was upon this rock that Christ was going to build his church. But the church could never have been the church without the cross. The cross has always been offensive to man. Even religious man finds it a 'stumbling-block', partly because it cuts all human pride from under his feet, and partly because it is a constant reminder that if we are to follow Jesus it must be for us the way of the cross. 'A servant is not greater than his master. If they persecuted him they will persecute you.'[18] The disciples soon experienced the truth of this. 'All who desire to live a godly life in Christ Jesus will be persecuted,' wrote Paul.[19] A disciple is a disciple only if he shares Christ's life, and this includes sharing his pain, his suffering, his rejection and his crucifixion. 'Do you not know that all of us who have been baptised into Christ Jesus were baptised into his death? . . . We have been united with him in a death like his . . . We know that our old self was crucified with him . . . We have died with Christ . . . I have been crucified with Christ . . . Those who belong to Christ have crucified the flesh with its passions and desires . . .'[20]

What does the way of the cross mean for us today when the majority of Christians will probably not be faced with crucifixion or any other form of martyrdom? A young man once asked an older Christian, 'What does it mean to be crucified with Christ?' The older man thought for a moment, and then replied: 'To be crucified with Christ means three things. First, the man who is crucified is facing only one direction; he is not looking back. Second, the man who is crucified has said goodbye to the world; he is not going back. Third, the man who is crucified has no further plans of his own. He is totally in God's hands. Whatever the situation, he says, "Yes, Lord!" ' That is a fair description of what it means to go the way of the cross. What, then, has to die – or, as the New Testament more frequently expresses it, what has already died – when we become true disciples of Jesus Christ?

First, our old self has died. This is the great truth that Paul expounds in Romans 6. In the first three chapters of Romans, Paul declares the universal fact of sin: all alike have sinned and are under the judgement of God. At the end of that section Paul asks, how can God both be just and the justifier of the sinner at one and the same time? How can a sinner be forgiven and accepted by a holy God? There is only one answer: it is by God's grace, received through faith – faith in Christ and in his death on the cross. In Romans 4 Paul goes on to expand on the nature of true faith, the faith that saves. Then in chapter 5 he draws the parallel and contrast between Adam and Christ. We might illustrate it in this way.

Since we are all 'in Adam', by virtue of Adam's disobedience we are all naturally in the kingdom of Satan where sin reigns. However, once we become 'in Christ', by virtue of Christ's obedience unto death we enter the kingdom of God where grace reigns. We have now passed from death into life. We no longer belong to that old life; we are now dead to it. By accepting the cross of Christ as the only means by which we can come from the kingdom of Satan into the kingdom of God, we fully identify ourselves with the crucified one, which means that we have died with him. And in so far as we have died with him, we have also died to the old world of self and sin. This should no longer have any part in us. 'You must consider yourselves dead to sin and alive to God in Christ Jesus. Let not sin therefore reign in your mortal bodies, to make you obey their passions.'[21]

Emil Brunner once put it powerfully in these words: 'In the cross of Christ God says to man, "That is where you ought to be. Jesus my Son hangs there in your stead. His tragedy is the tragedy of your life. You are the rebel who should be hanged on the gallows. But lo, I suffer instead of you and because of you, because I love you in spite of what you are. My love for you is so great that I meet you there, there on the cross. I cannot meet you anywhere else. You must meet me there by identifying yourself with the one on the cross. It is by this identification that I, God, can meet you in him, saying to you as I say to him, My beloved son".'[22]

Such identification, however, whilst bringing with us the unbelievable privilege 'that we should be called children of God', also guarantees our suffering for Christ's sake. Some imagine that, since Jesus has died for us once for all to bear away all our sin, we shall not be called to a life of suffering today. Certainly we shall never suffer to atone for our sins, since Jesus finished that work of atonement for all time on the cross. 'There is no longer any offering for sin.'[23] But the cross, far from being an escape from sufferings, is the promise of sufferings for all those who are Christ's disciples. Paul once said, 'Now I rejoice in my sufferings for your sake, and in my flesh I complete what is lacking in Christ's afflictions for the sake of his body, that is, the church.'[24] In no way was there anything lacking in Christ's death when it came to taking away the sin of the world. But the way of Christ is the way of the cross, and still today he suffers in his body, the church.

Although in Christ we are now in the kingdom of God where grace reigns – and in that sense we are freed from the authority of sin and Satan over our lives – the spiritual battle is very strong and powerful until that day comes when Christ will put all his enemies under his feet. We are free in Christ, yes; but we are free to fight. The writer to the Hebrews exhorted his readers not to give up this constant battle against the forces of evil: 'Consider him who endured from sinners such hostility against himself, so that you may not grow weary or fainthearted. In your struggle against sin you have not yet resisted to the point of shedding your blood.'[25] The Christian is certainly in the realm of grace, and has died once for all to the realm of sin. Paul therefore repeatedly exhorted his readers, 'Become what you are!'

That is the force of Paul's argument in Romans 6 and elsewhere in his letters. He expounds what Christians are in Christ, and then urges them to lead a life that is worthy of their calling. We must become what we are. The old self has died to sin through the cross of Christ. We must live in the light of our new life in Christ, refusing to allow that old realm of sin to have any dominion over us. In one sense, the Christian who sins is a fool! Of course we all do sin, either 'through ignorance, through weakness or through our own deliberate fault'. We still listen to the voice of the Tempter. We are still attracted to the deceptive pleasures of this world. Yet at the same time we are foolish when we sin, since the moment we do so we spoil our relationship with Christ (and almost certainly with others too), we lose peace of mind, we fall back into bondage, we become ineffective and unfruitful in the service of Christ, and we forfeit the joy of our salvation. God, in his infinite patience and mercy, longs to restore us, and will do so as soon as we truly repent. But we often have to learn the hard way that God's word is right; his instructions are good. We are free to ignore them if we want to, but we are not free to ignore the consequences.

To maintain our freedom and fruitfulness in Christ will neither be quick nor easy. That is why we need the mind of Christ, who humbled himself and became obedient unto death, even death on a cross.[26] We should note carefully the example of Christ's sufferings, and follow in his steps.[27] We should not be surprised at the 'fiery ordeal . . . but rejoice in so far as you share Christ's sufferings, that you may also rejoice and be glad when his glory is revealed.'[28]

At the heart of any self-denial or self-emptying is not a determination somehow to do away with our old self-life, since all that has already been crucified with Christ. It is rather a determination to do the will of God and to stand fast in the freedom that Christ has already given us through his own sufferings. We may lose that freedom by falling into either of two opposite errors, legalism or licence; but there is no need to.[29] We can win and come through the struggle; but it will be a struggle, and there is no way in which the disciple of Jesus can avoid suffering, in one form or another.

Second, the pull of the world must die. This is why Jesus insisted that the rich young ruler must give up all his selfish ambitions, sell all his worldly possessions, give to the poor; and then he could come to follow Jesus. Unless there is this death to the world, with all its values and standards, we remain in bondage to it and cannot be Christ's disciples. 'Do not love the world or the things in the world. If any one loves the world, love for the Father is not in him. For all that is in the world, the lust of the flesh, and the lust of the eyes and the pride of life, is not of the Father but is of the world.'[30] We need to let go all worldly attachments, which so subtly and powerfully draw our hearts away from Christ. Jesus wants us not to be 'out of the world', but to be kept from the evil one, as we move into the world to redeem it for him. We are free to do this only if we are free from the world's pull on our own life.

In every way God calls us to make a complete break from our former relationship with the world. In Christ we become a new person all together – 'the past is finished and gone, everything has become fresh and new.'[31] In this new realm, our relationship with everyone and everything must therefore be 'in Christ' if it is to be good and right in the sight of God. In the first century, the gnostics (who have their successors today under different names) taught a false doctrine concerning the duality of spirit and matter. They taught that God is interested only in the development of our spirits, and therefore we could either indulge in the desires of our flesh or seek to deny them altogether. The gnostics thus became known either for their gross permissiveness, especially in terms of sexual morality, or else for their extreme asceticism, 'Do not handle, do not taste, do not touch.' Paul rightly commented about this: 'These have indeed an appearance of wisdom in promoting rigor of devotion and self-abasement and severity to the body, but they are of no value in checking the indulgence of the flesh.'[32] Elsewhere he called all this the 'doctrines of demons', and wrote positively that 'everything created by God is good, and nothing is to be rejected if it is received with thanksgiving.'[33] In other words, there are many things in this world that are basically good, since they were created by God. But we live in a fallen world, which has come under the control of the evil one. Therefore we can enjoy the good things God has given us in his world only when they are redeemed by Christ and brought under his Lordship. As soon as this happens, they become 'in Christ' and can then be received and enjoyed with thanksgiving.

The classic example of this is in the life of Abraham. God called him to leave his country and his father's house, and to go to some unknown destination. He did not know where he was going, but he did know with whom he was going. Later he was challenged to offer up his only son, the son of God's promise, as a sacrifice to God. Because he was willing to let go his most precious possession, confident that God was able even to raise the dead, he was able to enter into God's promised blessings by faith. Concerning the remarkable incident with Isaac, Bonhoeffer made this comment: 'Abraham comes down from the mountain with Isaac just as he went up, but the whole situation has changed.' In New Testament terms, Abraham had brought his precious relationship with Isaac under the Lordship of Christ. It was now 'in Christ'. 'Christ had stepped between father and son. Abraham had left all and followed Christ, and as he follows him he is allowed to go back and live in the world as he had done before. Outwardly the picture is unchanged, but the old is passed away, and behold all things are new. Everything has had to pass through Christ.'[34] It is only when every part of our life has been through the same basic process that it can be redeemed for Christ, and received with thanksgiving to God.

Learning to be in the world but not of the world will often cause us a measure of suffering. 'Obedience to the gospel in a world where Satan is still active means living with tension. This is part of the meaning of the Incarnation. The Incarnation makes sense only through faith in God. If it is faithful, the church's career will largely parallel that of Jesus Christ. We, as Christians . . . are constantly forced back to total dependence on the incarnate Christ. We should be alarmed when we are at home in the world or have total "peace of mind". Christian life in a non-Christian world is tension, stress and at times even agony. A whole system of social techniques aim to adjust the individual to the world and eliminate tensions. But being a

Jesus-follower means accepting the scandal of Jesus' statements that he came not to bring harmony but discord; not peace but a sword. (Matthew 10:34–36) For only thus may true peace finally come.'[35] There is no escape from this suffering for the Christian. When the whole of creation is groaning, waiting to be set free from its bondage to decay, we ourselves as Christians must 'groan inwardly as we wait for adoption as sons, the redemption of our bodies'. But at this moment in time, we must wait in patience.[36]

The pain of relationships

No man is an island. Our lives are woven together, so that who we are and what we do always influences other people. The New Testament, therefore, knows nothing of the solitary Christian. Christ calls us into fellowship both with him and with all others who have become his disciples. Although he wants us to keep our God-given individuality, for God loves variety, he insists that we lose our independence, since this is the root of all sin. We are to submit to the authority of Christ, and we are to submit to one another out of reverence for Christ. It is only in this way, as members of the body of Christ 'joined and knit together', that the life of Christ can be manifest on this earth today. It is only when we are deeply united with one another in love that the world will begin to believe and know the truth about Jesus Christ. But it is precisely at this point that problems arise.

The German philosopher Schopenhauer once said that people are like a pack of porcupines on a freezing winter night. The sub-zero temperature forces them together for warmth. But as soon as they come close together, they jab and hurt one another. So they separate, only to attempt, repeatedly, to huddle together again. Our natural but sinful independence is largely a defence against close and painful relationships.

Many churches know little of the depth of Christian fellowship which the New Testament presents as normative. Many congregations consist largely of isolated and independent individuals who may select a small circle of like-minded friends with whom they share, if at all. But that is totally foreign to the biblical picture of fellowship. We are called, as disciples of Christ to share our lives together, and, if need be, our possessions together. We are to open our hearts to one another, take off our masks, become real and honest. And when fellowships of Christians try seriously to do this in the power of the Holy Spirit, they will soon discover two things. First, they will find deep and loving relationships as brothers and sisters in Christ, and this can prove enormously enriching and fulfilling. But second, they will also find pain, since we are still angular and sinful persons who, huddling together for warmth, hurt and jab one another. The temptation then will be to separate, to pull back to a safe and less painful distance, to erect little barriers, and to protect ourselves from those vulnerable deep relationships where we are likely to get hurt again and again. In so doing, we shall destroy, or at least greatly weaken, the love and unity that Christ commanded, prayed for, died for, and sent his Spirit to accomplish. In seeking to evade this particular cost of discipleship, we have denied our Master and grieved his Spirit. Had Jesus pulled back from his own disciples when they hurt him, the Christian church would never have been born.

Although Jesus became our sin-bearer in that unique sense of taking upon himself the sin and guilt of us all, he calls those of us who profess to follow him to be burden-bearers: 'Bear one another's burdens, and so fulfil the law of Christ.'[37] In the context this means bearing not only the anxieties of one another, but also the sins. In the previous verse Paul writes: 'Brethren, if a man is overtaken in any trespass, you who are spiritual should restore him in a spirit of gentleness . . . Bear one another's burdens . . .' And the only way that I can do this is by forgiving the sin that he has committed, which may be a grievous sin against me. In this way I release my brother from the burden of his sin and guilt, and at the same time release myself from the prison of my own unforgiveness. The essence of forgiveness is release. When Jesus said, 'Forgive, and you shall be forgiven', it could equally be translated, 'Release, and you shall be released.' To forgive someone who has hurt me, I shall need the grace and mercy of God which I find only at the cross of Christ. Forgiveness is never easy. It cost Jesus his life; and it may mean for me the crucifixion of pride, bitterness, resentment, or revenge. I may have numerous reasons for justifying my position of not forgiving. Some of those reasons may logically be right and humanly understandable. But God commands me to repent. There is nothing that so grieves his Spirit as lack of forgiveness. It destroys the health of his body. It hinders his work. The root of bitterness causes trouble, and by it many may become defiled. Reasons and excuses mean nothing at the foot of the cross. It is at the cross, when I begin to see how much God has forgiven me in Christ, that I am compelled by his love to forgive my brother, even if he has sinned against me seventy times seven. I may not have the grace to do it. But if I have the willingness, as a disciple of Christ, then God's grace will always be sufficient for me, not least in this vital area of forgiveness.

It is impossible to overstress the importance of all this. In the first letter of John, the apostle begins with the enormous excitement of having actually heard and seen and touched 'the word of life'. In Jesus 'the life was made manifest, and we saw it.' Peter too, in his second letter, was thrilled that 'we were eye-witnesses of his majesty.' But how can the life of Jesus be made manifest today? How can God's glory be seen when Jesus is no longer walking on this earth as he was two thousand years ago? The New Testament answer is quite clear. God's glory is to be seen today in the church.[38] 'No one has ever seen God,' writes John; 'if we love one another, God abides in us . . .'[39]

We may sometimes think of the cost of discipleship in terms of giving up all our sin. Certainly it will include that; but it will also include much more. Jesus had no sin, but he gave up his rights, and made himself weak and vulnerable towards others. It cost him his life, but in this way he brought life to others. If we, too, are to be obedient to God, remaining in unbroken fellowship with him and also with one another, we must lay aside not only our sin, but also our rights, making ourselves vulnerable and weak towards others. We may get hurt in the process. But this is the way in which the life of Jesus will be manifest and God's glory seen in the church.

Phil Bradshaw has expressed it in this way: 'Christ had no defences. In his life and death he absorbed the sin of the whole world without giving sin back in return. "When he was reviled, he did not revile in return . . ." (1 Peter 2:23) If we want to pursue this road (i.e. of maintaining that quality of fellowship amongst us that Jesus had with his Father) we do not even need to look to the world in order to know the cost. Our own

Christian brother will heap on us his sin – his anger, judgement, frustration, accusation, demands, fears. The challenge to
us is not to return our own sin . . . If we want unity in the
biblical sense, scriptural teaching is that it will cost us our lives
in givenness to the Lord and to each other. That kind of
fellowship is produced by gentleness, and the price of gentleness is brokenness of spirit. What produces brokenness is laying
aside our rights . . . So, unity does cost a lot. But . . . the
reward is something that has the power to heal and restore and
bring people to the knowledge of the truth. It is something that
will make the corporate life we share amongst ourselves the
glory of God on the earth.'[40]

Jesus had one supreme concern during his earthly ministry: to
glorify his Father in heaven.[41] It was for this reason that he
often seemed severe in making known his terms of discipleship.
His plan, both for his church and for his world, is so great that
he cannot afford to have half-hearted disciples. Christ once said
to the lukewarm Laodicean Christians, 'I will spew you out of
my mouth.' God's glory will be seen in those who are prepared
to accept the path of obedience, the way of the cross and the
pain of relationships. That is the life that Jesus lived, setting his
face like a flint, doing always those things that pleased his
Father. Only as we follow Jesus this way can there be salvation
for the world.

Notes

1. Luke 9:57
2. Hebrews 11:1
3. Matthew 7:29, NEB
4. Mark 4:41
5. Matthew 28:18
6. Acts 5:32
7. Preface to *The Young Church in Action*, Bles 1955, p. vii
8. Luke 14:26
9. Luke 14:27, 33
10. Hebrews 11:8
11. *The Cost of Discipleship*, SCM, pp. 54, 58, 63
12. John 3:36
13. 2 Thess. 1:8
14. James 1:22
15. Carl Wilson, op. cit., p. 273

16. Mark 8:31
17. Isaiah 53:3
18. John 15:20
19. 2 Timothy 3:12
20. Romans 6:2–8; Galatians 2:20; 5:24
21. Romans 6:11f
22. Source unknown
23. Hebrews 10:18
24. Colossians 1:24
25. Hebrews 12:3f
26. Philippians 2:5ff
27. 1 Peter 2:21
28. 1 Peter 4:12f
29. Galatians 5
30. 1 John 2:16f
31. 2 Corinthians 5:17, J. B. Phillips
32. Colossians 2:21–23
33. 1 Timothy 4:1–5
34. Op. cit., p. 89
35. Howard Snyder, *Community of the King*, IVP, 1977, pp. 115f
36. Romans 8:21–25
37. Galatians 6:2
38. Ephesians 3:21
39. 1 John 4:12
40. *Towards Renewal*, Issue 19, Autumn 1979
41. John 17:4

CHAPTER TWELVE

Abounding in Hope

F. R. Maltby used to say that Jesus promised his disciples three things: they would be absurdly happy, completely fearless, and in constant trouble! That is a fair summary of the New Testament church. In fact, almost everywhere in the biblical witness of God's dealings with his people we find this recurrent paradoxical theme:

> Joy and woe are woven fine,
> A clothing for the soul divine. (William Blake)

Like contrasting shades of light and darkness flecked together, dancing over the troubled waters of this earth, we see joy and pain, glory and agony, rejoicing and weeping, life and death.

We find this vividly expressed in the life of Jesus on this earth. At his birth, the exultant display of heavenly glory, bursting forth with angelic praise, was followed shortly after by the appalling massacre of the infants. At his baptism, the heavens were opened, the Spirit came down and God himself confirmed that this was his beloved Son; yet immediately after we see Jesus wrestling with his adversary in the wilderness for six exhausting weeks. The dazzling glimpse of eternity on the Mount of Transfiguration led on to casting out evil spirits and then rebuking the disciples for not being able to do this due to their lack of faith. When the seventy returned from their mission excited by their experience of God's power, 'Jesus was filled with rapturous joy by the Holy Spirit';[1] yet soon after he was accused by his critics of being demonically inspired in his ministry. The joyful enthusiasm of the crowds waving palm branches and shouting 'Hosanna!' contrasted sharply with Jesus weeping over Jerusalem for their spiritual blindness and coming judgement. The exquisite tenderness of the last supper was the prelude to betrayal, arrest, denial and despair: Peter wept bitterly and Judas hanged himself. Although Jesus healed the sick, raised the dead and had compassion on all in need, the Jerusalem mob thirsted for his blood, 'Crucify him! Crucify him!' Although he saved others, he would not save himself. Although he promised that he would never forsake those who trusted in him, in appalling agony on the cross he cried out, 'My God, my God, why have you forsaken me?'

The same pattern is also true of the New Testament church. The rushing mighty wind of the Spirit at Pentecost, leading to thousands of conversions, dramatic healings and 'many wonders and signs', was followed by imprisonments and beatings, and God's swift judgement on Ananias and Sapphira for lying to the Holy Spirit. The extraordinary multiplication of the church in Acts 6 preceded the martyrdom of Stephen in Acts 7 and the wave of persecution against the church in Acts 8. Bishop Cuthbert Bardsley once said, 'We hear marvellous stories of what happens when there is an outpouring of the Holy Spirit – conversions, speaking in tongues, miracles, large congregations. But it also brings fears, frustration and pain.'[2] Joy and woe were woven fine at Pentecost, and have been ever since when the Spirit has moved in refreshing and renewing power upon God's people.

Peter rightly warned the Christian refugees scattered throughout Asia Minor, 'Beloved, do not be surprised at the fiery ordeal which comes upon you to prove you, as though something strange were happening to you. But rejoice in so far as you share Christ's sufferings, that you may also rejoice and be glad when his glory is revealed. If you are reproached for the name of Christ, you are blessed, because the spirit of glory and of God rests upon you.'[3] Note the sequence of words: beloved, fiery ordeal, rejoice, sufferings, glory, reproached, blessed. This has always been the pattern of discipleship.

We see the same juxtaposition of contrasts in many of the Psalms. 'When the Lord restored the fortunes of Zion, we were like those who dream. Then our mouth was filled with laughter, and our tongue with shouts of joy.' Alongside this bubbling joy, however, is the sigh and cry for further refreshment: 'Restore our fortunes, O Lord . . . May those who sow in tears reap with shouts of joy.' In the midst of tears there is, however, abounding hope that he who weeps now 'shall come home with shouts of joy, bringing his sheaves with him'[4]

Our lives, personally and corporately, are like the seasons of the year. It cannot always be harvest. 'All sunshine makes a desert' is a wise Arabian proverb. We need the cold, hard winter; we need the rain. Yet through those bleaker days we also need the hope of spring and summer: 'If winter comes, can spring be far behind?'[5]

In many parts of the church today we have been through a long and barren winter: with bare branches, fruitless orchards, unyielding soil and not a hint of harvest. With all the spiritual deadness, however, coupled with the gathering gloom of today's hostile world, many people have been growing in their spiritual hunger. This is precisely the time when we should expect God to be doing something new in his church. Cardinal Suenens has expressed it like this: 'The church has never known a more critical moment in her history. From a human point of view, there is no help on the horizon. We do not see from where salvation can come, unless from HIM; there is no salvation except in his name. At this moment, we see in the sky of the church manifestations of the Holy Spirit's action which seem to be like those known to the early church. It is as though the Acts of the Apostles and the letters of St Paul were coming to life again, as if God were once more breaking into our history.'[6] God is certainly doing a new thing by his Spirit in the church. We see the first tender green shoots of springtime pushing through the hard soil; the dark clouds, blown by the wind, are being broken up by shafts of sunlight. 'The Spirit of God can breathe through what is predicted at a human level, with a sunshine of surprises.'[7]

Although there is much to encourage us and to stimulate our hope (if we look in the right directions), before there can be a harvest we must expect suffering: 'Unless a grain of wheat falls into the earth and dies, it remains alone; but if it dies, it bears much fruit.'[8] In practical terms, it means dying to our respectability, dying to our rights and privileges, dying to our prejudices, dying to our ambitions, dying to our comforts, dying to our independence and self-sufficiency, dying to our self-preservation. Unless we die to ourselves in these and other ways, there will be no fruit, no harvest, and no hope for this world.

Often our ideas about spiritual life and power are very different from the example shown by Jesus. Often we are like those first disciples who showed a natural but worldly understanding of values in life, and repeatedly Jesus had to stand those values on their head before the disciples could grasp the revolutionary concepts of the kingdom of God. For example, Jesus was perfectly filled with the Spirit from the moment of his conception, and anointed with the Spirit's power at his baptism. But what did this mean for him? Willingly he became as *we* are, in every way except sin. Often he was weak and vulnerable; he knew the pain of loneliness and rejection; he suffered mockery and misunderstanding; he experienced 'strong cries and tears'; he learnt obedience through suffering; he was tempted, beaten, bruised and crucified; he was 'a man of sorrows and acquainted with grief'. When we are filled with the Spirit, however, we sometimes want to become as *God* is: full of power, authority and glory, overflowing with spiritual gifts, reaching down to the weak and lifting them up in our strength. The apostle Paul chided the Corinthian Christians who thought they had 'arrived': 'Already you are filled! Already you have become rich! . . . We are fools for Christ's sake, but you are wise in Christ. We are weak, but you are strong. You are held in honour, but we are in disrepute. To the present hour we hunger and thirst, we are ill-clad and buffeted and homeless . . . We have become, and are now, as the refuse of the world, the offscouring of all things.'[9] To follow Jesus means to follow his way of suffering and crucifixion. As the Master was, so shall the disciple be.

Where there's death, there's hope

Jesus was willing to lay down his life for us, both in service and in death, for two main reasons. First, he knew that it was only through the untold agony of the cross that there could be forgiveness for men, and it was for this cause that he had come to this world. Second, 'for the joy that was set before him (he) endured the cross.'[10] He knew that the best was yet to be. Paul, along with the other disciples, accepted the pain of following Jesus for the same two reasons. First, although his sufferings could never atone for sin, he saw that 'in my flesh I complete what is lacking in Christ's afflictions for the sake of his body, that is, the church.'[11] His sufferings were necessary for the sake of others, that through his weakness, Christ's power might touch and transform many lives. Second, he knew that 'the sufferings of this present time are not worth comparing with the glory that is to be revealed to us.'[12] He was abounding in hope. In contrast, when we are not willing for the cost of discipleship and for the price of spiritual renewal, it reveals that we are holding on to our lives, clinging to our temporal privileges and insecure in the love of God. We are afraid that, if we let go, God may leave us with nothing but himself! What a terrible indictment about our faith, hope and love! Pascal once said, 'It is a happy time for the church when she is sustained by nothing other than God.'[13] We shall never know the security and reality of the Father's love until we come to that point of daring faith when we have to depend on him alone. Psalm 27 vividly illustrated this point.

The Lord is my light and my salvation; whom shall I fear?
The Lord is the stronghold of my life; of whom shall I
  be afraid?
When evildoers assail me, uttering slanders against me,
my adversaries and foes, they shall stumble and fall.
Though a host encamp against me, my heart shall not
  fear;
though war arise against me, yet I will be confident.
One thing have I asked of the Lord, that will I seek after;
that I may dwell in the house of the Lord all the days of
  my life,
to behold the beauty of the Lord, and to inquire in his
  temple.
For he will hide me in his shelter in the day of trouble;
he will conceal me under the cover of his tent, he will set
  me high upon a rock.[14]

Jesus today is looking for those who will follow him, what-ever the cost may be. When many thousands of others are willing to give their lives for their political or religious ideals, Jesus wants his world to be turned upside down by a revolution of love; but he can work effectively only through those who have lost their lives to him and who will put his kingdom as their absolute priority. In this world we have come to a moment of serious danger. We cannot boast of tomorrow, and we have nothing we can leave with confidence to our children. This is the time to lose everything for Christ and to stake our lives on the God of hope.

What hope has the disciple of Jesus when faced with suffering – suffering that is not a theoretical possibility, but a horrifying reality in many parts of the world today, and is likely to increase?

Knowing Christ

The apostle Paul had one supreme ambition, that of knowing Christ more and more. He knew also that, if such knowledge were to be deep, there must be suffering. He wrote that he counted everything as 'refuse . . . that I may know him and the power of his resurrection, and may share his sufferings, becoming like him in his death . . .'[15] He realised that when he and others 'were so utterly unbearably crushed that we despaired of life itself', it was 'to make us rely not on ourselves but on God who raises the dead'; and once he saw the value and significance of this, he added, 'he delivered us from so deadly a peril, and he will deliver us; on him we have set our hope that he will deliver us again.'[16] If we know God only when the sun is shining, our knowledge will be superficial, but when we trust him in the storms, the relationship will mature. The most distant object we can see in the bright light of day is the sun. But in the dark of night we see myriads of stars which are vastly more distant than the sun. 'I will give you the treasures of darkness.'[17]

Countless men and women down the centuries have experienced the truth of this. George Matheson, who was stricken with blindness and disappointed in love, wrote a prayer in which he asked that he might accept God's will, 'not with dumb resignation, but with holy joy; not only with the absence of murmur, but with a song of praise.' Richard Wurmbrand, who spent fourteen years in various communist prisons for his faith in Christ, was 'cold, hungry and in rags'. Over the years 'they broke four vertebrae in my back, and many other bones, They carved me in a dozen places, They burned and cut eighteen holes in my body.' Yet, 'alone in my cell . . . I danced for joy every night . . . I had discovered a beauty in Christ which I had not known before.'[18] Suffering, although evil, does not always mean tragedy. It can produce great depth and spirituality. God can use it to increase our knowledge of him.

Serving others

God is love, and such is the nature of God's love that he gave his only Son for the sake of the world. God's love always gives; it is marked by sacrificial service. We must open our lives to the love of God, and open our hearts to one another. Such vulnerability will lead to pain, but also to a living hope and to the possibility of God's love reaching those who are harassed and helpless. Jürgen Moltmann writes: 'A closed human being no longer has any hope. Such a person is full of anxiety. A closed society no longer has any future. It kills the hope for life of those who stand on its periphery, and then it finally destroys itself. Hope is lived, and it comes alive, when we go outside of ourselves and, in joy and pain, take part in the life of others.'[19] If Christ lived an open life for others, the body of Christ must do the same today. Sharing our lives with others is always a risky business. Sooner or later it will mean death to ourselves, with some of our old securities blown apart. But out of death comes resurrection: 'For while we live we are always being given up to death for Jesus' sake, so that the life of Jesus may be manifested in our mortal flesh. So death is at work in us, but life in you.'[20] This is both the mystery and the miracle of the gospel. As we open ourselves to one another we shall know pain, and probably crucifixion, but in this way the resurrection life of Christ is experienced in power.

A living hope in God means that we trust God with all that he is doing in our lives. A chef will beat a steak before he cooks it in order to make it tender; likewise, because sin creates in us a hardness of heart, God may take us through many painful experiences in order to make us tenderhearted and compassionate, like his Son. When our hearts are made tender through suffering we may find an enriched ministry towards those who suffer. Paul knew, for example, that his suffering could bring great encouragement to others: 'What a wonderful God we have – he is the Father of our Lord Jesus Christ, the source of every mercy, and the one who so wonderfully comforts and strengthens us in our hardships and trials. And why does he do this? So that when others are troubled, needing our sympathy and encouragement, we can pass on to them this same help and comfort God has given us . . . In our trouble God has comforted us – and this, too, to help you: to show you from our personal experience how God will tenderly comfort you when you undergo these same sufferings. He will give you the strength to endure.'[21] Paul was therefore willing to go through incredible hardships and sufferings, both that the power of Christ might rest upon him,[22] and also that others might become 'much more bold to speak the word of God without fear'.[23] When we have personally known the sufficiency of Christ in various trials we obviously have a right to speak to those who may be going through similar trials. Those who have suffered greatly, for whatever reason, and have come through their suffering full of faith and hope, have far more authority in their testimony to Christ than those who are simply trusting that God's word will be true when the trials come.

Do not lose heart

The devil loves to play on the discouragements of Christians. In many places Christian work today is extraordinarily tough. Christians are not immune from the depression which increasingly afflicts our society. People everywhere feel the meaningless muddle of their present existence, and face a hopeless future since they have no future hope. Our materialistic society is spiritually bankrupt. Consequently, a mood of resigned apathy and despair has settled over much of our world, although the affluent minority can afford temporary escapes into the fantasy of entertainment and travel – two industries that are flourishing in western society.

Paul, in his day, knew the strong temptations to discouragement. Twice in 2 Corinthians 4 he wrote 'we do not lose heart', which indicates that he was often tempted to do so. He mentioned the depressing spiritual blindness that kept so many from seeing the 'light of the gospel of the glory of Christ!' He referred also to the physical and mental exhaustion experienced by many dedicated Christian workers, and talked about being 'afflicted . . . perplexed . . . persecuted . . . struck down'. He discerned the immense spiritual battle that raged in the world, and felt the conflicts at every level. He also gave two good reasons why he was determined not to lose heart.

First, he was deeply aware that the immense privilege of Christian ministry had been given to him 'by the mercy of God'. Not only can we know God for ourselves, but God has called us to be ambassadors of Christ and to bring his love and mercy to others. We are entrusted with the word of God, the only true message in the world that can bring someone forgiveness for the past, a new life for the present and a glorious hope for the future; and just as God has scattered the darkness of our hearts with the light of Jesus Christ, so he can do the same for others. Therefore, wrote Paul, we do not lose heart; we continue to preach Jesus Christ as Lord, knowing that God can make anyone into a new creation in Christ.

Second, Paul always had before him a strong hope in the future glory. 'We do not lose heart,' he wrote again. 'Though our outer nature is wasting away, our inner nature is being renewed every day. For this slight momentary affliction is preparing for us an eternal weight of glory beyond all comparison, because we look not to the things that are seen but to the things that are unseen; for the things that are seen are transient, but the things that are unseen are eternal.' It was this confidence about the future that enables him to endure so much in the present: 'We are afflicted in every way, but not crushed; perplexed, but not driven to despair; persecuted, but not forsaken; struck down, but not destroyed; always carrying in the body the death of Jesus, so that the life of Jesus may also be manifest in our bodies.' Paul was willing to go through any trial, knowing that others would be helped ('it is all for your sake') and that the best was yet to be. It is sobering to reflect every now and then on Paul's 'slight momentary affliction' by turning to 2 Corinthians 11. There he spoke of beatings, shipwrecks, constant dangers, toil and hardship, many a sleepless night, hunger and thirst, cold and exposure – not to mention the pressure of his daily anxiety for all the churches. Yet he saw all this as nothing compared with the 'eternal weight of glory' that God had prepared for every true disciple of Christ.

C. S. Lewis once wrote: 'Hope is one of the theological virtues. This means that a continual looking forward to the eternal world is not (as some modern people think) a form of escapism or wishful thinking, but one of the things a Christian is meant to do. It does not mean that we are to leave this present world as it is. If you read history, you will find that the Christians who did most for the present world were just those who thought most of the next. The Apostles themselves, who set on foot the conversion of the Roman Empire, the great men who built up the Middle Ages, the English Evangelicals who abolished the Slave Trade, all left their mark on Earth, precisely because their minds were occupied with Heaven. It is since Christians have largely ceased to think of the other world that they have become so ineffective in this. Aim at Heaven and you will get earth 'thrown in': aim at earth and you will get neither.'[24] The old preachers often made the same point: you cannot live well until you can die well. When you are sure of heaven, you can spend yourself in the service of others here on earth. 'For living to me means simply "Christ", and if I die I should merely gain more of him.'[25] What a glorious hope to have! Rooted and grounded in the love of God, from which not even death can separate us, we can give ourselves unreservedly to Christ's work in God's world. Moreover, the Christian hope is not a pious dream. It is based on the solid evidence of Christ's own resurrection from the dead, together with specific promises that he repeatedly gave us.

More than ever today we need to hold fast our future hope. Christ warned his disciples that before the close of the age there would be much false teaching that would lead many astray. There would also be wars and earthquakes, persecution and wickedness. Cataclysmic events and cosmic signs would likewise precede that day: 'There will be signs in sun and moon and stars, and upon the earth distress of nations in perplexity at the roaring of the sea and the waves, men fainting with fear and with foreboding of what is coming on the world; for the powers of the heavens will be shaken. And then they will see the Son of man coming in a cloud with power and great glory. Now when these things begin to take place, look up and raise your heads, because your redemption is drawing near.'[26] We cannot say precisely what these words refer to, nor can we be dogmatic about the interpretation of Peter's description of the day of the Lord when 'the heavens will pass away with a loud noise, and

the elements will be dissolved with fire, and the earth and the
works that are upon it will be burned up.'[27] However such
poetic words are not inconsistent with a nuclear holocaust, and
the possibility of such a horrific form of total human suicide
grows with every year.

When Third World nations have nuclear weapons there is no
good reason why they should not use them. When the poor
have been oppressed and crippled for so long by the greed of
affluent countries, it is understandable if years of frustration are
unleashed in nuclear violence. Billy Graham said in 1980 that if
God does not judge our western society, he will have to
apologize to Sodom and Gomorrah. This was not a wild
statement. The sin of Sodom was not only sexual perversion –
though there is plenty of that in our western world. God
declared through his prophet Ezekiel: 'Behold, this was the
guilt of your sister Sodom: she and her daughters had pride,
surfeit of food, and prosperous ease, but did not aid the
poor and needy. They were haughty, and did abominable
things before me; therefore I removed them.'[28] Do we imagine that we who have acted with similar neglect and arro-
gance shall escape the judgement of God? In the past God has
often used the evil of man to accomplish his divine purposes.
There is little reason to be optimistic about the future. From
every perspective, in human terms, it seems extraordinarily
bleak.

The call to discipleship, however, is a call to God's promised
glory. In view of the urgency of the times, we are to live lives
that honour Christ, that heal the wounds within his body, and
that hasten the coming of the day of God. This is not a day in
which to play religious games. Time is running out fast. Christ
looks for disciples who are unashamed of him, bold in their
witness, obedient to his word, united in his love and filled with
his Spirit. There is no promise of an easy task. Joy and woe will
be woven fine; tears, pain and sweat intermingled with radiant
love and inexpressible joy. Christ wants disciples who will not
only have hope, but give hope. Whatever we receive we are to
give way, that others too may rise up through the darkness that
covers the earth. 'Arise, shine; for your light has come, and the
glory of the Lord has risen upon you.'[29] Christ's disciples with
such a hope can still change the course of this world. Following

St Francis of Assisi, we need to pray that where there is hatred, we may give love; where there is injury, pardon; where there is doubt, faith; where there is despair, hope; where there is sadness, joy; where there is darkness, light. 'Grant that we may not seek so much to be consoled, as to console; to be understood, as to understand; to be loved, as to love; for in giving we receive, in pardoning, we are pardoned, and dying we are born to eternal life.'

The disciple of Christ cannot lose: when he gives all, he gains all; when he loses his life, he finds it. Jim Elliott, who was martyred as a missionary amongst the Aucas in South America in 1956, summed it up like this: 'He is no fool who gives what he cannot keep, to gain what he cannot lose.'

The Lord reigns!

Notes

1. Luke 10:21. Weymouth
2. Quoted in the *Church of England Newspaper*, 13 September 1973
3. 1 Peter 4:12–14
4. Psalm 126
5. P. B. Shelley, *Ode to the West Wind*
6. *A New Pentecost?* Darton, Longman & Todd, 1975, p. 90
7. Cardinal Suenens
8. John 12:24
9. 1 Corinthians 4:8–13
10. Hebrews 12:2
11. Colossians 1:24
12. Romans 8:18
13. Quoted by Cardinal Suenens, op. cit., p. xi
14. Psalm 27
15. Philippians 3:10
16. 2 Corinthians 1:10
17. Isaiah 45:3
18. *Tortured for Christ*, Hodder & Stoughton, 1967, p. 19 and *In God's Underground*, W. H. Allen, 1968, p. 54
19. *The Open Church*, SCM, 1978, p. 35
20. 2 Cor. 4:11f
21. 2 Corinthians 1:3–7, Living Bible
22. 2 Corinthians 12:9f
23. Philippians 1:14
24. *Mere Christianity*, Collins, p. 116

25. Philippians 1:21, J. B. Phillips
26. Luke 21:25–28
27. 2 Peter 3:10
28. Ezekiel 16:49f
29. Isaiah 60:1

APPENDIX A

An Evangelical Commitment to Simple Lifestyle

For four days we have been together, 85 Christians from 27 countries, to consider the resolve expressed in the Lausanne Covenant (1974) to 'develop a simple lifestyle'. We have tried to listen to the voice of God, through the pages of the Bible, through the cries of the hungry poor, and through each other. And we believe that God has spoken to us.

We thank God for his great salvation through Jesus Christ, for his revelation in Scripture which is a light for our path, and for the Holy Spirit's power to make us witnesses and servants in the world.

We are disturbed by the injustices of the world, concerned for its victims, and moved to repentance for our complicity in it. We have also been stirred to fresh resolves, which we express in this Commitment.

1. Creation

We worship God as the Creator of all things, and we celebrate the goodness of his creation. In his generosity he has given us everything to enjoy, and we receive it from his hands with humble thanksgiving. (1 Timothy 4:4, 6, 17) God's creation is marked by rich abundance and diversity, and he intends its resources to be husbanded and shared for the benefit of all.

We therefore denounce environmental destruction, wastefulness and hoarding. We deplore the misery of the poor who suffer as a result of these evils. We also disagree with the drabness of the ascetic. For all these deny the Creator's goodness and reflect the tragedy of the fall. We recognise our own involvement in them, and we repent.

2. Stewardship

When God made man, male and female, in his own image, he gave them dominion over the earth. (Genesis 1:26–28) He made them stewards of its resources, and they became responsible to him as Creator, to the earth which they were to develop, and to their fellow human beings with whom they were to share its riches. So fundamental are these truths that authentic human fulfilment depends on a right relationship to God, neighbour and the earth with all its resources. People's humanity is diminished if they have no just share in those resources.

By unfaithful stewardship, in which we fail to conserve the earth's finite resources, to develop them fully, or to distribute them justly, we both disobey God and alienate people from his purpose for them. We are determined, therefore, to honour God as the owner of all things, to remember that we are stewards and not proprietors of any land or property that we may have, to use them in the service of others, and to seek justice with the poor who are exploited and powerless to defend themselves.

We look forward to 'the restoration of all things' at Christ's return. (Acts 3:21) At that time our full humanness will be restored; so we must promote human dignity today.

3. Poverty and Wealth

We affirm that involuntary poverty is an offence against the goodness of God. It is related in the Bible to powerlessness, for the poor cannot protect themselves. God's call to rulers is to use their power to defend the poor, not to exploit them. The church must stand with God and the poor against injustice, suffer with them and call on rulers to fulfil their God-appointed role.

We have struggled to open our minds and hearts to the uncomfortable words of Jesus about wealth. 'Beware of covetousness,' he said, and 'a person's life does not consist in the abundance of his possessions'. (Luke 12:15) We have listened to his warnings about the danger of riches. For wealth brings worry, vanity and false security, the oppression of the weak and indifference to the sufferings of the needy. So it is hard for a rich person to enter the kingdom of heaven (Matthew 19:23) and the greedy will be excluded from it. The kingdom is a free gift offered to all, but it is especially good news for the poor because they benefit most from the changes it brings.

We believe that Jesus still calls some people (perhaps even us) to follow him in a lifestyle of total, voluntary poverty. He calls all his followers to an inner freedom from the seduction of riches (for it is impossible to serve God and money) and to sacrificial generosity 'to be rich in good works, to be generous and ready to share'. (1 Timothy 6:18) Indeed, the motivation and model for Christian generosity is nothing less than the example of Jesus Christ himself, who, though rich, became poor that through his poverty we might become rich. (2 Corinthians 8:9) It was a costly, purposeful self-sacrifice; we mean to seek his grace to follow him. We resolve to get to know poor and oppressed people, to learn issues of injustice from them, to seek to relieve their suffering, and to include them regularly in our prayers.

4. The new community

We rejoice that the church is the new community of the new age, whose members enjoy a new life and a new lifestyle. The earliest Christian church, constituted in Jerusalem on the Day of Pentecost, was characterised by a quality of fellowship unknown before. Those Spirit-filled believers loved one another to such an extent that they sold and shared their possessions. Although their selling and giving were voluntary, and some private property was retained (Acts 5:4), it was made subservient to the needs of the community, 'None of them said that anything he had was his own'. (Acts 4:32) That is, they were free from the selfish assertion of proprietary rights. And as a result of their transformed economic relationships, 'there was not a needy person among them'. (Acts 4:34)

This principle of generous and sacrificial sharing, expressed in holding ourselves and our goods available for people in need, is an indispensable characteristic of every Spirit-filled church. So those of us who are affluent in any part of the world, are determined to do more to relieve the needs of less privileged believers. Otherwise, we shall be like those rich Christians in Corinth who ate and drank too much while their poor brothers and sisters were left hungry, and we shall deserve the stinging rebuke Paul gave them for despising God's church and desecrating Christ's body. (1 Corinthians 11:20–24) Instead, we determine to resemble them at a later stage when Paul urged them out of their abundance to give to the impoverished Christians of Judaea 'that there may be equality'. (2 Corinthians 8:10–15) It was a beautiful demonstration of caring love and of Gentile-Jewish solidarity in Christ.

In this same spirit, we must seek ways to transact the church's corporate business together with the minimum expenditure on travel, food and accommodation. We call on churches and para-church agencies in their planning to be acutely aware of the need for integrity in corporate lifestyle and witness.

Christ calls us to be the world's salt and light, in order to hinder its social decay and illumine its darkness. But our light must shine and our salt must retain its saltness. It is when the new community is most obviously distinct from the world – in its values, standards and lifestyle – that it presents the world with a radically attractive alternative and so exercises its greatest influence for Christ. We commit ourselves to pray and work for the renewal of our churches.

5. Personal lifestyle

Jesus our Lord summons us to holiness, humility, simplicity and contentment. He also promises us his rest. We confess, however, that we have often allowed unholy desires to disturb our inner tranquility. So without the constant renewal of Christ's peace in our hearts, our emphasis on simple living will be one-sided.

Our Christian obedience demands a simple lifestyle, irrespective of the needs of others. Nevertheless, the facts that 800 million people are destitute and that about 10,000 die of starvation every day make any other lifestyle indefensible.

While some of us have been called to live among the poor, and others to open our homes to the needy, all of us are determined to develop a simpler lifestyle. We intend to re-examine our income and expenditure, in order to manage on less and give away more. We lay down no rules or regulations, for either ourselves or others. Yet we resolve to renounce waste and oppose extravagance in personal living, clothing and housing, travel and church buildings. We also accept the distinction between necessities and luxuries, celebrations and normal routine, and between the service of God and slavery to fashion. Where to draw the line requires conscientious thought and decision by us, together with members of our family. Those of us who belong to the West need the help of our Third World brothers and sisters in evaluating our standards of spending. Those of us who live in the Third World acknowledge that we too are exposed to the temptation of covetousness. So we need each other's understanding, encouragement and prayers.

6. International Development

We echo the words of the Lausanne Covenant: 'We are shocked by the poverty of millions, and disturbed by the injustices which cause it.' One quarter of the world's population enjoys unparalleled prosperity, while another quarter endures grinding poverty. This gross disparity is an intolerable injustice; we refuse to acquiesce in it. The call for a New International Economic Order expresses the justified frustration of the Third World.

We have come to understand more clearly the connection between resources, income and consumption: people often starve because they cannot afford to buy food, and because they have no access to power. We therefore applaud the growing emphasis of Christian agencies on development rather than aid. For the transfer of personnel and appropriate technology can enable people to make good use of their own resources, while at the same time respecting their dignity. We resolve to contribute more generously to human development projects. Where people's lives are at stake, there should never be a shortage of funds.

But the action of governments is essential. Those of us who live in the affluent nations are ashamed that our governments have mostly failed to meet their targets for official development assistance, to maintain emergency food stocks or to liberalise their trade policy.

We have come to believe that in many cases multi-national corporations reduce local initiative in the countries where they work, and tend to oppose any fundamental change in government. We are convinced that they should become more subject to controls and more accountable.

7. Justice and Politics

We are also convinced that the present situation of social injustice is so abhorrent to God that a large measure of change is necessary. We do not believe in an earthly utopia, but neither are we pessimists. Change can come, although not through commitment to simple lifestyle or human development projects alone.

Poverty and excessive wealth, militarism and the arms industry, and the unjust distribution of capital, land and resources are issues of power and powerlessness. Without a shift of power through structural change these problems cannot be solved.

The Christian church, along with the rest of society, is inevitably involved in politics which is 'the art of living in community'. Servants of Christ must express his lordship in their political, social and economic commitments and their love for their neighbours by taking part in the political process. How, then, can we contribute to change?

First, we will pray for peace and justice, as God commands. Secondly, we will seek to educate Christian people in the moral and political issues involved, and so clarify their vision and raise their expectations. Thirdly, we will take action. Some Christians are called to special tasks in government, economics or development. All Christians must participate in the active struggle to create a just and responsible society. In some situations obedience to God demands resistance to an unjust established order. Fourthly, we must be ready to suffer. As followers of Jesus, the Suffering Servant, we know that service always involves suffering.

While personal commitment to change our lifestyle without political action to change systems of injustice lacks effectiveness, political action without personal commitment lacks integrity.

8. Evangelism

We are deeply concerned for the vast millions of unevangelised people in the world. Nothing that has been said about lifestyle or injustice diminishes the urgency of developing evangelistic strategies appropriate to different cultural environments. We must not cease to proclaim Christ as Saviour and Lord throughout the world. The church is not yet taking seriously its commission to be witnesses 'to the ends of the earth'. (Acts 1:8)

So the call to a responsible lifestyle must not be divorced from the call to responsible witness; the credibility of our message is seriously diminished whenever we contradict it by our lives. It is impossible with integrity to proclaim Christ's salvation if he has evidently not saved us from greed, or his lordship if we are not good stewards of our possessions, or his love if we close our hearts against the needy. When Christians care for each other and for the deprived, Jesus Christ becomes more visibly attractive.

In contrast to this, the affluent lifestyle of some Western evangelists when they visit the Third World is understandably offensive to many.

We believe that simple living by Christians generally would release considerable resources of finance and personnel for evangelism as well as development. So by our commitment to a simple lifestyle we recommit ourselves whole-heartedly to world evangelisation.

9. The Lord's return

The Old Testament prophets both denounced the idolatries and injustices of God's people and warned of his coming judgement. Similar denunciations and warnings are found in the New Testament. The Lord Jesus is coming back soon to judge, to save and to reign. His judgement will fall upon the greedy (who are idolaters) and upon all oppressors. For on that day the King will sit upon his throne and separate the saved from the lost. Those who have ministered to him by ministering to one of the least of one of his needy brothers and sisters will be saved, for the reality of saving faith is exhibited in serving love. But those who are persistently indifferent to the plight of the needy, and so to Christ in them, will be irretrievably lost. (Matthew 25:31–46) All of us need to hear again this solemn warning of Jesus, and resolve afresh to serve him in the deprived. We therefore call on our fellow Christians everywhere to do the same.

Our resolve

So then, having been freed by the sacrifice of our Lord Jesus Christ, in obedience to his call, in heartfelt compassion for the poor, in concern for evangelism, development and justice, and in solemn anticipation of the Day of Judgement, we humbly commit ourselves to develop a just and simple lifestyle, to support one another in it and to encourage others to join with us in the commitment.

We know that we shall need time to work-out its implications and that the task will not be easy. May Almighty God give us grace to be faithful! Amen.

'An Evangelical Commitment to Simple Lifestyle' was written and endorsed by the International Consultation on Simple Lifestyle, held at Hoddesdon, England on March 17–21, 1980. The Consultation was sponsored by the World Evangelical Fellowship Theological Commission's Unit on Ethics and Society (Dr Ronald Sider, Chairman) and the Lausanne Committee on World Evangelisation's Lausanne Theology and Education Group. (Rev. John Stott, Chairman)

I am grateful to the Administrative Secretary of the Theological Commission of the World Evangelical Fellowship for permission to use this statement.

APPENDIX B

A Basic Discipleship Course

All these twenty-four themes are available as 15-minute talks by David Watson on cassette. Each cassette has four talks on it, and comes as a pack with five copies of the outline of the talks and questions for study.

Numbers 2, 3 and 4 are available from
Falcon Audio-Visual Aids,
Falcon Court, 32 Fleet Street, London EC4Y 1DB
and from
Christian Foundation Publications,
45 Appleton Road, Hale, Altrincham, Cheshire WA15 9LP.
Number 1 is available from Christian Foundation Publications only.

1. *Live a New Life*
   How can I know?
   How can I grow?
   How can I show?
   How can I overcome?
2. *Christian Foundations I and II* (2 cassettes)
   I   What can we know about God?
       Who is Jesus Christ?
       Who is the Holy Spirit?
       Is the Bible the Word of God?
   II Why the Cross?
       Prayer
       Is there Life after Death?
       The Church
3. *Christian Living I and II* (2 cassettes)
   I   Helping others find God
       Common Questions

      Giving
      Guidance
  II Faith
      Suffering
      Forgiveness
      Love
4. *Spiritual Renewal* (1 cassette)
      Worship
      The Gifts of the Spirit
      Being Filled with the Spirit
      Spiritual Warfare

APPENDIX C

A Further Discipleship Course

(The author wishes to acknowledge that the basic format of this course was suggested by a study guide in evangelism called *In the Spirit of Love* by Bob Roxburgh and George Mallone of Vancouver, BC, Canada, 1975.)

The purpose of this course is to encourage personal study during the week, followed by group work based on the week's study. The following is offered only as a *sample*; other themes could be similarly developed.

1. The Power of the Holy Spirit
Note: Please go through your Readings and Questions during the week before the Group Study.

A) Daily Bible readings and study questions
Monday: Acts 1:1–14 – 'The Promise of the Spirit'
1. Even after 40 days, when Jesus proved his resurrection and spoke of the kingdom of God, his disciples still had a great need: (see also Luke 24:44–53)
   What was it?
   What must they do about it?
   When would it happen?
   Why was it necessary?
2. In what ways were their ideas about the future wrong? (see 6–8)
   What similar mistakes could we fall into today?
3. How did they prepare themselves for the coming of the Spirit?

Tuesday: Acts 2:1–36 – 'The Coming of the Spirit'
1. How can we be filled with the Spirit today? See Acts 2:38; 5:32; John 7:37–39.

2. How should the filling of the Spirit be worked out in our lives? See v.4, 11. 17–18, 22ff etc.
3. What is the place of tongues and other spiritual gifts in connexion with the Spirit's fulness? (4, 17f)
4. Is the filling (or baptism?) of the Spirit always something after conversion? How can we help (a) young converts; (b) other Christians who feel the need of 'something more'?

Wednesday: Acts 3:1–26 – 'Witnessing in Jerusalem'
1. Is it ever right to proclaim (or pray for) healing with such confidence, as Peter showed? (1–10) What part should healing have in the witness of the church today?
2. No doubt there were other sick people listening to Peter, but what was the main thrust of his sermon? What can we learn from this?

Thursday: Acts 8:1–25 – 'Witnessing in Judea and Samaria'
1. What 'helped' them to obey Christ's instructions in Acts 1:8? What can we learn from this about the Spirit's prompting?
2. What can we learn from Philip's ministry? (If time, read also verses 26–40)
3. How do you explain the coming of the Holy Spirit after the conversion of these Samaritans? (14ff)

Friday: Acts 28:16–31 – 'Witnessing to the end of the earth'
1. Paul had for years wanted to bring the gospel to Rome. What can we learn from this about God's working in our lives in answer to our prayers?
2. How did Paul witness to the Jewish leaders about Christ? When might such boldness seem right?

Saturday and Sunday:
1. **Personal**
   (a) How can we be continuously filled with the Spirit? What are your main obstacles or hindrances?
   (b) What are you doing, or could be doing, at present as a witness for Christ, in your area, in the city, and in the world?
2. **Corporate**
   (a) What hinders the power of the Spirit in your church?

(b) How should we expect the Spirit's power to be manifest in and through the church?

B) Group study

1. Share briefly some of the answers to your Bible Study Questions.
2. What inadequacies or difficulties do we have when it comes to sharing our faith with unbelievers? What can we do about this?

    e.g. I don't know the message

        I don't have the confidence that Christianity is always "true"

        I can't answer the questions people fire at me

        I find it hard to talk to people about my personal faith

        I feel guilty when I 'lay' things on other people

        You lose too many friends when you do this

        If just doesn't seem all that urgent to me

        I feel hypocritical talking about new life when I am so messed up myself

        I don't have a chance to relate to any non-Christians

        They never ask, so I never tell them

        I'm afraid to speak by myself, I need someone else along

        It's so unnatural for me

        I've never seen it done tastefully, it always seems tactless and offensive

    Any others.

C) Optional reading

One in the Spirit by David Watson (H & S)
I Believe in the Holy Spirit by Michael Green (H & S)

D) Verses to learn

John 7:37–39

2. The Body of Christ and the Gifts of the Spirit

Note: Please go through your Readings and Questions during the week before the Group study.

A) Daily Bible readings and study questions

Monday: 1 Corinthians 12:1–11 – 'Varieties of gifts'

1. How can we discern between true and counterfeit spiritual gifts? (1–3)
2. Give a brief 'definition' of each of the spiritual gifts mentioned in vv.4–11. In other words, how would you describe them to someone?
3. Do you think this is a complete list of the gifts of the Spirit? If not, what others would you include?

Tuesday: 1 Corinthians 12:12–31 – 'You are the body of Christ'

1. How should we recognise and encourage one another's gifts? (12–25)
2. Can you explain in your own words, verse 26?
3. What are the 'higher gifts' that we should earnestly desire (31)?

Wednesday: Romans 12 – 'A living sacrifice'

1. If we are to use God's gifts to his glory, what must we seek to do? (1–6)
2. What further gifts does Paul mention in verses 6–8? Can you explain them simply in your own words?
3. In the practical instructions of verse 9–21, what ones do you personally find to be most relevant or difficult?

Thursday: Ephesians 4:1–16 – 'Grow up . . . into Christ'

1. Why is the 'unity of the Spirit' really important? (1–6)
2. What ingredients make for the building up of the body of Christ into maturity? (7–16)

Friday: 1 Corinthians 3 – 'Only God gives the growth'

1. What problems did the Corinthian church face, and what similar dangers could we face today? (1–9)
2. What sort of test are Christians to experience? What does it mean to build with 'gold, silver, precious stones'? (10–23)

Saturday and Sunday:

1. **Personal application**
   (a) What gifts are you using in the fellowship?
   (b) What gifts are you praying for? How could you develop them?

2. **Corporate application**
   (a) Think of specific Christians whose gifts have helped you in the past, and thank God for them.
   (b) How is the church developing along the lines of Ephesians 4:7–16?

B) Group Study
   1. Share briefly some of your answers to Bible Study Questions.
   2. Discuss how gifts can be developed within the fellowship to edify the body of Christ.

C) Optional reading
   (See books for previous study)

3. The Great Commission

Note: Please go through your Readings and Questions during the week before the Group Study.

A) Daily Bible readings and study questions

Monday: Matthew 28:1–20 – 'Go . . . lo . . .'
1. What points of evidence do verses 1–15 contribute towards the fact of the resurrection of Christ? (briefly!)
2. What position does Jesus have in the world and in the church, resulting from his crucifixion and exaltation? (16–18; see Phil. 2:8–11; Eph. 1:20–23)
3. What does it mean to 'make disciples'?
4. 'Baptising . . . teaching . . .' What should be the place of Word and Sacrament in 'making disciples'?

Tuesday: Mark 16:9–20 (Not all manuscripts have this 'longer ending' of Mark, but at least it represents the Church's tradition, whether part of the true Word of God, or not)
1. What further evidence is there here for the resurrection? Why were the eleven slow to believe?
2. What place should baptism have in 'preaching the gospel'? See also 1 Corinthians 1:13–17.
3. What significance are these signs for today's evangelism? (17–20; see Romans 15:18f)

Wednesday: Luke 24:44–53; 1 Corinthians 15:1–11 – 'You are witnesses'

1. What is the essence of the gospel that saves? (see both passages)
2. What does it mean to be a witness 'to Christ' (Acts 1:8) or a witness 'of these things'?
3. What is the value of personal testimony? (1 Corinthians 15:6–11)

Thursday: 2 Corinthians 5:10–21 – Motivation

1. List at least 5 motives in evangelism in this passage. See, from these verses, what you can learn about them. Write down any common denomination, or any striking factor.

Friday: 1 Corinthians 9:15–27 – 'By all means save some'

1. What different ways can you (personally) 'preach the gospel' today? Do you have the same urge as Paul expresses it in verses 15–18? If not, why not?
2. Explain the principles in verses 19–23 in your own terms. How does this apply in your situation, for example?
3. What should we guard against, and how, from vv.24–27?

Saturday and Sunday:

1. **Personal**
   If someone you knew had just become a Christian, how would you follow them up, assuming you were given the responsibility? (Give as much detail as space and time allows!)
2. **Corporate**
   (a) How effective is your local church in 'making disciples'?
   (b) What more could realistically be done – by whom and how?

B) Group Study

1. Share some of your answers to Bible Study Questions.
2. Discuss some of the problems you have in evangelism. How could these be overcome?
3. What evangelistic work are you seeking to do outside your church buildings?

C) **Optional reading**
    I Believe in Evangelism by David Watson (H & S)
    The Christian Persuader by Leighton Ford (H & S)

D) **Verses to learn**
    Matthew 28:18–20

4. Sharing Good News
Note: please go through your Readings and Questions during the week before the Group Study.

A) Daily Bible readings and study questions
Monday: Luke 19:1–10 – Zacchaeus
1. What were the steps by which Jesus brought 'salvation' to his house?
2. What is the meaning of repentance; and how far should a person understand the implications of this before he comes to faith in Christ?

Tuesday: Acts 8:26–40 – Philip the evangelist
1. What lessons can you learn from this passage which indicate that Philip was such a good evangelist?
2. 'He told him the good news of Jesus'. (35) What steps would you use, with verses, in order to lead a person to Jesus?

Wednesday: John 3:1–21 – Nicodemus
1. How far is it necessary, from the example of Jesus, to answer a person's questions before leading him to personal faith in Christ?
2. What can we learn about the sovereignty of the Spirit in evangelism? Where does human will and responsibility come in?
3. 'He who does not believe is condemned already.' (18) Why? And why do some not believe? (19–21)

Thursday: 1 Corinthians 1:18; 2:5 – 'We preach Christ crucified'
1. In our message, what is the 'power of God'? See 1:18, 23f; 2:2, 5.
2. What is meant by preaching 'Christ crucified'?
3. Why can a sense of weakness, inadequacy and nervousness be an asset in evangelism?

Friday: Acts 20:17–37 – Evangelism and follow-up
1. Twice Paul said 'I did not shrink' (20, 27) – suggesting that sharing good news is not easy. What did he not shrink from?
2. How should we 'take heed to ourselves and to all the flock' (28) – the flock referring, at least, to anyone for whom God has given us a special responsibility?
3. What lessons did Paul teach by his life and example?

Saturday and Sunday:
1. **Personal application**
   Using John 4:1–37, check your position as a witness to Christ. Tick the appropriate evaluation:

	Developing this area	Weak	New idea
Sensitive to Spirit's leading (4)			
Willing to share at inopportune times (6)			
Willing to take the initiative (7)			
Willing to break social/cultural barriers (7–9)			
Sensitive to people's real needs (10–15)			
Frank and honest about personal problems (16–18)			
Able to avoid red herrings (19–21)			
Bringing people to a point of decision (25–36)			
Wanting to share Jesus with others (32)			

Having checked your position, pray that God will strengthen what is weak in your witness to Christ.

2. **Corporate application**
   (a) In what ways could your church strengthen its evangelism?
   (b) In what ways could your church improve its follow-up?

(c) How could Christians in your church be better trained
   and equipped for evangelism and follow-up?

B) Group study
1. Share briefly some of your answers to Bible Study
   Questions.
2. Discuss some of the opportunities for evangelism you
   have in your neighbourhood and/or place of work. What
   are you doing? What difficulties do you have? What
   more could be done?

C) Optional reading
How to Give Away Your Faith by Paul Little (IVP)

D) Verses to Learn
Romans 3:23; 6:23; Isaiah 53:6; Mark 8:34; Revelation 3:20

5. Answering Common Questions
Note: Please go through your questions during the week before
the Group Study. On this occasion you may need a concordance
and other aids, although a few verses are suggested as a start!

A) Daily study questions
What answers (with verses where possible) would you give
to the following?
Monday: 'I don't believe in God.'
   (See Romans 1:18–23; John 14:8–11; John 1:14–18; 1 John
   4:12)
Tuesday: 'I don't feel any need of God.'
   (See John 3:3–18; Ephesians 2:1–3, 12; Hebrews 9:27)
Wednesday: 'What about suffering?'
   (See Luke 13:1–5; Romans 8:15–25; 2 Corinthians
   4:16–18; Psalm 73)
Thursday: 'What about those who have never heard?'
   (See Luke 12:47–48; Romans 1:18–23; 3:19–24; Acts
   10:34f; Genesis 18:25)
Friday: 'What about other religions?'
   (See John 14:6; Acts 4:12; 1 Timothy 2:5–6; Hebrews
   1:1–3)

Saturday: 'I think I'm good enough as I am!'
   (See John 3:3–7; Romans 2:1–3; 3:9–20; Ephesians
   2:8–10; Galatians 2:16)
Sunday: Write down any other questions, objections or excuses
   you have commonly heard; and give, where possible, some
   passages in answer to them.

B) Group study
   1. Share briefly some of your answers to the Study
      Questions.
   2. Discuss ways of being equipped with answers – See
      1 Peter 2:15.

C) Optional reading
   How to Give Away Your Faith by Paul Little (IVP)
   Is Anyone There? by David Watson (H & S)

D) Verses to learn
   Any of the above!

6. Visiting and Counselling
Note: Please go through your questions the week before the
Group Study.

A) Daily Study Questions
Monday: Evangelistic visiting
1. Why is this necessary? Matthew 9:35–10:1; Romans
   10:13–15
2. From Luke 10:1–20 what principles can you learn that are
   relevant for today and in your context?
3. **Some general points:**
   When to go: Choose a likely convenient time. Avoid clash-
      ing with the most popular TV programmes, e.g.
   What to do: Knock (persistently), pray, wait, door opens,
      smile . . .!
   What to say: Announce immediately who you are (not JW
      etc.); where you are from; what you are doing.
   Try to get inside the house; develop conversation; don't be
      in a hurry; listen patiently; record information as quickly
      as possible afterwards (out of sight!).

Tuesday: Follow-up visiting (e.g. after an evangelistic service etc.)

1. From 1 Thessalonians 2:1–13, what should your attitude and approach be like – over a period of time?
2. From Acts 20:19–35, what should you aim to teach and watch for – over a period of time?
3. **Some general points:**
   Visit as soon as possible after the name has been passed to you – within 24 hours, if possible.
   Be friendly, and begin to establish a warm relationship.
   Go to someone of the same sex and approximately the same age.
   Be interested in them as a person.
   Read a short passage together – e.g. Psalm 103.
   Fix up a regular time to meet, but keep the sessions fairly short.
   Lend any useful literature.

Wednesday: Sick visiting

1. From James 5:13–16 what can we learn?
2. **General points:**
   Avoid being either hearty or gloomy.
   Sit down, but not always on the bed (pressure might be painful).
   If a person is deaf, speak up or write what you want to say.
   Don't be hurried, but don't stay too long.
   Don't make rash promises about coming again and then fail.
   Read some suitable verse(s) and then pray (briefly) – sometimes hold a person's hand (or lay hands on them) whilst praying.
   If a patient is very ill, read a well-known passage e.g. Psalm 23.
   If a patient is unconscious, still read and pray aloud.
   Leave suitable literature.

Thursday: Counselling those lacking assurance

1. From 1 John 5:13 we are meant to have assurance. How? See 1:1–3, 7; 2:3, 15, 29; 3:9, 14, 21; 4:13; 5:4, 19.
2. Try to discover why those doubts persist: see Chapter 8 in *Live a New Life* by David Watson. (H & S)
3. Show the nature of faith from Luke 1:30, 38, 46–49, etc.

Help the person to rest on the promises in God's word – see
  Matthew 7:24–27; 2 Peter 1:2–4, 19.
Pray for the person to be filled with the Holy Spirit – see
  Luke 11:9–13.

Friday: Counselling those who are depressed or defeated
1. Read Psalms 42–43 and Romans 8:26–39 as useful material.
   What can we learn here about God's answer to our battles?
2. Be very gentle and understanding. Pray for the gifts of
   knowledge and wisdom, so that the real problem may be
   revealed.
3. In some cases it may be necessary (gently) to give them time
   openly to confess (a) every sin, especially sin against others;
   (b) every way in which they have been hurt by others. It
   may be right for them to confess the sin of self-pity, and to
   begin to offer God the sacrifice of praise.

Saturday: Counselling those with wrong relationships
1. From Philippians 2:1–5; 4:1–7; Ephesians 4:25–32 and
   2 Corinthians 6:14–7:1 what can we learn in general terms?
   (Most of Paul's letters deal with this vast theme!)

Sunday: Evaluation
(a) **Personal:** In which areas –
         are you weak?
         would you appreciate further training?
         do you, in any way (however slight) feel called by God to
            serve?
(b) **Corporate:** In which areas could your church be strength-
       ened, and how?

B) Group study
   1. Discuss some of the answers to your questions.

C) Optional reading
   Live a New Life by David Watson (H & S)
   New Life, New Lifestyle by Michael Green (H & S)

D) Verse to learn
   Isaiah 50:4

7. Preparing and Giving Talks

Note: Please work on this during the week before the Group Study.

Introduction: Most people are very nervous at the thought of giving a talk, however brief! But most people are quite able to do so. However, a good simple talk does require careful preparation. Mark Twain: 'It takes me three weeks to prepare a good impromptu speech!' Preparing a talk is like building a house:

A) Select the site

With the 'ground' as the Bible, the 'site' will be some verse/passage, etc. 1 Peter 4:11 – Our ideas are unimportant; God's word is vital.

1. Use common sense.
2. Keep a 'Jottings Notebook' (especially if speaking fairly regularly)
3. Know the needs of your hearers, as far as possible.
4. Pray – before any specific preparation begins.

B) Lay the foundations

Study the verse/passage/theme as thoroughly as you can, until you really know what God is saying in his word. Without this there will be no conviction about your talk, and it may easily collapse!

C) Study the plan, or work out your message carefully.

Have ONE AIM: It is often useful to write out your aim in one short sentence, so that the rest of the talk can be referred back to that. Be ruthless! What is God's message for this occasion?

N.B. There are usually many different ways of tackling a passage

N.B. Remember Wesley's words, 'I offered them Christ.'

D) Erect the scaffolding

1. A simple plan: State your point (a heading), Explain, Illustrate, Apply.
2. Work out divisions and headings (usually about 2–3 points in a talk)

(a) Use words of verse (b) Ask questions (Who? What? Why? etc.) (c) 'Ask alliteration's artful aid' – but not too forced!

E) Build the walls

Give some substance to your talk. We are to 'stimulate', 'instruct', 'feed', 'stir', etc. Most talks will need some doctrine and teaching. Not just 'Put your trust in Jesus' – say why etc.

For this, study more than one translation
   have a Concordance
   use a well-chosen commentary.

F) Don't forget the windows – Illustrations are invaluable. Make a note of stories, quotes, topical news, etc. These often allow much light to fall on a path of solid doctrine.

G) Make it fit for living – This is to be –
   not a museum
   but a house to live in.
Thus the talk must be relevant; suggest practical action, where possible.

H) Check front and back doors

i.e. Beginning and ending of talks are of special importance. Some useful opening: A question, startling statement, topical news item, story, advertisement, puzzle or problem, etc.

Also know when to stop and how to stop!

Final preparation and delivery:

For most people (though not all) the following is probably wise, at least to start with:

1. Write out the talk in full, and then condense it to shorter notes.
2. Rehearse it – say it aloud (or whisper it!)
3. Be natural in
   (a) bearing – smile, stand still, avoid mannerisms
   (b) voice – 'enlarged conversation'
4. Use variety in pace and pitch. Use pauses.
5. At all times PRAY 1 Corinthians 2:1–5

Practical work: Prepare a short talk of not more than five minutes on any verse/theme from the Bible, and give this at the next Study Group.

Select Bibliography

Babbage, Stuart B., *The Mark of Cain*, Paternoster, 1966

Barclay, William, *More New Testament Words*, SCM, 1948

Baxter, James K., *Thoughts about the Holy Spirit*, Fortuna Press, 62 Friend St Karori, NZ

Beall, James Lea, *Your Pastor, Your Shepherd*, Logos 1977

Boer, H., *Pentecost and Missions*, Lutterworth

Bonhoeffer, Dietrich, *Life Together*, SCM, 1954

—— *Cost of Discipleship*, SCM, 1959

Bosch, David J., *Witness to the World*, Marshall, Morgan and Scott, 1980

Brown, Colin ed., *The International Dictionary of the New Testament*, Paternoster, 1976

Bruce, A. B., *Training of the Twelve*, Kregel, 1971

Coleman, Robert E., *The Master Plan of Evangelism*, Revell, 1963

Edwards, Jonathan, *Thoughts on the Revival*

Foster, Richard J., *Celebration of Discipline*, Hodder & Stoughton, 1980

Green, Michael, *I Believe in the Holy Spirit*, Hodder & Stoughton, 1975

—— *Evangelism – now and then*, IVP, 1979

—— *I Believe in Satan's Downfall*, Hodder & Stoughton, 1981

Griffiths, Michael, *Give Up Your Small Ambitions*, IVP, 1977

Harper, Michael, *Spiritual Warfare*, Hodder & Stoughton, 1970

—— *A New Way of Living*, Hodder & Stoughton, 1973

—— *This is the Day*, Hodder & Stoughton, 1974

Hartman, D. and Sutherland, D., *Guidebook to Discipleship*, Harvest House, Irvine, California, USA, 1976

Henricksen, Walter A., *Disciples Are Made, Not Born*, Victor Books, 1974

Hinnebusch, Paul, *Praise a Way of Life*, Word of Life, 1976

Hummel, Charles, *Fire in the Fireplace*, Mowbrays, 1978

Kittel, *Theological Dictionary of the New Testament*

Koch, Kurt E., *Christian Counselling and Occultism*,
—— *Occult Bondage and Deliverance*, Evangelization Publishers, 7501 Berghausen Bd, Western Germany, 1970

Lewis, C. S., *Screwtape Letters*, Bles, 1942
—— *Mere Christianity*, Collins, 1952

Lovelace, Richard F., *Dynamics of Spiritual Life*, Paternoster, 1979

Loyola, St Ignatius, *Spiritual Exercises*, Newman, 1954

Miller, Keith, *The Taste of New Wine*, Word, 1965

Moltmann, Jüngen, *The Open Church*, SCM, 1978

Morton, T. Ralph, *The Twelve Together*, Iona Community, 1956

Muggeridge, Malcolm, *Christ and the Media*, Hodder and Stoughton, 1977

Nevius, John, *Demon Possession*

Nida, Eugene, *Customs, Culture and Christianity*, Tyndale, 1963

Ortiz, Juan Carlos, *Disciple*, Lakeland, 1971

Packer, J. I., *Evangelism and the Sovereignty of God*, IVP, 1971
—— *Under God's Word*, Marshall, Morgan and Scott, 1980

Powell, John, *Why Am I Afraid To Tell You Who I Am?* Collins, 1969

Quoist, Michael, *Prayers of Life*, Gill, 1963

Richards, John, *But Deliver Us From Evil*, Darton, Longman & Todd, 1974

Richards, Lawrence O., *A New Face For The Church*, Zondervan, 1970
—— *A Theology of Christian Education*, Zondervan, 1975

Saunders, J. Oswald, *Problems of Christian Discipleship*, OMF, 1958

Sider, Ronald J., *Rich Christians in an Age of Hunger*, Hodder & Stoughton, 1977

Snyder, Howard A., *New Wineskins*, Marshall, Morgan and Scott, 1977
—— *The Community of The King*, IVP, 1977

Stewart, James S., *Heralds of God*, Hodder & Stoughton

Stott, John R. W., *Christian Counter-Culture*, IVP, 1978

Stott, John R. W. ed., *Obeying Christ in a Changing World*, Collins, 1977

Suenens, Cardinal, *A New Pentecost?* Darton, Longman & Todd, 1975

Taylor, John, *Enough is Enough*, SCM, 1975

Townsend, Anne, *Prayer Without Pretending*, Scripture Union, 1973

Tozer, A. W., *The Divine Conquest*, Ravel, 1964

Wagner, C. Peter, *Your Church Can Grow*, Glendale, C.A., Regal, 1976

Wallis, Jim, *Agenda for Biblical People*, Harper & Row, 1976

White, John, *The Golden Cow*, Marshall, Morgan, and Scott, 1979
—— *The Cost of Commitment*, IVP, 1976

Wilson, Carl, *With Christ in the School of Disciple-Building*, Zondervan, 1976
Wright, J. Stafford, *Christianity and the Occult*, Scripture Union, 1977
Wurmbrand, Richard, *Tortured for Christ*, Hodder & Stoughton, 1967
—— *In God's Underground*, W. H. Allen, 1968
Yoder, John Howard, *Politics of Jesus*, Eerdmans, 1976

Magazines
Evangelical Quarterly Mission, Box 794, Wheaton, Illinois, 60187, USA
New Covenant, PO Box 617, Ann Arbor, Michigan 48107, USA
Pastoral Renewal, PO Box 8617, Ann Arbor, Michigan 48107, USA
Third Way, 19 Draycott Place, London SW3 2SJ